Recoding the Muse.....

Why has it taken so long to make computers work for the museum sector?

Why are museums still having some of the same conversations about digital technology that they began back in the late 1960s?

Does there continue to be a basic 'incompatibility' between the practice of the museum and the functions of the computer that explains this disconnect?

Drawing upon an impressive range of professional and theoretical sources, this book offers one of the first substantial histories of museum computing. Its ambitious narrative attempts to explain a series of essential tensions between curatorship and the digital realm.

Ultimately, it reveals how through the emergence of standards, increased co-ordination, and celebration (rather than fearing) of the 'virtual', the sector has experienced a broadening of participation, a widening of creative horizons and, ultimately, has helped to define a new cultural role for museums. Having confronted and understood its past, what emerges is a museum transformed – rescripted, recalibrated, rewritten, reorganised.

Ross Parry is a lecturer in the Department of Museum Studies at the University of Leicester, and a historian of museum media and technology. Much of his research focuses on the proximity of computing to the management of information and construction of knowledge.

Museum Meanings

Series editors
Eilean Hooper-Greenhill and Flora Kaplan

The museum has been constructed as a symbol of Western society since the Renaissance. This symbol is both complex and multi-layered, acting as a sign for domination and liberation, learning and leisure. As sites for exposition, through their collections, displays and buildings, museums mediate many of society's basic values. But these mediations are subject to contestation, and the museum can also be seen as a site for cultural politics. In post-colonial societies, museums have changed radically, reinventing themselves under pressure from many forces, which include new roles and functions for museums, economic rationalism and moves towards greater democratic access.

Museum Meanings analyses and explores the relationship between museums and their publics. 'Museums' are understood very broadly to include art galleries, historic sites and historic houses. 'Relationships with publics' is also understood very broadly, including interactions with artefacts, exhibitions and architecture, which may be analysed from a range of theoretical perspectives. These include material culture studies, mass communication and media studies, learning theories and cultural studies. The analysis of the relationship of the museum to its publics shifts the emphasis from the museum as text, to studies grounded in the relationships of bodies and sites, identities and communities.

Also in the series:

Evolution in the Museum
Envisioning African Origins
Monique Scott

Recoding the Museum
*Digital Heritage and
the Technologies of Change*
Ross Parry

Museum Texts
Communication Frameworks
Louise Ravelli

Reshaping Museum Space
Architecture, Design, Exhibitions
Edited by Suzanne MacLeod

Museums, Society, Inequality
Edited by Richard Sandell

**Museums and the Interpretation of Visual
Culture**
Eilean Hooper-Greenhill

Re-imagining the Museum
Beyond the Mausoleum
Andrea Witcomb

Museum, Media, Message
Edited by Eilean Hooper-Greenhill

Colonialism and the Object
*Empire, Material Culture and
the Museum*
Edited by Tim Barringer and Tom Flynn

Learning in the Museum
George Hein

Liberating Culture
*Cross-Cultural Perspectives on Museums,
Curation and Heritage Preservation*
Christina F. Kreps

Pasts Beyond Memory
Evolution, Museums, Colonialism
Tony Bennett

Recoding the Museum

Digital Heritage and the Technologies of Change

Ross Parry

Routledge
Taylor & Francis Group

LONDON AND NEW YORK

First published 2007
by Routledge
2 Park Square, Milton Park, Abingdon, Oxon OX14 4RN

Simultaneously published in the USA and Canada
by Routledge
270 Madison Ave, New York, NY 10016

Routledge is an imprint of the Taylor & Francis Group, an informa business

© 2007 Ross Parry

Typeset in Sabon by
The Running Head Limited, Cambridge
Printed and bound in Great Britain by
MPG Books Ltd, Bodmin, Cornwall

British Library Cataloguing in Publication Data
A catalogue record for this book is available from the British Library

Library of Congress Cataloging in Publication Data
Parry, Ross.
Recoding the museum : digital heritage and the technologies of change / Ross Parry.
p. cm.
Includes bibliographical references and index.
1. Museums—Data processing. 2. Museums—Technological innovations. 3. Museums—Information
technology. 4. Museums—Curatorship. 5. Museums—Philosophy. 6. Virtual museums. 7. Digital media.
I. Title.
AM7.P33 2008
069.0285—dc22
2007022718

ISBN10: 0–415–35387–4 (hbk)
ISBN10: 0–415–35388–2 (pbk)
ISBN10: 0–203–34748–X (ebk)

ISBN13: 978–0–415–35387–8 (hbk)
ISBN13: 978–0–415–35388–5 (pbk)
ISBN13: 978–0–203–34748–5 (ebk)

For Frank and Jean Colson

Contents

Figures

Preface

This book is about two stories. One of the stories is about a sector that has, over the past four decades, struggled with the opportunities offered by new digital media. This is a story partly about strategic weaknesses and a lack of resources, but, more deeply, it is about how a more essential *incompatibility* between the idea of the museum and the idea of the computer might be seen to have stymied the adoption of some of these new technologies. However, the other story is more encouraging. It is a story about agreed standards and increased co-ordination and partnership between organisations. It is a story about exponential growth, the broadening of participation and the widening of creative horizons. This is a story where any incompatibilities between *museum* and *computer* appear to be resolved, and where new futures for the museum are made possible.

These stories represent two histories of museums and new digital technology, and, through the pages that follow, they will weave in and out of each other. They are not alternatives, nor are they sequential, and they are certainly not intended to be comprehensive or definitive. Rather they represent contrasting readings of the evidence available. Both stories in their own way are valid. When told together, they illustrate how varied the sector's experience of institutional change has been over the past forty years and how difficult it is (inappropriate even) to try to build a single narrative of what has happened.

I have always been an admirer (if somewhat guiltily) of the confidence with which Martin Kemp introduced his study on *The Science of Art*. In an unsettling, but at the same time quite reassuringly honest way, he explained how he was

> in favour of the historian chancing his or her arm by framing wide-ranging generalisation on the basis of the evidence as far as it is known and understood. This is not an excuse for inaccuracies in particulars or generalities that will inevitably appear in this book. Rather it is an acknowledgement that some issues are sufficiently important and 'big' to justify taking the risk of being wrong in a spectacular manner.
>
> (1990: 2)

To offer an ambitious panoptic view of four decades of museum computing (reflecting on different professions around the world and different types of technology) means that omissions and oversights, of the sort Kemp alludes to, are inevitable – and, sure enough, these will be for subsequent reviewers and writers to add to and correct. In some respects, therefore, the book is a challenge to others to offer alternative readings, of different contexts or other technologies – to tell other stories of museum computing. For as the rebuttals, responses, comments and critiques of this book appear, so (excitingly) will our new historiography on this subject also appear.

There is also an important message in the title of the book. The 'recoding' at play here is not only the *coding* with which software developers are familiar, but is also culture's *codifying* of behaviour and the way we (and technology) give meaning to things. This double reading exemplifies the fusion of cultural studies and technology studies that lies at the heart of the analysis presented here. Moreover, by styling itself as a 'recoding' of the museum, there is also a self-conscious attempt to align the debates here to the mainstream of museological study. We allude here to Stephen Weil 'rethinking' the museum, Andrea Witcomb's 'reimagining' of the museum, Suzanne MacLeod's 'reshaping' of museum space and Richard Sandell's 'reframing' of difference. To fashion my arguments here as a 'recoding' of the museum is knowingly to wear the clothes of orthodox museology, and to bring museum computing in from the margins of museum studies.

The timing of this book is also not accidental. It is intended to mark the fortieth anniversary of the birth of computerisation in the museum. In 1967 the Smithsonian Institution's landmark information retrieval project formally began, exploring and demonstrating what could be possible with automation. In the same year a number of natural history curators congregated in Mexico and discussed computer-assisted information retrieval. In Germany previous experience of using data management programs with library and bibliographic records began to focus upon cataloguing museum objects. Also in that year the founding of the Museum Computer Network in the US represented a critical mass of activity and advocacy for the standardisation and computer-interchange of museum information. In the same year ICOM's International Committee for Documentation (CIDOC) established a Documentation Working Party, following a recommendation to explore mechanisation in information retrieval. And in this same year the Information Retrieval Group of the Museums Association (IRGMA) was established in the UK – and its first meeting was held in the Department of Museum Studies at the University of Leicester. In other words, 1967 was the touchstone moment for museum computing. It seems appropriate, therefore, forty years on, to step back and begin to piece together what has (as well as what hasn't) happened in that time.

Finally, and perhaps most of all, the stories in this book are about helping to forge the creation of a new sub-discipline of museum studies. There is an aim here to illustrate the complexity of the confluences and collisions that continue to take place at that intersection between cultural heritage and digital media. That place, today, we call *digital heritage*.

Ross Parry, Leicester, May 2007

Acknowledgements

My arrival in 1998 in the Department of Museum Studies at the University of Leicester (a crucible of innovative research and leading-edge practice) came at a time when it was novel for a curatorial training programme to include a substantial engagement with the theory and practice of museum computing. Today, however, a decade later, we are witness to a flowering around the world of modules and programmes in what is variously called 'museum informatics', 'digital heritage' and 'cultural technology'. In such exciting times for our subject, it remains a privilege to work in an academic environment where one is surrounded not only by highly motivated postgraduates from a range of countries and subject disciplines, but also by colleagues who all relish our intellectual milieu here at Leicester which is constantly interdisciplinary and always folding practice on to theory and vice versa. I am grateful to these colleagues (past and present) who have never failed to reveal new angles of approach on the myriad ideas and issues confronted in this project. Specific thanks are due to three successive heads of department whose encouragement has sustained me: Eilean Hooper-Greenhill, Simon Knell and Richard Sandell.

Like anyone teaching and researching in a university, I owe one of my greatest debts for this project to the successive cohorts of students who have questioned, amended and encouraged (and, I suspect, sometimes *endured*) my rehearsals on the various theses contained in this book. Without their patience and their enthusiasm this book would be considerably impoverished. Dissertation supervisions with Lauren Parker (on liminality) and Oliver Douglas (on what we might mean by 'in-reach') are just two examples of countless memorable encounters that have helped to direct me. (After all, learning is best when it can be two-way like this.) I am particularly grateful to – and proud of – three of my former students who not only engaged more deeply than most in the discussions described here, but who have also gone on to build their own careers researching and practising in museum computing. They are Nadia Arbach, Konstantinos Arvanitis and Areti Galani.

I continue to respect and value the two-way transfer of knowledge that can take place between academia and the museums sector. A subject such as museum studies can mean and achieve very little unless there is this focus on praxis, this coupling and dialectic between theory and practice, each informed by the other.

In this respect I am particularly grateful to the hundreds of members of the Museums Computer Group (MCG) who over the years have supported these synergies. A great deal of my thinking represented in these pages has been constructed in and around the work of this long-established community of practice. It seems fitting, therefore, bearing in mind its scope, that this book appears in the year when the MCG celebrates its twenty-fifth anniversary. Special thanks must go, in particular, to Nick Poole, Jon Pratty and Mike Lowndes for the collaborations and discussions that they have framed and fuelled. Equally, I have been fortunate enough to benefit from a number of strong relationships with industry; a number of the research projects that underpin this book are built upon knowledge transfer partnerships with the commercial sector. For many years of dialogue, debate and practical help (not least important insights into the levers and drivers of the new media marketplace) I am particularly grateful to MWR and Simulacra – specifically their museum specialist, Andrew Sawyer.

For the not inconsiderable amount of travel that has been required to undertake the research for this book, I would like to offer my thanks to the British Academy for an Overseas Conference Grant, and the Department of Museum Studies at the University of Leicester for two travel grants (to Washington, DC, in December 2005, and to San Francisco in April 2007). There have also been two significant research grants for which I have been principal investigator, that have evidenced significant sections of this book: the award of an HEROBC 'Innovations Fellowship' to explore the development of in-gallery media (2005–6); and an Arts and Humanities Research Council Research Workshop grant to fund a thinktank (2006–7) on museums and the Semantic Web.

The research within this book draws extensively from three key archives: the Smithsonian Institution Archives in Washington, DC (specifically the Museum Computer Network Records and the Automation Development Records), the MDA library (formerly in Cambridge and now in Leicester), and the archive of the Museums Computer Group (now also in Leicester) – all of which have helped to build an invaluable 'warts and all' perspective on forty years of museum computing. I would like to offer my thanks to each of these organisations as well as to Ellen Alers, Gordon McKenna and Charles Pettitt for their assistance in accessing these collections.

Importantly, early drafts and iterations of parts of this book were aired and tested at a number of conferences and events. In particular, I am grateful to the invitations and acceptances from the organisers at the following for allowing me to speak and develop my thinking on the discussions covered in this book: the American Association of Museums Annual Meeting, Dallas, Texas, 15 May 2002; 'Museums and Technology: an international conference on the application of new technology in museums', Graduate Institution of Museology, Tainan National College of the Arts, Taiwan, November 2004; 'Technology for cultural heritage: management, education, communication', 2nd International Conference of Museology, University of the Aegean, Greece, 28 June 2004; EITEC 2006, University of Coimbra, Portugal, 20 October 2006; and XIVth National Congress of Educational and Cultural Action Departments, Las Palmas de Gran

Canaria, Spain, 10 November 2006. Parts of the discussions on LIVE!Labels were first presented as part of a paper: Parry, R., Ortiz-Williams, M. and Sawyer, A. (2007) 'How Shall We Label Our Exhibit Today? Applying the principles of on-line publishing to an on-site exhibition', in J. Trant and D. Bearman (eds) *Museums and the Web 2007: Proceedings*, Toronto: Archives & Museum Informatics. Similarly, small parts of the discussion here on virtuality and virtual reality appeared as: Parry, R. (2002) 'Virtuality, liminality and the space of the museum', *MDA Information*, vol. 5, no. 5: 67–70, and in Parry, R. and Hopwood, J. (2004) 'Virtual Reality and the soft museum', *Journal of Museum Ethnography*, no. 16: 69–78. I am grateful to Archives and Museum Informatics, MDA and the Museum Ethnographers Group for granting permission to re-present and rework parts of these papers here. I must also thank Jim Roberts for his help in preparing the line drawings that appear in the book.

Finally, a number of individuals kindly agreed to be interviewed (sometimes at considerable length) for this research. I am extremely thankful for their time and insight. They are: David Bearman, Robin Boast, David Bridge, Mick Cooper, David Fleming, Geoffrey Lewis, Richard Light, Frances Lloyd-Baynes, Fiona Marshall, Jonathan Moffett, Susan Pearce, Charles Pettitt, Phil Philips, Joyce Ray, Andrew Roberts, Debbie Schaefer-Jacobs, Alan Seal, Jane Sledge, Matthew Stiff and Raelene Worthington. Each of them will, I am sure, be able to see how their thoughts have contributed to this text. However, any errors or oversights remain, of course, my own.

Museum/computer

A history of disconnect?

The dilemma at the heart of this book is perhaps captured by these two fragments, from two different speeches, by two different speakers:

> the future coordination of digitisation activity [. . .] with the vision of cre-
> ating a European Cultural Information space [. . .] will provide rich and
> diverse cultural resources [. . .] to enable digital access by all citizens to
> the national, regional and local cultural heritage of Europe.

> this project [. . .] anticipates the eventual recording of all museum collec-
> tions [. . .] within a single integrated system, it is principally concerned at
> this stage with designing a national information system for art museum
> resources which will later serve as a model for compatible 'data banks'
> covering scientific and historical institutions.

Both comments come from individuals working in or with the museum sector,
and both of these individuals have an expert and professional interest in cultural heritage. More significantly, here, both individuals are reflecting upon
digital heritage, in particular the possibilities for expanded access that can come
from a distributed but co-ordinated digital network of on-line cultural content,
be it national or international. Both are presenting a vision of increased accessibility brought about by the thoughtful deployment of network technology.
Both commentators, it would seem, could be writing about the same moment.
The scenarios they describe could be contemporaneous, part of the same discourse. And yet, the reality is that whereas the first piece is taken from a speech
made by the UK's Culture Minister in November 2005 (Lammy 2005), the
second is derived from a paper delivered to a conference in Munich of the International Council of Museums, in August 1968 – almost four decades earlier
(Ellin 1968a). We are left wondering, therefore, why it is that we have taken
some forty years to realise these visions. Why has it taken the museum sector
quite so long to begin to build these integrated information systems to which
both speakers refer? Or, to put it another way: why are we still having these
same conversations that we began in the late 1960s?

There are, of course, some pragmatic explanations that would no doubt immediately spring to mind for many museum practitioners – especially those involved

in museum computing over this period. In times of economic recession, and well before the age of 'e-government', political expectations and priorities were frequently elsewhere (Lewis 2007). There was not the anticipation to see computers in the museum as there is today – where now, apparently, 'visitors expect technology' (Dierking and Falk 1998: 67). Museums themselves perhaps underestimated the resource and skills needed to go digital.[1] Equally, the software has itself frequently been a barrier – shielded by a counter-intuitive interface, the preserve of the expert (Worthington 2005). In 1992, confronted with many incompatible platforms, and chasing the state of the art, even curators with considerable expertise in the area of museum computing lamented how 'the technology has not settled down' (Moffett 1992b: 7). Consequently, for all of these reasons (many of which will be explored in detail in Chapter 7), organisational structures did not adapt, time was not allocated, and money was never readily available. Moreover, not all museum sectors around the world had the infrastructure, the environment or even the justification to accommodate the new computing. Many were confronting, instead, more fundamental aspects of their vision and development (Koujalgi 1974), or freeing themselves from a curatorial practice that belonged to an increasingly irrelevant colonial past (Abungu 2002). In these contexts 'automation' was not always the priority. As one early manual on museum computing put it, describing the 'difficult, expensive and often frustrating process' of going digital:

> today – and for many years to come – our expectations of automated cataloging must be in tune with practical constraints imposed by the limited resources and technology available to museum collections. Further, there is the welter of problems that must be solved with respect to data standards, preparing collections for cataloging, and training adequate personnel for the task of computer cataloging.
>
> (Humphrey and Clausen 1976)

However, this explanation (an explanation largely based on resource, priority, structures, skills, time and money), although difficult to refute, perhaps tells only part of the story. To some extent these may be the symptoms rather than the root cause of why museums responded to the computer revolution in the way they did. In other words, this explanation (this history) might be expedient and recognisable, but it might not acknowledge some deeper reasons as to why computers, during this time, followed a sometimes bumpy and circuitous road into the museum. There may, in short, be a more essential tension at work here between this technology and the institutions into which it has slowly been adopted. What we might call (to reach for a moment for a word from information technology itself) a more fundamental *incompatibility*[2] between the concept of a museum and the concept of a computer. Looking beyond the day-to-day and localised obstructions and difficulties, there may have been more inherent problems between museum and computer that might reveal and explain any perceived *disconnect*. And it is this disconnect that this book will explore.

Museum histories

But before we even begin to tell histories we have to make some decisions, as authors, about history-making itself. Any history – including those of museums, and of digital media in museums – requires a number of assumptions to be made about how history-writing works. The moment we choose to look back, to reflect upon the past, we find ourselves making choices not just about the questions we decide to pose, but also about the places we choose to look for answers. Not only do we privilege and select narratives and theses based on the (sometimes) fragmentary evidence available, but, subsequently, these are filtered further by the medium (the book, hypermedia, television documentary, exhibition) through which we choose to convey these histories (Colson et al. 2003). The preface, for instance, to the sixteenth edition, 1995, of E. H. Gombrich's canonical *Story of Art* reviews the changes the author has made to this classic study since its initial publication in 1950. We see that in his original preface, Gombrich (1995: 9) had identified the 'space allotted to the various arts in this book' as a contentious issue. He went on to attribute the bias towards painting within his narrative to the fact that 'less is lost in the illustration of a painting than in that of round sculpture, let alone a monumental building'. As a consequence of this prejudice, some formats (particularly those that are two-dimensional) have arguably been artificially foregrounded in this and subsequent histories of art, whereas others, specifically the three-dimensional, have been consciously under-represented. In other words, one of our canonical stories of art is (self-admittedly) constrained by the limitations of its medium.[3] Likewise – but some forty years later – Martin Kemp's survey of optically minded theory and practice in art confronts this same limitation of the flat illustration. Acknowledging how the format of the printed book inevitably distorts readers' impressions of works of art (particularly in terms of scale), Kemp (1990: 2) apologises for the way in which 'a great illusionistic room decoration from the Italian seventeenth century appears on roughly the same scale as a Dutch cabinet containing a peep show'. The 'space allotted' to the historian for interpreting the past is as important now as it has been to writers such as Kemp, and as it was for Gombrich back in 1950.

Furthermore, to some writers historical certainty remains conspicuously impossible – almost to the point of self-congratulation. 'I am well aware', Foucault asserted, 'that I have never written anything but fictions'; so quotes Hunt (1989) as she laments where we will be 'when every practice, be it economic, intellectual, social, or political, has been shown to be culturally conditioned'. Consequently, some have worked to turn the attention of historians to the fictional and literary quality of some of their narratives on the past. To White (1978), for instance, historical narratives are but verbal fictions, 'the contents of which have more in common with their counterparts in literature than they have with those in the sciences'. Such are the reservations of modern commentators who, approaching 'meaning' as a text to be read, identify an essential contention within attempts to write about a localised knowledge. The description may be 'thick', but it is only ever of the *here* and *now* rather than the *then* and *there*. Amid this high intensity of self-examination, we are, perhaps, becoming more familiar with our histories being fixed within the frames of the present as well as (or indeed, *instead of*) the past – and more sensitive to the ways in which the historical models we build are of ourselves rather than of a distant historical locality.

Even when they are in their most pragmatic form, when we allow ourselves to admit that the past 'really happened' (Evans 1997), our modern sensibilities to historiography continue to sow doubt into what, today, is possible as a historian – what we can genuinely and authoritatively say about events past. To write history today is, it seems, to make choices about the flow of time (and the arbitrary divisions we make within it), the value of representations (and the limits of what can be educed from them), the nature of society and power (and the strata and operators that may or may not work within them), as well as the historical contingency of our institutions, values and world views. Consequently, as narrator, director and stage-manager to these interpretations of the past, historians are also understood to be visible and active in these productions. Both reader and writer are made aware of the inevitability of each historian's bias to any given array of evidence, and received orthodoxy has it that there are no value-free judgements in the act of history-making. Therefore, just as history-making in the museum is riddled with decisions and judgements on the use of narrative, the selection of evidence, and the choice of subject (Kavanagh 1990) so, likewise, historicising the museum itself demands a moment of reflection on how that history will focus and function.

So how will our histories of museums and computing be presented in this book? To answer this question, it might be easier to start by saying what sort of history this book will not be. First, as has already been made clear, this is not intended to be a general or survey history – but rather a specific thesis on compatibility and incompatibility between museums and computers. Second, it is not intended to be a history of museums and technology within a broader narrative of emerging 'civilisation'. Our narrative here will work hard not to slide into deterministic readings of technology; that is, readings that see technology such as digital media as an external force exerting change on society (Lister et al. 2003). As we acknowledge the 'transformative impact' that technology has had on culture (Druckrey 1996: 13), there is a risk, after all, of seeing museums and digital media, temptingly, within this context of progressive, incremental improvement – with the technology itself as the main driver. In contrast, a more constructionist ('anti-realist') stance may help us to see, instead, that a technology such as digital media does not actually have a use inherent within it, but rather that this use is always constructed and constantly contested by the society that chooses to use it (Kuhn 1970). For instance, the monumental work of Elizabeth Eisenstein (1980) on the advent of the printing press provides an exemplar of how the synergy between new technology and society can be illustrated. In her analysis of Christianity's shift from 'pen to press' in Europe during the fifteenth and sixteenth centuries, Eisenstein makes the case for new technology inciting revolutionary change. Print ended what was understood by some Protestant divines to be a 'priestly monopoly of learning', by allowing religious dissent to leave a 'much more indelible and far-reaching impression than dissent had ever left before' (ibid.: 305–17). The new technology of printing brought about a higher exactitude of scripture and allowed liturgy to be standardised and fixed for the first time in a more or less permanent model. Eisenstein's thesis, in other words, is one in which a new technology helps to bring about not only a new learning and erudition, but also new forms of intellectual property rights and new concepts of authorship. Communication technology emerges as a profound agent of literary, spiritual and linguistic change. However, as much as her thesis on the printing press shows the impact of a specific technology on the foundations of a society, so it (importantly) also demonstrates how society and culture, at once, affect this technology. For the cultural uses of the new printing technology added meaning to (and allowed a specific set of meanings to permeate into) the medium of the press, to the extent that Eisenstein asserts that printing revolutionised all processes of transmission. To place something in print was to perform a 'kind of disruption' (ibid.: 327). Within this view of 'cultural technologies' (Flew 2002) – culture shaped by technologies that are themselves cultural constructs – the relationship between technology and society (digital media and the museum) emerges as something more reciprocal and complex. To take one small, but poignant, example: as the library sector began to work through the requirements and functionality of its new machine-readable catalogue system in the mid-1960s, some commentators at the time had seen human (rather than technical) factors as a brake on the development of the new automation. When considering the way the initial specifications had been overloaded with elements that would satisfy very localised and personalised needs it was suggested (as it turns out, with undue pessimism) that:

> They [other librarians] loaded up the Library of Congress group with requirements that today it appears unlikely that the project will ever get off the ground. I am not sure the limitation there is a basic flaw in computerisation; it may be an impassable flaw in human nature.
>
> (Taube 1966: 1158)

We remain mindful, therefore, of the central role human actors (what Taube saw here as the role of personal interest and 'human nature') play in the ideation, development and uptake of new technologies. I acknowledge that seeing technology as a 'prisoner of culture' can itself be culturally specific and beyond the categorisation by one catch-all model, as writers (such as Winston 1998) are moved to construct. Nevertheless, my assumption here will be that society allows technological progress to happen, that it controls the forming of the idea (the imagination within which the technologist is allowed to think), as well as the circumstances in which the prototype is formed. Crucially, from this intellectual perspective, where technology is not allowed to lead the story, the museum is understood to have greater influence on its own development.

There are also schools of historiography from which my approach here will borrow – particularly with respect to its interdisciplinarity and its choice of evidence. First, informed by the New Cultural History (Hunt 1989), the histories here assume that museums should be seen within a complex array of histories, which are themselves in a state of flux and part of a wide structure of meaning and events. The assumption here is that the concept 'museum' sits at the nexus of a number of different histories and discourses – and certainly not just those concerning technology. In one respect 'the museum' is part of a history of objects – of material culture, the specimens, artefacts and art that both define, and are themselves defined by, society (Pearce 1995; Šola 2004). In another respect it is a history of individuals – of the collectors who bring together these objects, who arrange them, classify them, and give them meaning (Knell 2000; Martin 2004). Similarly, we can fashion the story of museums as a history of buildings – of spaces that provide a framed exhibition and production of knowledge, of thought made three-dimensional and physical (MacLeod 2005; Parry and Hopwood 2004). The history of museums is also a history of institutions – of private societies and national repositories (Cowtan 1872; Crooke 2000). However, museum history can also be seen as a history of society itself – of cultures struggling with their own identities, riding on the ebb and flow of politics, finding ways to socialise, to remember, to play and to learn (Bennett 1995; Hooper-Greenhill 1992). 'Technology', therefore, is only one of many lenses through which this book reads the museum's past.

The narratives I present in this book aim to be aware of these different directions to which we can cast our historical gaze. However, the discussions here also endeavour to remain mindful of the nature and variety of evidence upon which we are able to draw. Here the approaches of the British historian Lewis Namier are a key point of reference. Namier, and the scholars in this tradition who followed him (such as Conrad Russell and Kevin Sharpe), sought to smash some of the meta-narratives of their predecessors by stressing flux and difference in their histories of British parliament. They did so by demonstrating the power and influence of the individual on a day-to-day basis. In this way, the iconoclasm of their 'Revisionism' (Sharpe 1978) was built upon a firm foundation of liberal humanism, in which historical actors (rather than social theories) shaped history. Rather than a history of institutions, what emerged was a history of individuals following a personal agenda, not anachronistic ideologies, in lives characterised by conjunction and chance, not inevitability. Rushing to the archives, the Revisionists offered a plethora of different narratives within the historical localities to which they looked. It is this approach to historiography that informs the narrative of this book. Consequently, from text to hypertext, from theoretical treatises to computer manuals, and from unpublished memoranda and interviews to formally accessioned archival material, the *evidence horizon* I present here is intentionally broad.

Histories of museum computing

To date there have been very few histories of the technological and curatorial changes that have taken place from the second half of the twentieth century onwards. Museology has been reluctant, it seems, to give the story of museum computing (a story of technological and professional change) the same academic scrutiny as has been bestowed on other parts of our curatorial and museographical past. This may partly be to do with historical distance. Being proximate to these events (perhaps even being a historical actor within them, *being part of the story*) might make it difficult for us to step out of this timeline or to see these events as worthy of study – leaving events instead for the realm of reverie, anecdote or personal resumé. But perhaps our history of museum computing has now a beginning that is suitably distant from us and, as it enters its fifth decade, an archive that is suitably full, that we can be more comfortable and able to offer it more serious historical treatment. Maybe, until now, we have been too close, too much in the moment itself, to take our vantage point as the historian looking back meaningfully on what has happened. The irony is, of course, that the further away we come from the historical period on which we are writing, the more dislocated we are from that moment, from that locality, and the harder it becomes to appreciate the pressures and the personalities that may or may not have affected events. Equally, there is a danger that our aerial view – on the historian's hilltop – seduces us into building longer narratives and teleologies, spotting broader patterns that may (or may not) be there.

A number of specific museum computing projects have been given a historical treatment by authors. Vance (1973) outlined the history of the Museum Computer Network. Katherine Spiess (from the National Museum of American History) had compiled a list of 'selected great moments from 1965 through 1985', and Jonathan Bowen (1997) would later describe the birth and development of the Virtual Library museums page (VLmp). We can also find brief histories of Canada's National Inventory Program and the role of technology in the establishment of the Canadian Heritage Information Network and the Virtual Museum of Canada (CHIN 1992; Dietz et al. 2004), as well as summaries of the work of CIDOC in the area of automation, standardisation and computerisation (Roberts and Light 1980). Most notably, perhaps, there have been some very successful attempts to write the first histories of museums and their use of the Web (Bearman and Trant 1999; Rellie 2006). Sarasan (1981) has sought to understand recurring problems that museums faced in applying computer technology, partly by locating recent failings in a longer context of development and change. Similarly, in his detailed primer for beginners in museum computerisation, David Williams began with an essay outlining key historical developments in museum computing (1987: 1–7). Even if one reviewer did complain of how long was spent dwelling on past difficulties and past technologies (McLaren 1988), this was a valuable and thoughtful way to introduce a step-by-step guide. In recent years, the most referenced history has been Jones-Garmil's introductory chapter to her edited volume, *The Wired Museum* (1997), taking stock, as it did of (then) thirty years of museum computing. A testimony perhaps to the speed at which digital technology has changed, and to the developments in the museum sector in responding to this change, is the fact that this book, only ten years on, appears very much of its time. This important volume came at a moment in the mid- to late 1990s, before the bursting of the dot.com bubble, when the focus in the sector was on the 'emerging' technology of the Web and when Internet usage was growing at a staggering and exponential rate, and its influence appeared unstoppable. Discussions on network and telecommunications technologies, consequently, figure large in the book. And less, therefore, is said about information management – the subject that had preoccupied museum computing for the previous two decades. Instead, the language here ('encounter', 'impact', 'challenge', 'the heady transitions', 'experimentation') is that of collision and flux and of a sector looking for 'guidance' at a time of rapid change. Published the following year, Thomas and Mintz's *The Virtual and the Real* (1998) presented itself as a complement to *The Wired Museum*; whereas Jones-Garmil's book looked towards 'internal issues' inside the museum, *The Virtual and the Real* saw itself looking, instead, outwards to the ways 'media affects the external relationships between museums and their audiences' (Thomas and Mintz 1998: ix). But as it does so, there are useful glances to history. Current practice is understood by reflecting on laser disk projects of the early 1990s, just as museum computing in general is set within the wider historical contexts of the invention of printing, and the display technologies of the Victorian Great Exhibition in the Crystal Palace.

A number of broader histories of museum computing have been interleaved, and sometimes tucked away, within larger manuals and guides. Although not widely published, Everett Ellin was by 1967 outlining to specialist groups 'a brief history of computers in relation to the humanities'. Also, tucked away in an appendix to his 'manual' *Computers in the Museum* (1973: 41–51), David Vance provided a brief summary (if from quite a technical perspective) of the key projects that had driven the first decade of automation and machine-assisted information retrieval. Two years later Robert Chenhall opened his book on *Museum Cataloguing in the Computer Age* (1975) with a short chapter on technological change that placed museum computing in a longer historical context: from Leonardo da Vinci to the 1850s, and from the Ling-Temco-Vought computer centre to the Vietnam War.[4] Interestingly, by 1988, when Chenhall returned to the task of providing the sector with a highly informed – and even more far-reaching – guide, these historical strands had fallen away. Likewise, in the other key books on museum computing from this period, 'history' only ever really achieved the status of context and background, at best the stuff of appendix case studies – best demonstrated in the impressively compiled works by Orna and Pettitt (1980; 1998) and Roberts (1985). Subsequently, it was this emphasis on practical advice, rather than historical reflection, that came to characterise the literature in this area for the next ten years (Fahy 1995; Gill 1996; Gordon 1996; Keene 1998). Keene's volume, in particular, exemplified this. Offered as a self-admittedly 'optimistic view' (ibid.: 115) of the practicalities and possibilities facing museums in the information age, the book was an example of one very experienced practitioner providing a whirlwind tour of a current situation, advising on best practice along the way, and projecting an image of the challenges and new approaches that might await. Written with the relaxed tone of collegial advice, it offered a very clear, accessible, economic and no-nonsense approach.[5]

It would be only in this current century that the 'cultural turn' in museum computing would begin to manifest itself fully, as authors (practitioners and academics alike) began to reach for the intellectual frameworks and critical tools of other subjects – especially cultural studies – to inform their readings of cultural technology and the 'cultural complexes' they generate (Parry 2005; Cameron and Kenderline 2007). It is indeed into this last school of writing on museum computing (writing that is both historicised and theorised, the school of *digital heritage*) that this book is strongly located.

The language of museum computing

Consequently, with our attention here on theory, as well as on history, it is important at this point to be clear of our understanding of media themselves. It is, after all, in the rudiments of media theory that both the extent and the complexity of digital technology's influence on the museum might best be comprehended. And where better to start than with Marshal McLuhan? Some parts of McLuhan's seminal 1964 essay 'The medium is the message' (taken from his anthology, *Understanding media: the extensions of man*) may sound discordant to modern readers. On the one hand the ease and confidence with which the discussion moves between different cultural references (from *King Lear*, E. H. Gombrich, and E. M. Forster, to Cadillacs, cornflakes and baseball) may be received well by the polyphonic sensitivity of the post-modern ear. And yet, McLuhan's transition between his examples can be quick (indeed, as instantaneous as some of the media messages he describes) and disorienting for a reader waiting to be led through a sequential argument. Moreover, his language is very much of its time, and occasionally can jar against (even offend) today's sensibilities.[6] And yet, despite the challenges that his text sets us today, it is McLuhan and the re-versionings by others of his original ideas that have followed in subsequent decades that still loom large in studies of media and communication. It is at our own risk that we disregard the enduring importance of his famous statement on media agency: 'it is sometimes a bit of a shock to be reminded that, in operational and practical fact, the medium is the message' (McLuhan 2001: 7). His point was, in many respects, a simple one: that, far from being a passive and putative vessel merely carrying content, the medium used (be it television or telephone, t-shirt or text) has a vital role to play in the construction of any communicated message. Any media technology carries in fact its own set of associations for the recipient – a series of what he calls 'personal and social consequences'. In the case of, say, one individual communicating to another through the medium of a book, there will be 'consequences' associated with the use of text (perhaps associations with literacy, rules of grammar, linearity, authorship and so on) as well as with the notion of a book itself (maybe related to its tangible, portable, fixed quality, or the fact that it can be consumed privately, or even the fact that it is a published commodity). The media (the book and its text, as well as other media elements within it, such as perhaps images) will, in other words, carry personal meanings for the reader, all of which contribute to the message that he or she will construct from reading

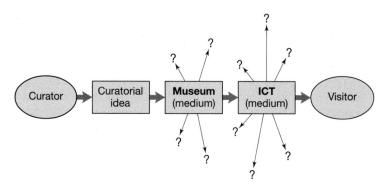

Figure 1.1 Identifying the personal and social consequences of using both the museum and the computer as medium.

the author's work. On this point, writers such as Šola (1997) have suggested that museums have been somewhat neglectful in their understanding of the museum as *medium*. Asserting that the knowledge of the medium 'is the first prerequisite of any correct action and use of its full capacity', he issues the rebuke that while many people working in museums have excellent knowledge of the museum institution and its working process, 'they are unable to use it beyond its inherent administrative logic, they do not perceive it as a tool, as a means, as medium to achieve effects outside of the immediate institutional logic' (ibid.: 24). In other words, as soon as we decide to use the 'medium of the museum' to convey a message, we ought also to think about what the 'personal and social consequences' of that medium (the museum) are going to be for the visitor.

Extending McLuhan's thesis, we might also usefully remind ourselves of how this process of meaning-making is culturally and historically contingent. In other words, that the meanings (the *agency*) associated with any given media are never fixed, but rather that they change according to the experiences and knowledge of an individual and the shifting values and discourses of any given community or society. For instance, within computing, we might identify this agency even within the Graphical-User Interface system that relies upon windows-icons-menu-pointer, the WIMP system, as it has been called (Cubitt 1998: 2). This system (which has a history traceable back to 1945) is predicated upon the idea that it represents a 'familiar' environment – that it projects a metaphor of a desktop that we recognise, and within which we, as a user, can quickly feel comfortable. And yet this ubiquitous North American interface system (a mainstay of modern personal computing) is culturally specific text. Its so-called 'familiarities' are far from universal. Instead it represents only one commercial analogy of corporate-bureaucratic work-patterns determined by one specific concept of global technology – it glamorises one vision of 'bureaucratic, capitalist deskskills' (ibid.: 3). In his excellent wide-ranging critique of modern technological culture, Sean Cubitt suggests that the WIMP system attempts to impose a normative behaviour (a 'normative visual vocabulary') upon the interpretive communities that use it. In this respect, he suggests, the North American interface purports a political 'vocabulary as powerful as colonial English'. Drawing upon writers such as Ranajit Guha, Cubitt introduces an argument that places the use of the WIMP (as well as the use of English as the standard language of the Internet) as a significant player in the longer history that has seen 'the geographical spread of English as a racist instrument of exploitation' (ibid.: 2). Effectively, Cubitt forges powerful links between the Windows operating system, capitalism and the cultures of colonialisation. Whether Cubitt's impassioned thesis is valid or not is open to debate. However, what is less contentious is the way in which his analysis demonstrates the critical apparatus we can assemble to identify the meanings of media. In short, Cubitt reminds us how to read new media critically in the museum.

Importantly, therefore, McLuhan and others alert us to how profoundly implicated and active media are to any act of communication – that a medium can send its own messages, that the medium is part of the message, and that, moreover, the reciprocity between medium and content is compounded in the use of modern media (such as digital media) where the act of communication is so instantaneous. For museums, museum studies and the study of digital media, these ideas seem particularly pertinent. Museums, after all, are a medium – in their most common state a unique, three-dimensional, multi-sensory, social medium in which knowledge is given spatial form. However, they are also themselves *full of* media. (To McLuhan the content of one medium is always another medium.) We might even go as far as to say that media define the museum. Through their histories museums have taken their varied shapes and functions from the communications technologies that they have chosen to deploy. In fact, it is difficult (if not impossible) to imagine a museum without media technologies of some description – be it text panel, display case, or gallery space. As soon as we accept museums in this way (as a medium), and recognise that it is media that make up the museum, we set in place assumptions that make possible certain ways of thinking about its communication technology. For instance, Macdonald reminds us how in the museum '[p]olitics lies not just in policy statements' but also in media such as 'glass cases or interactives, and the presence or lack of voice-over on a film' (1998: 3). This is the same point that attracts the attention of Wallace, as he warns us of the extent to which interactive displays 'can foster the illusion that a machine is providing value-free interpretations when of course it's presenting pre-programmed perspectives' (1995: 113). In their analyses, we begin to see the interactive machine in the gallery as a medium, and consequently far from value free. At once the media of the museum become something responsive to cultural and historical analysis. Suddenly, with this *agency* acknowledged, museum media are open to new levels of critical study. Consequently, for practitioners and students of museums the challenge today is not only to explore the potential of these new technologies (and how they might support or enhance current practice and provision), but also to identify and acknowledge the 'personal and social consequences' of their use. It is imperative that we ask ourselves, therefore, what the implications are of choosing to communicate and work with digital media in the museum. To do this, however, we need to discover the ideologies and assumptions that are connected with these media. This means understanding where this technology has come from and how it has developed. It is this line of enquiry that provides an important rationale for this book.

The narrative of this book

New media studies has also grappled with the extent to which any given new medium is reliant upon (derivative of) previous existing media, and/or to what extent it is 'remedial', an improvement on, and identifiably distinct from these older technologies (Lister et al. 2003: 53–5). Whatever stance writers on digital heritage may choose to adopt, understanding the properties of new media will be essential. Digital media are articulated with, and used according to, many of the modes and codes of existing technologies, but their qualities and applications are, to many commentators, unique. Flew, for instance, cites this uniqueness (in part) in new media's manipulability (how easy they are to adapt), networkability (how easily they can be shared), denseness (what little space their information occupies), compressibility (how this space can be reduced even further), and its impartiality (how indifferent new media are to what forms their digital information represents, who owns or created this information, or how it is used) (2002: 10–11). However, it is Lev Manovich (2001) who provides a seminal way of identifying, differentiating and articulating the qualities of new media. His 'principles', as he calls them, can provide a way of dismantling what digital media are, and more importantly what distinguishes them from other media. According to Manovich's schema, new media are *numerical, modular, automated, variable* and *transcoded*. New media are *numerical* in that they reduce our corporeal, four-dimensional world to a string of 1s and 0s. The continuum of our analogue experience is sampled to the granularity of a binary digit (ibid.: 28). New media, however, are also *modular* in that they are composed of discrete logical 'objects' with separate identities. These inherently independent and interchangeable blocks of content can then be assembled into 'media elements'. New media are *automated* in that, unlike some other media, they process data and can undertake certain assigned actions. In other words, new media have an inherent functionality and operational quality – the discipline is active, it does things. *Variability* means that, again, unlike many other media, new media have a mutable and 'liquid' quality (ibid.: 36). Their content, in other words, is rarely fixed and static but, rather, open to editing and reversioning. Manovich's last 'principle' is perhaps the most opaquely termed and most challenging of the five to grasp. Simply put, new media are involved in a process of *transcoding* in the way in which computers are shaped by society, and elements of society are shaped by the presence of computers. Like all technology, computers are a construct, historically and culturally contingent. They are, therefore, as part of culture coded (given meaning, referents, significance) by the cultures that use them. And, likewise, the values, actions and meanings within these same cultures can themselves be *coded* by the presence and usage of computers. Each has the capacity to code the other – hence *trans-coding*.

Crucially, it will be these five principles (of numerical, automated, modular, variable and transcoded new media) that will inform the assumptions, the language and the logic of this book. What will be presented here will not be a straight chronology – if indeed such a thing is possible for this subject. Nor are the chapters here differentiated by their choice of technology – foregrounding, as that would, the technology too much and making technology (rather than the institutions, practitioners and visitors) the protagonist. Neither will this be a book structured by museum type, subject disciplines, geographical location or some other arbitrary division. Instead, each chapter will take one of Manovich's principles and hold it up as a different frame, a different filter through which to watch the interplay between museum and computer. It will be through the five components of new media that some of the fundamental incompatibilities (the historic lack of fit) between the museum and the computer will begin to come into focus.

By way of context, Chapter 2 lays down some markers in the broad history of museum computing. By looking at the rise of computing in the 1960s, the building of a machine-readable catalogue in the library, the expansion in collections, the striving for a new professionalism and the influence of systematic thinking and philosophy, the chapter attempts to identify some of the reasons why the first adopters in the sector took to computing when they did and in the way they did. Taking the concept of 'automation' as its starting point, Chapter 3 compares the ways museums and computers process data. It suggests that the standardisation and systematisation of the new approach to computer-oriented documentation were sometimes inconsistent with the traditions of the 'creative cabinet', where the curator had been able to develop quite personalised and idiosyncratic methods for understanding and ordering a collection. It asks whether standards imposed an inelegant and unsympathetic homogeneity on collections description, whether these standards made certain (Linnaean) assumptions about the ordering of the world, and to what extent the demands of the machine were allowed to dictate practice. Chapter 4 takes its inspiration from the 'numerical' quality of new media. It sets out the ways in which museums have, through their histories, privileged the material world, and considers the extent to which this cultural materialism may have been at odds with the uncompromising granularity of the binary code that is the essence of computing. Some of the bi-polarities set up by the museum sector between 'real' and 'virtual' are unpacked, and the role of trust and authenticity, mimesis and simulacra in these dialogues is drawn out.

Subsequently, it is the principle of 'modularity' that helps to inform the approach taken in Chapter 5. Here, the centrifugal and localising qualities of Web content and the Web experience are contrasted with the credentials of the museum as a circumscribed experience centred on the visit event. The main part of the discussion relates to the mismatch between the traditional on-site museum as contained microcosm (as singular space), against the fragmentary and distributed characteristics of museums' new on-line channel. In Chapter 6 we fly across our subject yet again, but this time with the principle of 'variability' in mind. The chapter investigates the extent to which the liquid and editable qualities of digital media have been harnessed (or is that just tolerated?) within the physically and intellectually controlled environment of the museum – where fixity has always been prized. Here the discussion considers the receptiveness of the new museology (especially its emphasis on audience advocacy and visitor-centred design) to the coming of user-driven software and user-generated content. The last of Manovich's five principles – 'transcoding' – is used in Chapter 7 as the basis for a discussion on the ways the museum institution has coped, as an organisation, with the advent of computing. The discussion works through a number of the barriers that (in resource and organisational terms) have prevented computing from developing inside the museum: from the cost of the computers to the skills deficit of the workforce; from the time commitment needed to develop the new technical functions to the unreliability of the technology itself; and from the opaqueness of expert jargon to the 'factory culture' that came associated with automation. It considers the extent to which museums have (or have not) adapted their structures to accommodate new media, as well as the role played by increased collaboration, the development of strategy, the emergence of communities of practice, the provision of funding and the growth of confidence in the museum curator as 'informed customer'.

What emerges, in Chapter 8, is a museum recoded. By drawing out strands that run through the five preceding chapters, the book concludes by showing how any fissures or tensions between the concept of the computer and the concept of the museum have, in recent years, been moving to a point of resolution – of compatibility. It highlights how our notions of visit, of object, of collection, of expository space, of curatorial authority, have all become recodified (rescripted, recalibrated, disaggregated, and rewritten) by the presence and influence of four decades of digital technology.

However, to begin this long story of 'recoding' we must start by looking back to the 1960s as it is here that we can begin to identify the technologies and institutions, the people and places that were at the very beginning of museum computing.

2

From the 'day book' to the 'data bank'

The beginnings of museum computing

If we felt the need to give the history of museum automation a beginning, then perhaps the date might be 1963 and the place Washington, DC. Certainly, other forays in automation were also beginning around this time.[1] However, it was at this particular date and in this particular location that the then Director of the Museum of Natural History, Smithsonian Institution, appointed a scientific staff committee, chaired by Donald Squires, to develop through a series of meetings, consultations and training courses a 'general understanding of the potential of data processing for the museum community' (Smithsonian Institution 1967: 6; Squires 1969a: 2). Subsequently, in 1965 the Management Services Division of Peat, Marwick, Mitchell & Co. undertook a major study into the potential utilisation of computers by the Smithsonian Institution. The resulting report made specific recommendations for the development of a data processing system in the Museum of Natural History. Following this, in July 1967, the museum embarked upon a programme of research into the automation of documentation.[2] The work was carried out in conjunction with the newly founded Information Systems Division of the Smithsonian Institution and through the support of the Office of Education Department of Health, Education, and Welfare (Squires 1969a: 14). For the first 18-month phase of development the Smithsonian (1967) had requested $292,927 of federal funds. Essentially, the Smithsonian was attempting to understand whether it could apply computer technology to the management of museum collections and what the benefits might be. In its endeavour, the project used as its sample data, specimen records from the national collections of sea birds, marine crustaceans, and rocks. By January 1969 a data processing system had been developed and implemented, which included the standardisation of input procedures for cataloguing using punched paper tape units, as well as the creation of data entry and query software. By 1970, as the second of the two grants from the Office of Education was drawing to a close, personnel involved in the research and development were quick to ensure the legacy of the project. 'Your accomplishments', wrote Donald Squires to his team, 'are part of a task which is increasingly being recognised as a major accomplishment in the field of information storage and retrieval [. . .] there is now every reason to believe that our collective labors will bear fruit and that a major renovation is in store for the museum community' (1970). These not only proved, in the long term, to be somewhat prophetic words, but, more practically, this evidence (and no doubt this rhetoric) also had an impact on the museum's directorate.[3] For in that same year the National Museum of Natural History created its new Automatic Data Processing program, demonstrating a clear commitment by the museum to take this research and development further (Bridge 2005). Shaped by Reginald Creighton, the next more flexible iteration of the Smithsonian's system – SELGEM[4] – described itself as a collection of general purpose programs developed for information management. 'SELGEM can handle any type of information about anything', so one user manual explained, 'provided that it is organised according to some basic rules'.[5] By the mid-1970s the system consisted of about twenty-five computer programs written in COBOL. To run, it needed a minimum of four tape drives, 20,000 characters of core and a COBOL compiler. The Smithsonian was using a Honeywell 2015 computer, though other institutions running SELGEM used platforms such as IBM 360, CDC 3100, CDC 6400, UNIVAC 1110 and GE635. Once data had been submitted to the system (either through keypunch worksheets, or punched paper tape or typed according to conventions for machine-optic recognition of characters) the data could then be retrieved via indexes, occurrence tallies or even labels. From the USDA Forest Service to the University of Alaska, and from Florida State University to the University of Cape Town, by May 1972 the SELGEM system was being used in almost a dozen institutions across the US and beyond. By November 1974 this number had risen to around fifty – with the Museum of Natural History itself, by then, boasting over 2 million specimens referenced through the system (Creighton and King 1974). A year later the number of institutions using SELGEM was over sixty, and included institutions as varied and as dispersed as Arizona State Museum, the Field Museum of Natural History, Maine State Museum and the Museum of New Mexico. With its early start, innovation, thoroughness, productivity and substantial federal investment, the Smithsonian was probably justified, therefore, in claiming to government that it had 'assumed leadership in this area' (Smithsonian Institution 1967).

Unsurprisingly, by September 1968, the Smithsonian's work had caught the attention of the other major museum automation project that had also begun in the US in the late 1960s (Ellin 1968c). However, this was a project with its roots in New York, rather than in the capital, and aligned more self-consciously to humanities computing than with the natural sciences. This was the Museum Computer Network (MCN). The central force behind the MCN 'project' was the Institute for Computer Research in the Humanities (ICRH), part of New York University since 1963. Growing out of a small computing centre that had been established on the University Heights campus, it claimed to be the first group of its kind to combine (the then) new computer technology with research in the arts and humanities (Heller and Wasserman 1967: 1). Evidently undaunted by the complexities of applying the systematic processing of computing to the arts, Jack Heller and his team had already been working on linguistic and musical analysis, and had explored with faculty members the ways computing could assist in 'auto-abstracting and auto-describing'. Projects in the mid-1960s had included computer analysis of the works of Haydn, a study of tonality in the works of Corelli, stylistic analysis of works attributed to Defoe, and the collection and organisation of data related to London theatre (ibid.: 2). Seeking a sum of just over $2 million, a proposal dated 6 February 1967, written by Heller and his assistant, made it clear that the Institute had aspirations to be (and, more importantly, to be funded to be) 'the center of a humanities-oriented computer network, representing the most important organisations in the arts and humanities today' (ibid.: 5). Museums (including the Metropolitan Museum of Art, the Museum of Modern Art, and the Museum of Natural History, all cited in the proposal) were already part of Heller's vision for this humanities computing network. Crucially, it was New York University that had invited the museums. And by the spring of 1967, key members of the group had already realised that the project's success was reliant upon the role played by the ICRH and New York University: 'it is becoming increasingly clear to us', one member concluded, 'that our museum consortium would, in probability fall short of its goal without the financial and managerial assistance of NYU and the expertise of Jack Heller's group' (Ellin 1967c). The Museum Computer Network, at its inception, was, in other words, born from the higher education sector and computing – not from museums and curatorship.

With institutions pooling resources and sharing costs, the plan for the MCN was to establish a large computer known as the 'Data Bank Computing Center', located at the ICRH facility in the Bronx. The computer would be at the disposal of the group of museums in the New York area through a network of terminals. Indexes and catalogues of information stored in the data bank would then be compiled by the Institute. Unlike the birds, rocks and crustaceans being processed at the Smithsonian, the MCN looked instead to painting, sculpture and drawing. Specifically, the data bank was based on the works of Picasso (including 500 from the Museum of Modern Art; and a number from the Solomon R. Guggenheim Museum), Pre-Columbian Mexican stone sculpture (including some 600–1000 from the Museum of the American Indian/Heye Foundation; 50–60 pieces from the Brooklyn Museum; and 100 from the Museum of Primitive Art), and drawings (including 52 from the Frick Collection; approximately 600 from the Whitney Museum of American Art; 1740 from the National Gallery of Art; approximately 200 from the Jewish Museum; approximately 200 from the New York Historical Society; approximately 300 from the American Academy of Arts and Letters) (IBM and Ellin 1969: 1.7– 1.8). In time, and with the help of its original funding (from the Old Dominion Foundation and the New York State Council on the Arts), and with assistance from the Federal Systems Division of IBM, the focus of the network began to evolve and extend – addressing the creation of a nationwide information system for art museums, if not all museums.

> The sponsoring groups are convinced that, eventually, we must create a single information system which embraces all museum holdings in the United States (including those of science and history museums). Therefore,

this project is being approached with consideration of the requirements of interdisciplinary data compatibility.

(ibid.: 1.1)

One of the MCN's early workshops organised with the University of New York, had been held at the Metropolitan Museum of Art, and had considered data collection and data dissemination in museums. Typical of the new networks and connections that were being forged at this time through events such as this, one of the sessions in the workshop was run by a representative (John Cutbill) from the team at the University of Cambridge in the UK. Cutbill had been working with the UK Museums Association on standardisation and automation within collections management (Smithsonian Institution 1970: 1). The Cambridge work was already known not only to the MCN but also to the Smithsonian's team; in September 1969, just two years into their development, Donald Squires had visited Cutbill in Cambridge (Squires 1969b), and there was subsequent correspondence comparing the standards of the two systems; in fact, writing in November 1971, Cutbill was struck by the 'reassuring' similarities between the two standards being developed on either side of the Atlantic (1971a). Initially working with the 40,000 specimens that made up the collection of Lower Palaeozoic fossils in the Sedgwick Museum, Cutbill's attempts to develop general programs for files of specimen-oriented data had been running since 1967 (Crovello and MacDonald 1969). With 'extensive use of computers', his focus had been on introducing automatic data processing techniques into the management of geological data during research and into the subsequent communication of results (Cutbill 1971b: 2). Cutbill had received funding from the Office for Scientific and Technical Information (later the British Library Research and Development Department) to create software to document the Sedgwick collection. Hierarchically structured catalogue card information was typed on to to paper tapes, which were then read into a computer, and then produced into catalogues, indexes and collection statistics (Nuttall 2000: 4.1. iv). With the support of further (and larger) funding, Cutbill and the Sedgwick were then able to establish a computer-based cataloguing team for which a key focus was the development of a specification for a package that could be used more widely within the sector. Subsequently, the museum's existing internal computing system (the Cambridge Geological Data System) evolved into a system called GOS written in BCPL (Basic Combined Programming Language).

The work of the Sedgwick project (and the later emergence of GOS) became closely linked with another key development in automation and standardisation – the establishment of the Information Retrieval Group of the Museums Association (IRGMA). In the late 1960s and early 1970s the objective of IRGMA was the definition of a Museum Communication Format (MCF) (Cutbill 1970). This meant

creating an absolutely general information structure, able to accept information from any source in any machine-readable form, to combine such information with data from other sources, and to transmit it to any other system, subject only to the ability of the receiving system to accommodate that data.

(Vance 1973: 48)

From 1967 the steering committee looked at standardised classification and terminology for museums. Effectively a lobbying group attempting to make the Museums Association respond to the crisis in information retrieval that some practitioners saw (Lewis 2007), IRGMA generated two working parties. One looked at humanities, the other at natural science, but both – initially at least –worked towards the long-term goal of a standardised national index (Nuttall 2000: 4.1. ii). Essentially, IRGMA was attempting to form a single interdisciplinary system usable across museums with different sorts of collections (Ellin 1968a: 66). When it finally produced its results in 1969, crucially, it was not a piece of software, but a standards document that was presented to the sector. It described a data definition language, a simple syntax for how to hold information (Roberts 2005; Light 2005).

By 1967 a number of national museums in the UK were either considering the use or had already begun to use digital technology for the processing of collections data (Lewis 1967: 90). A year later, and even though they may have been 'separate and largely uncoordinated', there were at least fifty projects under way worldwide in the area of automation, standardisation and the machine-oriented systematisation of documentation (Ellin 1968a: 68). By 1978 it was observed (if, perhaps, by two advocates) that 'virtually everyone connected with museums seems to have developed a greatly increased awareness of the need for systematic documentation' (Chenhall and Homulos 1978: 43). The question is why this explosion of activity took place. What made museums suddenly move to 'automate' on this scale and in this way?

The rise of computing

From the early 1960s the business and research communities were beginning to confront the possibilities associated with a new form of resource in which many users were able to 'share' one main central computer seemingly at the same time and perhaps even with the convenience of a teletype machine at one's own desk. Despite the cost of long-distance telecommunications and problems over queuing and peak times for use, the 1960s marked a period when this concept of 'time sharing' was beginning to evolve from an academic concept and demonstrator to a viable commercial service, which in the right environment could be 'immensely useful' to curators (Peters and Collette 1968: 75). The promise for institutions involved in informational processing and retrieval, was that the cost, the time, and the inconvenience of using computer processing could (potentially) be renegotiated within a new digital environment. Equally significant was the arrival in 1964 of IBM's System/360, an event that radically altered the shape and reach of the computer market. The S/360 was essentially a family of six mainframe computers that, in their scalability, offered flexibility to organisations, including museums, which were entering, or contemplating entering, automation for the first time. For instance, James Sweeney's GIPSY program (a generalised information handling system) used from 1968 within the University of Oklahoma's inventory of ethnographic collections project, was written in IBM S/360 Assembler Language (Vance 1973: 49). Consequently, the landscape of data processing was changing, and governments were quick to realise that they needed new maps and new compasses. An unclassified report by the United Kingdom Atomic Energy Authority published in 1964 made it clear that national governments had already by that point been investigating, and in some cases applying, the use of computers in major reference-providing retrieval systems. As administrations sought to brief their professional and research communities on the way ahead, the overloading of existing search services, the opportunity to provide more layers of indexing to a body of information, the widening of potential uses of the current data and increased productivity were all established as factors favouring the use of computers (Barnes 1964).

Seeing these potentials, persuaded by these arguments, and (most importantly of all) gaining access to this equipment, many academic disciplines were, by the mid-1960s already exploring the potential of the new computational technologies. Computing had become particularly prevalent in the sciences. For instance, despite admitting that most palaeontologists, by 1969, did not have firsthand experience with computers and were not fully aware of the possibilities and limitations inherent in palaeontological computer applications, individuals from the US Geological Survey were enthusing on the potential of the new technology (Mello 1969). 'There is little doubt', Mello declared, 'that the computer will become a most potent tool in paleontology and that exploitation of this potential will give new impetus to paleontology for many years to come'. It was evident how a machine might allow for tedious or time-consuming tasks to be performed more efficiently. More significant, however, was the way in which a computer could allow for a much freer and more critical analysis of the structure of much palaeontological data which could lead, so it was thought, to the establishment of new levels of relationship (then indiscernible) between and among fossils (Mello 1969). Similar reasoning was being made in biology and its related subjects. As far back as 1958 the McLean Paleontological Laboratory in Alexandria, Virginia, had been developing a system for storing and retrieving biological, ecological and geological information. In time, these had involved the use of a 1401 Computer, 14,000 IBM cards and a number of Friden Flexowriter 8-channel tapes (Crovello and MacDonald 1969: 15). As early as 1959 the Bureau of Commercial Fisheries at the Exploratory Fishing and Gear Research Base in Pascagoula, Mississippi, had been working on utilising electronic data processing (Bullis 1967). From 1966 the Department of Botany and Plant Pathology at Michigan State University had been developing software systems for automating routine procedures involved in plant identification (Morse 1968). Supported by the Food and Agriculture Organization of the United Nations and the International Atomic Energy Commission, Washington State University had begun a project in 1965 to 'establish an international communication system for plant breeders, geneticists, explorers, curators, tax-onomists and others to disperse information about crop plants and related species'. The standardised systems and international crop data centre was being constructed with the help of an IBM 360/30 hardware configuration (Crovello and MacDonald 1969: 13). In South Africa, using an ICT 1301 computer, the Bolus Herbarium at the University of Cape Town had in 1967 begun a pro-ject to develop a Fortran IV-based system for identifying incomplete biological specimens in difficult groups for which specialists' advice was not available locally (ibid.: 10). The Herbario Nacional del Instituto de Biología at the Uni-versidad Nacional Autónoma de México, had from 1967 begun a project to encode taxonomic, ecological and geographical data in order to automate the recovery of information about specimens originating in the state of Veracruz (ibid.: 16). Evidently, in the late 1960s the Department of Herpetology at the American Museum of Natural History, New York, was also making use of elec-tronic hardware (including a 3M Uniprinter 086, 3M Reader-printer, and Telex machine) in the collation and production of data on reptile and amphibian col-lections (ibid.: 8). By 1969 at least forty major electronic data processing and information retrieval projects were running internationally in the area of bio-logical systematics.

Computers had been used in the humanities since the 1950s (Feeney and Ross 1993: 3). At New York University, Jack Heller (who would later become a museum computing pioneer) had in 1963–4 worked with Alice Pollin on a com-puter-assisted index to the *Revista de Filologia Espanola*. As Director of the Metropolitan Museum of Art, Thomas Hoving remarked how as far back as 1956, as a graduate student at Princeton, he had been thinking about the ways in which computer technology could be harnessed in the museum. On read-ing Norbert Wiener's book *The Human Use of Human Beings*, Hoving says he was struck by the thought that 'perhaps computers were better suited than the brain to deal with masses of fragmented material, to work out difficult schol-arly typologies and manuscript recensions, to help in the study of iconography and iconology' (1968: vii). If perhaps not on a par with the sciences, uptake and activity was at a level that by 1968 the IBM Corporation was describing computers as a 'well-established if not indispensable tool' for certain types of problems within the humanities (Bowles 1968: xv).

Many curators, therefore, were part of research communities in which comput-ers were being adopted. And yet, as if to waylay concerns over technology-led innovation (or innovation for innovation's sake) museums, at this time, were surprisingly cautious at foregrounding the computer as a driving factor in the coming of automation. Frequently, the rise of automation in the late 1960s was presented as computer-*assisted*, rather than computer-*led* change. There was reference to the 'coincident strides' in adapting the computer to the diverse requirements of the museum profession (Ellin 1968a: 65). Some looked back on how 'fortunately' a new tool had appeared to make the need for system-atic documentation of museum collections economically feasible (Chenhall and Homulos 1978: 43). To others this was a 'coming together' (Roberts 2005) of a drive to standardise and systematise, to make cataloguing more efficient and ordered, with the arrival of more affordable and programmable computing. Computers were the 'opportunity for people to do what they wanted to do [. . .] the tool that would allow the ideas to be put into place' (ibid.). And yet, it was undeniable that the computer had opened up possibilities of processing information more efficiently in ways that would have been undreamt of with earlier techniques (Light 2005). 'Some of the intricate problems of our time', gushed Hoving, 'can be analysed instantaneously by computers' (1968: vii). The appearance and promise of new computer technology itself was, of course, key to the new automation. However, this was by no means the only factor that explains why museum computing emerged at just this time and in the way it did.

Machine-readable catalogues in the library sector

Another influence on museums in the mid-1960s, that helps to explain the sector's adoption of computing, was the emergence of new machine-readable standards in libraries. At just the same time, in the mid- to late 1960s, that museums around the world felt moved to explore automation, new international standards were emerging for the interchange of computer-based information in the library sector. From the mid-1960s the library sector was working in a co-ordinated way in assessing the feasibility of standardisation, central preparation, and distribution, as well as the desirability of certain bibliographic and machine features of the record (Library of Congress 1966: 2). The machine-readable catalogue (MARC) pilot project came from a series of studies that had investigated the possibilities of transferring cataloguing data to machine-readable form. Pulling together representatives from the higher education sector, private industry, and from government, a conference held in January 1965 reached the conclusion that the Library of Congress should proceed in developing a machine-readable format for use in supplying cataloguing information on magnetic tape (Information Systems Office 1968: 1). Significantly, this development had the new computer technology at its core. Computer functionality was a key determinant of the design of the standard:

> The concept of a man–machine dialogue with a central store of bibliographical information is an area which requires a great deal of further study. The requirements of such a dialogue will certainly influence the final system design.
>
> (Library of Congress 1965: 11)

In the two or three years prior to the work of the Smithsonian, MCN and IRGMA, the MARC systems development in the US had placed computers at the front of this development. In the preliminary work three Library of Congress staff members were delegated to analyse cataloguing data 'from a machine processing viewpoint' (Information Systems Office 1968); MARC was at its birth machine-led and computer oriented. Libraries were, of course, presented with a different problem. For libraries it was largely the conspicuous information of the title page that needed to be captured, and once written a record was largely static. Contrastingly, in museums a record had to keep reflecting the ongoing knowledge about that item. Museums had unique objects, not standard and duplicated items. And museums (unlike libraries) needed to document the history and the meanings of that object. As the Smithsonian's information retrieval project would later explain to its funders, 'unlike a book which is written, bound and shelved, specimen data is continually enriched by subsequent study and the importance of the specimen increases almost geometrically with its utilisation' (1968a: 6).[6] Furthermore, MARC itself was a standard for input methods. It did not represent the 'hard and fast design for data within an actual computer memory' – the information architecture (Library of Congress 1965). And yet, libraries were demonstrating to museums how new technology could be brought into play, and what standards, underlying that new technology, needed to be built. They showed museums how it could be done and the value of doing it. Moreover, these discussions in the library sector were taking place under the noses of those individuals and those institutions that at the time were leading museum automation. The Fourth Conference discussing the MARC pilot project took place in Washington, DC at the Library of Congress on 4 December 1967. It was here that Quincy Mumford (the Librarian of Congress) had announced that MARC had been received enthusiastically by the library community in the US and abroad, and that consequently records on magnetic tape were expected to be available on a subscription within eight months (Library of Congress 1968: i). Less than a mile away from Mumford as he made his announcement on this key development in the utilisation of machine-readable cataloguing, the government-funded pilot project into information retrieval of museum specimen records at the National Museum of Natural History was already under way. And certainly, the Smithsonian had already acknowledged how a computerised system of collection management was essential not only to the efficient utilisation of museum resources but also as 'an interface' (as it called it) with conventional libraries and other subject-oriented facilities (Smithsonian Institution 1967: 2).

Museums' needs may have been quite different from those of libraries, and by 1968 their paths may have diverged. They may also have said little (and looking back remember little) of the influence of libraries on the move to standardisation (Bridge 2005; Lewis 2007; Roberts 2005; Sledge 2005). And yet, the thought processes that developed MARC shared a heritage with the pioneering work in museum computing. Back in 1965 they were part of the same conversations – with archives and with other research institutions – on the potential of the new computational technology (Bearman 2007). The difference was that libraries already had a registration data standard and an established practice of producing a unified catalogue dating back to the early decades of the twentieth century. Consequently, when the technology developed sufficient capacity to process these catalogues in a helpful and meaningful way, libraries had the pre-existing practice that simply allowed them to move quicker and more decisively.

Expanding collections

However, whereas the influence of the library sector may have been a more subtle external influence, there was also a more conspicuous driver (in the building) pushing museums to automation. This was the expansion in collections and, in some quarters, an increased loss of control over their management (Ellin 1969: 25). The 1960s and 1970s were a period of 'considerable flow' (Pearce 2005) in acquisitions, with certain types of collections growing at an accelerating rate. In the United States both the civil rights movement and the women's movement had a bearing upon how social history was beginning to be viewed and evidenced, as attention turned to stories that had never been collected (Ray 2005). At this time, whether through the new Marxist histories 'from below', or the social interest of the *Annales* generation, the way history was written, who got to write history, and the focus that history took, were all being negotiated, effecting not only history making (historiography) in the museum but also what could and should be collected by curators (Hunt 1989: 1–4). American history generally, and the Smithsonian in particular, experienced an 'explosion of collections' in the early 1970s, as it prepared to showcase the United States bicentennial in 1976 (Schaefer-Jacobs 2005). Consequently, there had to be ways to document and manage that tide of new acquisitions (both collected and donated) flooding into institutions such as the National Museum of American History at this time.

Changes were also taking place in the field of archaeology that were having implications for the size of museum collections. An explosion in excavation work in the UK had been driven, in part, by the sudden arrival in the 1960s of young graduates with archaeology degrees, a product of the expansion in higher education that had taken place in Britain at that time (Pearce 2005). Equally important was the rescue movement. The pace of 1960s development (new houses, new roads, new trading estates) as well as the innovation and growth of deep ploughing, all posed a threat to archaeological heritage. One response was a tremendous drive to excavate sites before they were developed and before that heritage disappeared (Pearce 2005; Lewis 2007). Not only did this mark the beginning of field units in archaeology (many of which were attached to museums, or were run by curators of archaeology), but it precipitated the accumulation of more artefacts for museum collections. At the same time, curators in the natural sciences were also reporting on their collections 'growing at a rapid rate' (Manning 1969: 671). The sharp increase in the numbers of specimens being housed by many museums was in part attributed to 'the thrusts of today's larger science' (Squires 1969a: 5). Furthermore, the 1960s 'literature explosion' within the scientific community had meant that the natural sciences were experiencing an increase not just in the number of specimens, but in the accumulation of data associated with individual specimens (Smithsonian Institution 1968a: 6). Significantly, the Smithsonian's original application for federal funds to support their development of an automated information storage and retrieval system had painted a vivid picture to the US Commissioner of Education of 'the acceleration of today's scientific effort and resulting enormous increase in size of collections' (Smithsonian Institution 1967). It was estimated that by 1969 the Smithsonian's Department of Invertebrate Zoology alone was experiencing an annual increase in collections of 200,000 specimens (Manning 1969: 671). Startlingly, as an institution as a whole it was understood that the collection was growing by the rate of about one million specimens each year (Creighton and King 1969: 3).

The result of this continued growth was that some museum holdings were expanding beyond control. A report charged with reviewing the state of the information management in one institution alerted its director to how 'the danger of museums withering is reaching a crisis stage' (Kochen et al. 1970: 7). Using the traditional cataloguing methods at their disposal, by the late 1960s, many museums were finding it increasingly difficult to keep proper records of their own holdings; 'it is a prodigious effort', reported the Museum Computer Network in its first press release announcing its establishment, 'to conduct even the simplest study of a given body of material' (Ellin 1967d). Other museums went from new accessions being well documented to a period when in some cases large numbers of objects (particularly within social history) were coming into the museum with curators having no time to document them thoroughly (Roberts 2005). In many instances museums were finding that manual cross-referenced files were not adequate to keep pace with the rapidly growing collections (Smithsonian Institution 1967: 4). To some, therefore, information loss was probably at its greatest (Smithsonian Institution 1968a: 6). Already 'badly behind in documenting' their collections, museums were suddenly being confronted with larger backlogs than ever before – backlogs that many museums would then spend the next twenty years trying to eliminate (ibid.: 3). Addressing the Federal Government in October 1968, the Smithsonian Institution painted a bleak picture of how 'museum personnel may not fully understand the dimensions of their own despair, so fully submerged in the bewildering backlogs are its curators' (1968a: 6). It was, therefore, into this 'crisis' and 'despair' that the computer appeared.

> In an effort both to keep abreast of the information relating to their expanding collections and improve their research and educational services, museums everywhere are looking in increasing numbers to computer technologies for the storage and manipulation of the data to be found in their libraries, files and catalogues.
>
> (Ellin 1968a: 65)

By the late 1960s it was already understood by government and the research community that the most promising applications for computers, at least in the field of information retrieval, was where the information threatened to outgrow the existing filing methods (Barnes 1964: 21). In short, many museum collections were in trouble, and computers provided the promise of part of the solution.

New demands and new audiences

However, when the Smithsonian Institution submitted its proposal for substantial public investment into the development of its automated information retrieval system in 1967 (and then again in 1968) the expansion of collections was only part of its rationale. An important plank of its case, in fact, was 'access'. Automated collections, it was argued, would 'permit greater accessibility of fundamental resource materials of specimens and related data to students at all levels as well as senior scholars' (Smithsonian Institution 1967). Evidenced by the growth in loans requests being made to the museum, the Smithsonian stressed how it was being called upon to supply more information to the academic community than ever before (1968a: 3). By the late 1960s the increasing costs of collection upkeep had also forced many educational institutions, in the US at least, to abandon the study collections amassed during years of collecting. Part of the early development of automation was, consequently, justified in terms of making information about the Smithsonian collections more accessible to these educational audiences who were finding such resources becoming less accessible in many university museums (Squires 1969a: 5). Later, when reporting in 1969 to the US Government's Department of Health, Education, and Welfare on the progress of their research and development into collection automation, the Smithsonian again stressed that a key motive for their work was the objective 'to make the information about these specimens more accessible through data processing'. It was, therefore, 'the requirements of the student, the researcher or other requester' that were (apparently) shaping the system specification (Squires 1969a: 6). Like other museums, the Smithsonian were becoming acutely aware of the 'vital role' they had to play in the communities they served, and the responsibility, consequently, they had to make their collections accessible (Bowles 1968: xix). Addressing a meeting of the International Council of Museums in ICOM Munich, in August 1968, Everett Ellin had been unequivocal on the link between the current state of collections documentation and museums' responsibilities for public access:

> As museum audiences everywhere continue to grow, we are coming to recognise that the textual and visual data descriptive of our public collections of art and of scientific and historical material must be made more accessible and employed in far more imaginative ways than are possible by conventional means. Museums are fast approaching the point of stagnation in serving their own requirements for information, not to mention the intensified demands made of them by the scholarly community and the public.
>
> (Ellin 1968a: 65)

Museums now found themselves within a new climate of accountability; this was the moment when the shift began from the curator as researcher with 'their' collections, to the curator holding the collection in trust for a public who really had a right to know. A concern to give access to information about the collections went hand-in-hand with major developments in the sector that were beginning at this time in some parts of the world. In the UK there would follow a period of major government changes, local authority restructuring (with the consolidation of museums into bigger units), increasing pressure on national bodies to demonstrate value for money and relevance, a considerable increase in size and staffing of the organisations, the beginning of specialisation, and the great increase in the awareness of how valuable museums could be as an educational resource (Roberts 2005). The pressure (the 'problem' as it was called by some) was to provide access to the collection and information about that collection, to those other than the curator, in a timely and accurate manner (Smithsonian Institution 1967: 7).

In the late 1960s museums were operating in a time of considerable social change. In its first interim report to its funders, the Museum Computer Network described the 'inability of the museum community to serve its own needs for information or the intensified demands of a society attuned to new modes of communication' (Ellin 1968b). As they tried to respond to this change, museums soon came to realise that their mechanisms for managing and retrieving information on the things they collected were sadly wanting. And, again, automation and computing appeared to present an answer.

The new professionalism

The problem was that many museums had scanty documentation and, with the lack of any enforced standards, a great deal of trust was bestowed upon the conscientiousness of individual curators (Lewis 2007; Philips 2005). In the early 1970s a provincial museum might contain mostly handwritten records, to a large extent personal notes and not necessarily organised thoughts or ideas observing a particular form or format (Sledge 2005). Even among some of the larger museum institutions, by the late 1960s there was a perception that the current methods of record keeping were not adequate for a vast information resource such as a museum (Manning 1969: 671). Some museums were confronted with a chaotic situation; an internal appraisal of one national collection in the United States in 1967 had concluded that a professional approach has been lacking, and methods used could be described as 'amateurish' or 'antiquated'. 'It would seem', the report concluded, 'that x number of people, keeping records in y number of ways, for z number of years leads inevitably to x times y times z or a sort of geometric progression toward chaos' (Ruffin 1967: 3). Museum records were missing key information. There were ambiguities over the information entered, duplication of catalogue cards, only occasional cross-referencing, missing cards, or cards for which objects were missing (ibid.: 6). More specifically, there were profound difficulties in accessing collections on a multi-disciplinary basis. Reflecting back on the experience of working with archaeological collections in the mid-1960s, Geoffrey Lewis (the key force behind the UK's move to standardisation) recalls where the shortfalls frequently were to be found:

> Your card indexes were inevitably structured to a certain concept, which was quite often, in an archaeological sense, chronological. Whereas enquiries would typically come with a location priority. In those cases you simply could not answer the query from your documentation.
>
> (2005)

Consequently, museums were becoming aware of how low their standards of documentation were. During the initial period of development (in the late 1960s) into automation and standardisation at the Smithsonian, investigators reported on the significant amount of collections data that was simply not being recorded due to (as they put it somewhat colourfully) 'the inability of existing systems to capture data and because of the complete breakdown of existing retrieval systems (the curators)' (Squires 1969a: 13). Quite simply, for institutions such as the Smithsonian there was a perception, even before the technology was a reality, that machine-based data entry and information retrieval systems would improve data acquisition procedures by museum curators, which, it was thought, would lead to better and greater use of collections in both education and research. Certainly, by the mid-1970s, and the time it was marketing its SELGEM information management system, the Smithsonian had developed a persuasive 'pitch' to the museum community on the importance of automated processes for locating a specimen from a catalogue card or ledger entry; for the preservation of collections data; for making accurate statements about the collections' condition; for determining the economic feasibility of collections-based research; and even for space planning. In the UK this necessity and willingness to collaborate in order to solve the problem and improve collectively as a sector was captured by Lewis in a rallying call in a paper in the *Museums Journal* in 1965. Highlighting the 'urgent need for a national lead in the standardisation of museum indexing', Lewis articulated how the need for an efficient method of obtaining information from museum collections could not be overstressed (1965: 21–2). The colloquium of thirty-nine practitioners and researchers that followed two years later (Lewis 1967: 90) led to the forming of a working group by the UK Museums Association to see how museums could work together to improve the way in which they retrieved information. Although a kind of professionalism had existed and flourished already in museums, what Lewis and others were instigating was part of a new 'managerialism' and a common sense of responsibility by museums for the collections that were entrusted to them. However, some of the conversations that took place and some of the personnel who were invited to these early discussions were as much concerned with new digital technology as they were about standards, inventories and accountability. As it reflected on Lewis's challenge, and began to frame its response, the group listened to presentations on 'computer printout indexes', 'the automatic typewriter' and 'Flexowriters'. Crucially, this vision of professionalism and managerialism was, already by 1967, envisaging a role for the state-of-the-art in information processing. The computer was already in the room.

Systematic philosophy

The new computing appeared to offer the order, efficiency and processing power that museums required as they struggled to cope with ever-increasing accessions as well as the more complex demands being made on their growing collections. For museum communities that had the resources, commitment and information to pursue them, computers were the obvious candidate – the right tool for the job. However, while this might all be evidential, we might also argue for another, but less expedient and perhaps more conceptual explanation as to why at just this time museums sought to order and systematise their management of collections in the way they did. It may, in other words, be relevant here to consider also the ways in which many academic disciplines in many societies were, just at this time, reflecting on *the order of things*. It is important to remember that the 1960s was a period in which a number of deeply influential schools of philosophy and academic practice were addressing the ways scholars (if not society) conceptualised the production of knowledge. This, for instance, was a key moment in the development of systems analysis and the building of systemic over-views of the world through the application of mathematical methods. Likewise, under the influence of General Systems Theory, the positivism of the 'New Archaeology' was defining the social world in a systemic way. Archaeologists in this new school saw a society (its institutions, its knowledge base) as something that could be categorised. Inductively or deductively, societies, and the fragments of those societies, could then be mapped out and linked. A consequence of these assumptions was a form of working in which data were assiduously recorded in order to be processed and patterned, in order for conclusions to be extrapolated.

Beside (although not consistent with) these tabulating, systemic and quantifying approaches of the new systems thinking stood 'structuralism'. At first in the French-speaking world, but soon afterwards in Anglo-Saxon discourse as well, the mid- to late 1960s witnessed a revolution in philosophical thought, specifically in ways of thinking about meaning. We can comfortably identify a moment, just at this time, when philosophers, inspired by linguistic metaphors and linguistic ideas, were trying to understand patterns of thought and patterns of meaning. It was a moment when the technologies of modern linguistic science were applied to cultural studies (Burgin 1996). In a sense, interested in words and in the systemic nature of language, the prevailing philosophical thought of the time was looking at the world through a certain lens, 'setting certain problems to do with structure, to do with pattern, to do with, essentially, the rules of being human' (Pearce 2005). Although profoundly different philosophically, the systemic thinking (of systems analysis and the new archaeology) and structuralism shared a predisposition to naming and patterning (Radford and Radford 2005). What catches the historian's eye is how these both become compelling ways of thinking (and ways of studying), at just the same time as the museum sector began to think about its collections in a profoundly more systemic and systematic way. Museums sought new standards, designed new automated systems. Museums began to think in terms of patterns, reducing

Figure 2.1 Butterfly collection, Eton College Museum. Copyright 24 Hour Museum.

parts of curatorial work to a naming exercise. They tried, in a sense, to find the logic within the collections. As if in tune with these pervasive *modi operandi*, museums began systematising their understanding of collections through term lists and thesauri just as the dominant philosophical traditions were using the systems of language to understand meaning-making. Or to put it another way: when we step back and view five hundred years of museums using different ways of keeping in control of their collections (whether through curatorial memory, the drawers of a cabinet, or the physical proximity of objects to one another), the act of reducing collections to hierarchies, of imposing data control or standardising data entry, of containing documentation to specific codes and terms, does all seem a peculiarly late twentieth-century solution to the production of knowledge.

Such connections remain, of course, elusive to the materialist historian searching for hard evidence (although it is noteworthy that one of the three dozen curators and researchers who attended the landmark colloquium in 1967 that set the British museum practice on a trajectory to standardisation and automation was Colin Renfrew – one of the architects of the systematising 'new archaeology' (Renfrew 1967)). Perhaps what we can conclude with more confidence, however, is that this interplay of information science, systematics, new archaeology and structuralist modes of thought – and, crucially, the assumptions that each made about naming, patterning and ordering – provided the intellectual backdrop to the formation of the new collections management. At the very least, these tantalising connections between philosophy, curatorship and computing might remind us of the sometimes creative and unexpected lines of enquiry that our thinking should be prepared to follow in its attempts to present the many facets of museum computing.

3

Disaggregating the collection

The museum as creative cabinet: idiosyncrasy and 'enigma'

In his 1958 series of essays *Brave New World Revisited*, Aldous Huxley described a primary and fundamental urge of the human mind to 'bring harmony out of dissonance and unity out of multiplicity'. He called this intellectual instinct the 'Will to Order' (1994: 30). Looking through history we can identify countless examples, in different times and different places, of individuals and communities using visual and physical technologies in order to find or fix order on their world, seeking the harmony and unity to which Huxley referred. To look, for instance, at the Sephirot of Jewish mysticism is to see at first a complex schema of ten circles interconnected by thirty-two lines. However, it is also to witness one faith community capturing and presenting the all-encompassing elements of its physical and metaphysical life, and the secret paths within them that lead to wisdom. This is an instantiation, in one sense, of 'systematic' thought (Manguel 1996: 8). Likewise, to look at a twelfth-century kinship table is to see one historically and geographically localised community attempting to determine possible consanguinity between marriage suitors by means of a horizontally and vertically tabulated schema. Here again, an individual's sense of identity (in this case defined in terms of blood-line and genealogy) is given order through a standardised and visual system (Duby 1988: 118–19). Equally, the 'reading wheel', as conceived by Agostino Ramelli (1987) in the late sixteenth century, was essentially a desk attached to a rotating series of hinged shelves each carrying a different book. In a practical sense it represented an ingenious solution to the proliferation of reading and ownership of books that followed the invention of the moveable typeface and printing press at the end of the fifteenth century. And yet, it is also a system, a technology, for containing and ordering the expansion in the printed word that took place at that time; it was an active desktop, an information management system. Similarly, to look at the intricacies of one of Robert Fludd's seventeenth-century concentric ring images is to glimpse a historical moment where intelligent society thought it could diagram all that was to be known in art and nature, in heaven and earth. However, what we also see is a portable mnemonic – a memory system, reducing all experience and knowledge to an ordered, condensed and memorable form (Belsey and Belsey 1990). In these examples (and others like them) sometimes the order is imposed, sometimes it is discovered. Sometimes it is used to remember, sometimes to control. Sometimes it is linear, circular or tabular; sometimes it is three-dimensional, sometimes physical, and sometimes mental. But in every case we see a culture attempting to make sense of its material surroundings, its knowledge and its experience, by containing them within a closed, ordered and logical system.

Museums belong to this history of structured knowledge. In a sense the museum project represents the endeavour of many societies, in their own time and cultural context, to extract and then give meaning to fragments of their past and present. Antonio Giganti's museum in Bologna, in the second half of the sixteenth century, managed the placement of objects and the arrangement of exhibition space according to rules of visual symmetry (Laurencich-Minelli 1985: 19).[1] We even find co-ordinating schemes based on colour; the cupboards that dominated the Kunstkammer in Ambras were organised partly under a colour-coded system, with different materials corresponding to (and, aesthetically, being complemented by) different background colours within eight of the eighteen cupboards (Scheicher 1985: 31). Museums' systems for ordering may vary from period to period, culture to culture, discipline to discipline (Murray 1904: 211–15). But whatever the details of their ordering principles might be, museums, by definition, gain their shape and identity through these rationales of collecting, storing and displaying objects. Consequently, it is very difficult – if not impossible – to think about museums without thinking about classificatory and ordering systems. In a sense, the museum represents just another instantiation of Huxley's 'Will to Order'.

This influence of information schemes and information technologies over space is seen as vividly within the institution whose history intertwines with that of the museum – the library. Like the history of the museum, that of the library is characterised by reading and display technologies guiding the hand of the architect and librarian alike. From the totalising compass of the library of Alexandria (its collection representing, in the words of one editor, 'the memory of the world'), to the voluminous seventh-century library of Isidore, Bishop of Seville (with its fourteen presses, all with portrait-busts and verses above them), and to the seventeenth-century library of the University of Leiden (with its bookcases labelled and organised into subjects such as 'Philosophi' and 'Mathematici'), we can trace a story of space shaped by information and communication technologies (Manguel 1996: 189; Clark 1894: 55 and 45). These pre-modern spaces were designed and contrived with the functions of information management technologies (such as reading wheels, rotating desks and chained books) in mind (Black 1996: 248). Though perhaps not on the scale as that which had seen the emergence of the great Italian collections (such as that compiled by the Duke of Urbino at the end of the fifteenth century), it was in the seventeenth century that countries such as England witnessed a flourishing of libraries. By the 1650s individuals such as Sir Henry Chetham were bequeathing prodigious amounts for the single purpose of setting up libraries. In Chetham's case, the £15,139 left by him 'for the use of scholars and others well affected' made provision for a substantial public resource, with its first holdings including works by Calvin, Aristophanes, Camden, Galen, Euclid, Aristotle, Galileo, Copernicus and Kepler, as well as texts such as Walter Raleigh's *History of the World* and Francis Bacon's *Advancement of Learning*. Much later in the century a visitor described the large library with its

> 2 long walls full of books on each side there is also the globes at the end and maps, there is alsoe a long whispering trumpet and there I saw the skinn of the Rattle Snake 6 foote long with many other Curiositys, their anatomy of a man wired together, a jaw of a sherk; there was a very fine clock and weather glass.
>
> (Fiennes 1888)

What visitor Celia Fiennes saw was an exemplary library, containing the seminal texts on history and science of the period, amid the other accoutrements of this assembled knowledge. This was not simply a repository of books, but a space of knowledge – the 'Curiositys' a tangible manifestation of the ideas contained within the volumes, a testimony to the accomplished learning they contained. As much as the objects endorsed and advertised the knowledge within the books, so the books provided the evidence, rationales, contexts and interpretation for the objects. A similar proximity of printed material to objects characterised the library of the co-founder of the Society of Antiquaries, Sir Robert Cotton. Cotton set his collection of coins and inscribed stones among the presses of his four hundred or so books (Sharpe 1979: 66–7). Through this arrangement Cotton was 'assembling a library in which each of these various forms was expected to complement the others' (McKitterick 1997: 105). By 1622 Cotton's library had settled in a narrow room thirty-seven feet by six feet in a house next to the Palace of Westminster, and by the time of his death in 1631, the library was ordered into thirteen presses (*scriniae*) with up to six shelves (*classes*) per press (Sharpe 1979).[2] Though a full subject catalogue was not produced until 1674, Colin Tite (1994) has argued persuasively for Cotton's direct involvement in a completed classificatory system as early as 1626. Subsequently, Tite has suggested that a manuscript held in the British Library made up of a series of strips cut up from a larger sheet, is, in fact, the catalogue for Cotton's collection of printed books. The taxonomy reduces the collection to subjects such as: 'Religio', 'Historia Ecclesiastica', 'Politicae', 'Ethicae', 'Astronomia' and 'Chronologiae'.[3] If the collection was as comprehensive and as ordered as Sharpe's initial research and Tite's more recent findings suggest, then it comes as no surprise that Cotton's library was a mainstay of the Jacobean cognoscenti. Even the king and queen borrowed from the collection.[4] It is likely that the king and queen's own collections were also organised according to a royal classification system used since the time of Henry VIII. The system involved the formation of an alphabetical inventory of books (both printed and manuscript) against which a corresponding number was set. By the early seventeenth century, however, library classification was being transformed by the work of Frenchmen Pierre and Jacques Dupuy, and Gabriel Naude, the librarian of Cardinal Mazarin and author of a treatise entitled *Advis pour dresser une bibliothèque*. Influenced by these new continental methods individuals such as John Evelyn set about establishing private libraries based upon fully comprehensive classification systems for organising knowledge (Homans et al. 1995: 168–9). Encyclopaedic projects such as this rendered the private library as a tangible manifestation of the structures of an individual's personal thought.

Therefore, whether through the new ordered presses of the king and queen, or through the (then) modern continental approaches to library classification shaping the collections of Evelyn, or even through the complementary relationships set up between texts and objects (as exhibited in the libraries of Cotton and Chetham), these organised reading systems were in each case presenting (to use Alberto Manguel's phrase) a 'nursery universe in which everything has its place and is defined by it' (Manguel 1996: 199). Much as in the (cognate) cabinets of curiosity, these libraries of early modernity were being categorised and systemised, then realised in physical space. In its most extreme form, this sort of knowledge architectonics would give rise to something on the scale of the oddities such as that produced by Giulio Camillo for Francis I. However, whereas Camillo's 'Memory Theatre' (a wooden model based on a Vitruvian-like theatre that provided *loci* within which the spectator could apparently read off at one glance the whole contents of the universe[5]) the libraries of England's intellectual elite drew less upon hermetic codes, and more upon the classificatory rigour that within a century would help shape the scientific programme of the Royal Society.

Three hundred years later, England's libraries reoriented their practices and spaces yet again as they imported (from the United States) other new technologies for managing their information – this time the Dewey Decimal Classification and the concept of 'open access' (Black 1996: 202–4). Significantly, it was the information management technology – the inventory systems, the presses – upon which they were centred that affected the arrangement and appearance of these spaces. In many ways, the history of our library spaces can be written and read as a 'conquest of space' by these technologies (Irwin 1958: 5). And – in common with the library – it is the technologies of display and information management that have, likewise, been inherent within the museum. It is these technologies (colour, symmetry, alphabet, numerical progression) that have provided rationalising schemes for the arrangement of museum objects. These technologies have become an essential element of what a museum is.

Moreover, working with schemes, museums had become places where scholars and curators could collect and construct in three dimensions theses and views on the world. As it was difficult to build multiple indexes of collections, the way, typically, a curator built taxonomy or typology was by proximiating objects to one another. Consequently, when a collection was interrogated – when 'information retrieval' was performed – a curator was not at a desk looking at a screen, or in front of a filing cabinet, but instead was physically moving within that collection. The practices of documentation may have been methodical but, more often than not, they were also idiosyncratic, required a considerable amount of human intervention and had very few outputs (Roberts 2005). Both the evidence they amassed, and the indexing and cataloguing systems they built to marshal this evidence were invariably personalised and localised. In fact, so overwhelming was the variety and colour of these creative documentation practices that by 1967, when one employee of the Smithsonian was charged to review the records management of the institution, her final report drew attention to this fact in no uncertain terms. 'As of now,' she concluded, '[the museum's] records, taken as whole, can only be described as an awesome enigma' (Ruffin 1967).

It was, therefore, this 'enigma' into which the order and logic of computer technology entered from the late 1960s onwards. The new managerialism that characterised the workplaces of the 1970s, museums' drive to improve their access and accountability, the curatorial and logistical pressures that accompanied the rise in acquisitions, the increased use of computers in many research disciplines, and the advances in the use of digital technology within the library sector, had all contributed to the innovations in standardisation, systematisation and automation within the museum. Unfortunately, this was not to be a bloodless revolution. Advocates for the new automation were frequently confronted with resistance, reluctance and inertia within their organisations. When automation was still in its infancy, the team at the Smithsonian's National Museum of Natural History found their colleagues 'generally unenthusiastic', and even discussions with groups who would potentially be more receptive had been 'inconclusive' (Smithsonian Institution 1967: 6). Advocates in the organisation published papers on the problems of dealing with the 'antipathy of museum curators toward mechanization and modernization' – and antipathy, it was concluded, built largely on fears 'often poorly understood' (Squires 1966: 216). Just yards away, at the Museum of History and Technology, other discussions with curatorial staff over the potential computerisation of collection records and exchange of information across the institution were – with a few exceptions – met by a lukewarm response. Evidently, many curators 'preferred to obtain information of this kind, when it was necessary, by personal contact' (Ruffin 1967: 9). Others found many of their research and communication needs already adequately met by existing media such as journals and published catalogues. At the Sedgwick Museum in Cambridge (at the vanguard of the new automation in the UK) the local impact of its innovation ultimately was mixed: 'when we finished the three year project, and we had racks of magnetic tape containing the Sedgwick's holdings, by and large the curators ignored it', was one developer's recollection, 'they just used the manual system' (Light 2005). To be fair, the Sedgwick project had been, to a great extent, an experiment – a research project exploring and testing how computers might cross-reference museum information in hierarchically organised ways. And yet, this response, and those that other projects experienced elsewhere, were symptomatic of a more widespread reticence to the new automation. Clues to why this reticence occurred can be found in the way parts of the sector responded to the emergence of standardised ways of working, how it questioned some of the assumptions that lay behind some of the structures being advocated, and how it reacted to the concept of a machine determining aspects of curatorial practice.

Were standards homogenising curatorship?

Automation came hand-in-hand with standards. Standardisation in knowledge capture delivered not only the parity and clarity of the new professionalism within the sector, but also the predictability that computer processing required. Therefore, it was standards that stood at the heart of the new systematisation of collections management. 'Standardization', explained Gautier, was about 'getting one's house in order to meet some need for better acquisition, organization and accessibility of data' (1976: 1). Indeed, the case for standards continues to be powerfully made. To many strategists, the development of workable, sensitive, shared standards in information management and computing remains central to the success and sustainability of museums (Poole 2007: 5). If developed well (with a clear vision of what the outcomes are intended to be, and balancing benefits against risks), a standard and a standard-based strategy can

> help individual museums acquire information less expensively and with greater functionality, but its real pay-off is for the cultural heritage community as a whole. There it promises to make our information collectively useful, enabling us to become players in the emerging communications environment.
>
> (Bearman 1995: 281)

Some of the early adopters of computing in the heritage sector were already mindful of these issues. Henriette Avram, Information Systems Office, Library of Congress and Director of the MARC project was, by 1968, stressing the fact that standardisation was basic to any communications network and any principle of sharing information (Library of Congress 1968: 2). Equally, within months of the project's inception it had already become a matter for discussion that the steering committee of the computer network project (later the Museum Computer Network) should approach the International Council of Museums seeking to enlist its cooperation in establishing uniform (or at least interchangeable) standards and methods of classification (Koch 1967). Other groups of practitioners outside the MCN were already beginning to raise concerns over the considerable amount of duplication of effort that was already taking place in this burgeoning community of automation. A delegate at one of the first (if not the first) international conferences that gave serious consideration to museum automation, concluded that:

> Many different institutions or individual workers are preparing methods for encoding locality data, scientific names, bibliographic information, and

in many cases the methods will not be compatible with each other in the future. Worse still, errors are made again and again that have been experienced and solved by earlier workers, but require repeated laborious solutions by the next generation.

(Smithsonian Institution 1968b: 2)

One member of this 'next generation' would be David Bearman. Effectively in the role of a chief information officer, from 1981 to 1986, Bearman was at the Smithsonian, the creator and deputy-director of the new Office of Information Resource Management, and moving the Institution from the Honeywell mainframe computing environment to a distributed computing environment. To an expert in knowledge systems and information architecture such as Bearman, the landscape of museum computing by the mid-1980s was 'a disaster'. The root cause was the unilateral approach that many individuals and institutions had taken and, most importantly, the lack of agreed unifying standards.[6] Faced, in the US at least, with several large-scale multi-institutional databases each conceived completely differently, Bearman was echoing sentiments from Chenhall and others a decade before.

Until such time as museums begin to use some minimal data standards for recording their collections, it will not be easy for one museum to communicate to another museum information about its collections in precise and understandable terms.

(Chenhall and Homulos 1978: 48)

Evidently, to the team at the National Museum of Natural History in Washington, DC, who were developing the SELGEM system, the establishment of standards was the key to bringing various collections and various museums together under a single conceptual and operational program. Later, to one Keeper of Documentation (Martin Norgate, at the Hampshire Museums Service) the equation was quite simple: 'bad data structure + no terminology control + computer = DISASTER' (Moffett 1992a: 2). In Hampshire's case, it was the MDA standard (with its data model and associated term lists) that was to be the key to avoiding this fate. When in the late 1970s the IRGMA cards (and precursor of the MDA standards to follow) began to appear in the UK, it was indeed their 'multidisciplinary standard' that was heralded; the professional press billed them as the 'first multidisciplinary computer catalogues and indexes in the UK and probably the world' (Nuttall 2000: 4.1. iii).

Standards, in other words, were not only seen to be the key to capturing core pieces of information of which museums were accountable and responsible, but they were core to the function of computers. Moreover, contrary to some perceptions, standards were seen by their champions as flexible. A key feature of SELGEM, its proponents emphasised, was the 'ease with which users can learn the basics and begin building their own files' (Gautier 1978: 3). This is what allowed, for instance, the National Museum of American History, to 'put its own interpretation on to the code' (Worthington 2005) when it was encouraged to use SELGEM. The philosophy of SELGEM (mirroring the philosophy of the library sector's MARC system) and that which underpinned IRGMA's work in the UK, was of standards that could be self-declarative. IRGMA's ambition for its 'Museum Communication Format' was to create a structure that could 'take all types of information and impose no restriction on the researcher or recorder' (Cutbill 1970: 259). In SELGEM data could be stored either hierarchically or in unit-record format, and records and fields could be variable in length – the maximum records size being 999 fields, each 6,330 characters long. Moreover, in theory, the model was understood to be generalised and flexible enough to allow a record to be tuned to the needs of that particular collection or subject. Apologists for the new standards continued to see that curators could be liberated (rather than shackled) by standards; 'there are beautiful things that you can do with well-applied standards that may not be possible otherwise' (Stiff 2005).

However, not all curators saw standards in this same way. Writing in 1966, the curator of anthropology at the Dartmouth College Museum wrote of the museum catalogue – I suspect without any hint of irony – that 'if it is not completely uniform, or if all the numbers are not used, or if the pages are littered with comprehensible cross references – WHO CARES?' (Whiting 1966: 87). Clearly somewhat weary with what modern technology had by that point presented him, his view was that all that mattered with a museum catalogue was to maintain the data which related to a numbered specimen. Evidently, standards and standardisation were not entirely un-open to criticism. When applied inappropriately or insensitively, there could be inelegance within standards – a point not lost on one of the Smithsonian's former chiefs of its Automatic Data Processing Program:

> Standards may develop spontaneously, or as the result of a planned effort, and may be formed for personal use by a single individual, or by groups for broader purposes. The characteristics of standards vary with the nature of the problem to be solved, and the means of handling the data; and the formality of statement and control of standards ranges from subconscious, unverbalized guidelines to enforced legislation.
>
> (Gautier 1976: 2)

Moreover, and as Sandra Scholtz, in her 1974 Museum Data Bank Research Report was at pains to make clear, those involved in converting a museum's catalogue data to machine-readable form had always maintained that their aim was to devise techniques for maintaining (and not compromising) the integrity of data structure of the original catalogues. And yet, worrying language could be found deep in the technical descriptions of the new data bank systems. For instance, as Vance and Heller described the structure developed by the Museum Computer Network between 1967 and 1970, they also revealed the dangers of working to unified parameters. 'The definitions must be constant', they explained:

> This requirement is easily met in the context of a limited set of data from one source. It becomes critical when data from various institutions and several disciplines are combined, for some meaning must inevitably disappear whenever data sets using the same annotators in different senses or different annotators in overlapping senses are merged.
>
> (1971: 71)

For a shared system to be compatible and meaningful, there had to be, in other words, complete agreement on the function of each entry point or field and the terms to be used in each of these entries. However, this had to be achieved without imposing a homogeneity of practice on the heterogeneity of collections. The concern some curators felt, related (again) to Huxley's fear of the 'will to order', and what he saw as human beings' desire 'to impose a comprehensible uniformity upon the bewildering manifoldness of things and events' (1994: 153). To standardise the point of knowledge capture might be seen to hold up a homogenising filter to the world. This, in turn, raised the question of what assumptions underpinned and informed the standard. After all, the database and the data model were themselves part of the long history of structured knowledge. And just like the sephirot, the kinship table, the reading wheel, the concentric ring mnemonic, or indeed the cabinet of curiosity, or the tabulating classificatory tables of the Royal Society, the new systems being proposed in the 1970s were part of a history of societies devising ways to structure knowledge. As such, the architectures of the new museum automation were equally loaded with culturally specific ideology and assumption (Poster 1990). The question, therefore, was what sort of ideology and what sort of assumptions.

Was this essentially a Linnaean standard?

Standards, and the terminology control they brought, had the potential to present a mirage of certainty; this is the fiction Gere refers to, the illusion of structure and standardisation (1999). Moreover, this was something of which David Vance, one of the architects of the new automation, was all too aware. As much as the new computer-oriented information management systems called for an 'overriding need for definition and rigorous vocabulary control', these terms concealed 'traps':

> Does 'France' include Martinique? Tahiti? Did it formerly include Algeria? How does the sense of this word change in a medieval context? Does it always include Burgundy – retroactively? What will be the consequence of calling Picasso Spanish but including him in the School of Paris?
>
> (1974: 10)

It was a similar discomfort that David Scott felt as he reflected on Vance's machine-readable catalogue record of the *Three Musicians* by Picasso. Reflecting upon the system's demand for meaningful entry under a series of hierarchical fields, he slowly unfurled the uncertainties that lay within:

What, indeed, *is* the subject matter of the picture? All shapes are highly distorted and abstracted, but there appear to be three seated figures, in costume and masks. Two hold musical instruments and the third, a musical score. There also appears to be a table in the foreground, with objects on it, and a dog in the background. Because of their musical accessories, the figures can be termed 'musicians', but they can as well be labelled 'actors' or 'masks', or 'a pierrot, a harlequin and a monk', on the basis of their costumes. The musical instrument of the left-hand figure is perhaps more like a recorder than a clarinet. The musician to the right holds a musical score, not an accordion, and is perhaps shown as singing . . .

(1976: 4)

The frustration that Scott felt in the reading of the painting was that the system appeared to objectify the uncertainty, the contested meanings, and the complexities of iconography that might be read into it. The system, in other words, appeared to expect a level of discrete and accurate identification of subject matter that (while maybe workable within the holotypes and classifications of the natural sciences) was unsympathetic within the polyvalence of art history. After all, it was not uncommon for a geologist or a botanist at the time to view their collection, ordered in taxonomic sequence, as 'self-indexing' (Philips 2005). In contrast, Scott was experiencing the presence of a system predicated upon one system of thought, but applied to a discipline that worked within a noticeably different conceptual framework. He saw himself 'as a spokesman for art museums in the company of botanists, biologists, anthropologists, archaeologists, social historians and computer scientists', and in that context found it 'necessary to illustrate most explicitly the distinctive nature of the concerns of the critic-historian as they are shaped by the uniqueness and the unique nature of the object of art' (Scott 1976: 5). Consequently, if the registrar and the curator were unable to work together in building a machine-readable catalogue that was tuned to art curatorship, then, Scott reasoned, art museum staff were going to be less likely to be interested in such a catalogue than staff of a history or science museum.

However, even a subject such as archaeology, where records were comparatively more complete than many other subjects and where the needs for systematic analysis were at times similar (if not congruent) to many of the natural sciences, there were questions still to be answered. As a newly appointed lecturer at the University of Sheffield, Colin Renfrew (the future Baron Renfrew of Kaimsthorn and later holder of the Disney Professorship of Archaeology at Cambridge) had attended the colloquium in 1967 to which the Information Retrieval Group of the Museums Association owed its origins. Renfrew commented to the forty or so other researchers and curators on the 'difficult problem' that was related to trying to define archaeological 'types' cleanly and accurately within any new machine-based indexing systems. Stressing how 'there are no species in archaeology', he explained how any 'types' might be arbitrary and open to change. And even then 'a "type" often shows a bewildering range of forms, and types merge promiscuously one into another' (1967: 113). Any coded system would, consequently, need to cope with this fluidity, subjectivity and lack of finality. In a sense, to Renfrew – just as to Scott after him – there were evaluations within scholarship and curatorship whose import appeared to evade the computer. There would continue to be a steady rise of archaeological computing, particularly the embracing of statistical processing of excavation data (cluster analysis, mapping), of storing data (data banks of finds and artefacts) and later of visualisation (pattern perception, shape analysis and 3D modelling). Nevertheless, there was in the mid-1970s (and to an extent there remained for some time) a caution about using computers for qualitative analysis. Questions remained on how computers could store and utilise detailed archaeological knowledge, and how their failure to do so was a 'general and major limitation' on the use of computers as aids to archaeological interpretation (Doran 1974: 69). As one author had it, these were the concerns of 'the many archaeologists who, with some justification, feel that all the computer can do for them is to simplify their problems to the point of absurdity' (ibid.: 70).

It can be revealing to note the background and specialist subjects from which the authors and promoters of the new automation and the new systematisation came. Strikingly, the overwhelming majority of those leading the move towards standardisation were professionals whose training, experience and intellectual apparatus had been assembled in the new disciplines of the computer and information sciences or subject disciplines with deep-rooted 'systematic' and taxonomical approaches. Around the Cambridge group in the UK were individuals such as Karen Spärck Jones, who had worked in automatic language and information processing research since the late 1950s. Richard Light worked on the original IRGMA data models, and had a background in mathematics and the natural sciences and a degree in theoretical physics. Andrew Roberts joined this circle of activity at the Sedgwick Museum while still working on a Master's degree in Information Science at City University. Roberts had been taught by Jason Farradane (1906–89), a pioneer of information science, instrumental in establishing the first academic courses in information science and founder member of the Institute of Information Scientists. Farradane was instrumental in the approach of looking at information and breaking it down into so-called facets and concepts, and looking at the relationship between those concepts. Information science at this time was itself being influenced by computer science, and, through the presence of individuals such as Roberts, this had an influence on the standards that were emerging in UK museums in the 1970s. In the United States, the Museum Computer Network project, initiated by Jack Heller at New York University, was consistent with (and a continuation of) a trajectory on which his research group were already heading – that is 'formulating new programming languages and methodology for direct-access storage, organisation and retrieval of humanities data' (Ellin 1967a: 2). At the Smithsonian, it was Reginald Creighton who was manager of the Information Storage and Retrieval projects. Creighton came from outside the museum sector, with twelve years' experience of systems design and programming, previously working as a systems research programmer, methods analyst and computer programmer for the US national security agency. His research, therefore, was not on artefacts, artworks and specimens, but in the area of computerised systems for telemetry simulation modules and in-flight information retrieval systems for Air Force satellites (Smithsonian Institution 1967: II iv). And, significantly, Creighton's team was recruiting young computer specialists from the NASA Scientific and Technical Information Facility.

These were the specialist individuals who could understand the demands of the conversion of data from the language of museum practice into the language of machines (Chere and Polyakov 1978: 1). This was a new breed of professionals who were finding themselves in museums. Or to put it another way, those museums at the forefront of the automation and standardisation revaluation were recruiting and putting at the centre of this work individuals who did not come from a curatorial background and had no experience of collections care and management. They were a new generation of graduates and professionals who called themselves 'information scientists' and 'systems analysts' and 'computer programmers'. As significant as the fact that individuals with these competencies and experiences were now working in (some) museums was the fact that it was the same individuals (with all the assumptions they made about information) who were embedded in the development of standardisation and automation.

Just as significant, however, was the subject background of many of the curators leading and driving many of these projects. In particular, a very large number of the early adopters of the new automated, standardised, systematised approaches were taxonomists and those working with taxonomy – be it the stratigraphy of geology or the grand hierarchy (of domain, kingdom, phylum, class, order, family, genus, species). The majority of the first collections and departments to automate in Europe and North America were located within the disciplines of geology, biology and botany. In the very early days of museum automation, some practitioners could see how the hierarchical logic and tabulated ordering of the first generation of mechanised and digitised information management systems mapped well on to the Linnaean taxonomy and systematics of the natural sciences. Working with IBM punch-cards, the Department of Herpetology at the American Museum of Natural History, for instance, had already identified what they called 'the advantages inherent in the hierarchical system of zoological classification' within their punch-card bibliographic index. Alphabetic and numeric codes had been used, therefore, to identify systematic categories from within this 'well-known system' (Dowling and Gilboa 1967). In the late 1960s it was biologists and geologists who formed the so-called 'Leicester Group' discussing data processing in museums and universities (Cutbill 1970: 256). Based on a shared vision of a common approach to documentation, they aimed 'to develop an index of specimens and set up a centre for data-processing in systematics' (Nuttall 2000: 4.1. i). Members of the Leicester Group had been included in the Natural Sciences group of the Museums Association's lobbying body on information retrieval (Lewis 2007), and later the Group became part of IRGMA. And, of course, John Cutbill, leading the Sedgwick project, was an academic within the Geology Department at the University of Cambridge, and a field archaeologist. Tellingly, when Cutbill came to publish results on the machine-exchange of museum data it was to systematics literature that he naturally turned (Cutbill 1970). Indeed, it was in that particular publication that he made clear that the communication format devised by IRGMA in the UK had originally been 'devised for specimen information' (ibid.: 268). In fact the MDA data model, the roots of which were partly in Cutbill's work some ten years before (much like the generalised flexibility of the Smithsonian's SELGEM), had the capacity, in reality, to be self-declarative. This meant, in theory, that it was perfectly capable of holding humanistic data. And yet, owing to the museum that hosted its development, the collections that initially populated it and the professionals who advocated it, the application that was presented could all too easily be seen to wear the mantle of the natural sciences. For this reason the 'new documentation' appeared predisposed to scientific taxonomy and systematics. Subsequently, for institutions such as the Royal Botanic Gardens in Kew (London), the new tabulations and hierarchies of automated collections management were highly consistent with existing scientific mappings of their extensive collections. Consequently, even by 1986, when for many museums computer-based collections management was still several years (if not a decade) away, Kew was boasting a database of living plant collections with over 86,000 records, connected to a dead specimen database of 4,000 records and the National Trust's arboretum records of some 26,000. As well as a further 60,000 records of taxonomic data, the institutions also already had built specialist bibliographies containing some 160,000 records (Pettitt 1986). Likewise, from 1977 to 1986, 190,000 records were created based on the natural history collections data and documentation archives at the Hancock Museum, Newcastle (UK) using the SPIRES package on its university's AMDAHL mainframe (Brewer 1986). In each case the curators involved were all very familar with the systematisation, standard nomenclature and hierarchical structure that the new automation preferred.

As if to advertise this link, it was telling that some early conferences on museum automation were even being consciously scheduled to coincide with national curators' meetings in the natural sciences: 'the date has been selected', explained one newsletter from March 1969, 'because it falls between the meetings of the American Society of Ichthyologists and Herpetologists [. . .] and the American Society of Mammalogists [. . .] and offers the maximum opportunity for members of both societies to participate' (Smithsonian Institution 1969a: 1). It was abundantly evident that the SELGEM project at the Smithsonian had its roots deep within the systematic and taxonomical logic of the natural sciences. At the core of its initial application and pilot work was Dr Donald Squires, at the time the author of some forty-eight publications in invertebrate palaeontology, invertebrate zoology, marine biology and marine geology. The original project was principally an investigation into the possible uses of electronic data processing for computer storage and information retrieval of specifically *specimen*-associated data. The system that effectively later became the Smithsonian standard for information management was not initially a pan-institution creation, nor was it born from research and development from both the arts and sciences. Rather, the system came very much from within the assumptions and practices of the systematic sciences – in fact, three separate areas of the

Museum of Natural History: marine rocks, oceanic birds and marine crustaceans (Manning 1969). Furthermore, the system was designed in such a way that taxon was understood to be the 'focal point' for entry and retrieval of data (Manning 1969: 678). The language of an interim report on the first phase of development (the so-called HEW project) of what later became the SELGEM system is testimony to where – in intellectual terms – the project was aligned. The Smithsonian reported that:

> Consideration of, and preliminary implementation of formats of output and protocols by which stored data will be recalled and presented to the scientist has been undertaken. Involved in the techniques, has been the development of a satisfactory numerical expression for classical Linnaean taxonomic binomials and hierarchy and the automated procedures by which such numericlature is assigned.
>
> (Squires 1969a)

Any museum practitioner following the work of the Smithsonian would have been left in little doubt that this was a meeting of scientific systematisation and taxonomy with computational codification and tabulation. The taxonomic hierarchy used by the system was conceived as a working hierarchy and was not intended as a definitive scientific list (Creighton and King 1969: 7). And yet, in its description of how the pilot projects were progressing, we can see how the Smithsonian Institution were finding a neat fit between the taxonomic language of the natural sciences and the tabular fields of the computer system:

> In defining the descriptors of these collections, it was recognised that the questions posed to the data bank developed in the project would invariably contain either a unity of taxonomic hierarchy by which biological classifications are structured, and/or some geographic designator. Thus, these two characteristics become the primary cross-reference subject fields, with secondary fields including parameters of vertical distribution (depth, altitude, or geologic age), name of collector and date of collections. All other data would be structured as subsidiary files. By the means of unique catalogue numbers for each specimen or groups of specimens, data are associated directly with the specimen.
>
> (Squires 1969a: 6)

The 'hierarchy' of the Linnaean taxonomy appeared to have mapped well into the precisely differentiating and ordered computational world that the machine required – and more so as the 1970s progressed and the world of computing changed and 'the triumphal age of the hierarchical database' began (Bearman 2007). There was, in short, a 'good fit' (Philips 2005) between the approach the computing systems required and the approach that many curators trained in the natural sciences were familiar with. The taxonomic nomenclature and differentiation of some of the museum's disciplines dovetailed well into the tabulated processing of the new automation; after all, to many practitioners this existing system of natural science classification was 'already something of an encodement' (Swinney 1976: 3). Therefore, for curators already thinking and working in this way, the further step to the ordering protocols of the new automation was not a step that far.

And yet, for others it was. For those working in the humanities, for instance, the 1960s was a time where the tabulated and quantified world of technology did not feel as familiar and consistent with existing intellectual processes. Then – as now – it was all too easy, perhaps, to build overly simplified images of how the humanities and sciences both worked. 'There they were, the Two Cultures', cried Hoving, painting a dramatic picture for one museum conference audience, 'the humanistic and the scientific, dug in at the heels and distrustful of each other, and God prevent them from ever coming together' (1968: vii). Nonetheless, to those leading the innovation it was undeniable that 'the electronic structure of the computer's brain' closely paralleled 'the metric patterns of mathematic and scientific thought' (Ellin 1967a: 1). The plain truth was that people trained in the arts and humanities were not used to scientific nomenclature and a systems-oriented approach; the approach of systematically codifying and categorising was, for instance, alien to many art historians and historians (Marshall 2005). Computers had, it seemed, the potential to 'impose a rigorous and perhaps a harsh discipline upon us' (Hoving 1968: ix). The risk for humanities was that computational content analysis could take the place of the '*ad hoc* impressionistic ways of observing frequencies of occurrences of content variables (such as words, symbols or concepts or images)' that curators might be using in their research (Bowles 1968: xvii). The cause for much of this concern belonged to how computers worked – and their reliance on code.

Was curatorship being reduced to code?

In a paper prepared for the 8th General Conference of the International Council of Museums, and delivered before the session on Collections and Research in Munich on 7 August 1968, the director of the new Museum Computer Network in the US referred to 'the museologist and his understandable opposition to the machine intervention in the performance of his traditional functions' (Ellin 1968a: 65). This 'intervention' that Ellin had shrewdly already identified related not just to the physical presence of these new machines, or the relocation of tasks and resources that their arrival precipitated, but to the transliteration of records that they necessitated. In short, for a museum to automate its collection, the information of the day book, the catalogue and the index card now had to be readdressed to a machine-readable form. The issue was, as Poster reminds us, that just as the act of writing in some ways reduces and shapes experience by its internal structure, so 'digital encoding also imposes its limiting grid and changes its material by doing so' (1990: 94). Computers would require curators to describe their collections in a different way, and in a way that would have its limitations.

As far back as 1969 IBM and the Museum Computer Network were explaining to the sector the realities of the terminology control that automation required.

Figure 3.1 Acts of Parliament stored in the Parliamentary Archives, Great Charles Tower, House of Lords, London. Copyright Jon Pratty.

This included dictionaries of 'approved words' with which the system could cope – particular vocabularies that were generated, processed, printed and maintained by the system, and that formed the 'control device for indexing and searching' (IBM and Ellin 1969: viii). Whereas previously curators described objects and collections in ways that were meaningful to them or their institution according to conventions that may have been personal and probably were adaptive, the era of standardisation heralded by the coming of automation resulted in a less object-oriented and more system-oriented approach. The problem was that the system, by definition, was usually prescriptive. When, for instance, the British Museum first introduced its MAGUS collections management system, simple groups such as 'inscription' were broken down into as many as eight separate data fields – *type, position, script, language, inscription, translation, transliteration* and *inscription description*. 'People don't need such an arrangement', a member of the documentation team admitted at the time, 'and [they] resent the complexity of it' (McCutcheon 1993: 3).

Another (perhaps more subtle) illustration of the way computing was shaping and changing the way curators recorded their collections came in the development of MODES – the collections management system launched by the MDA, in the UK, in May 1987, and closely allied (in its development and functionality) to the documentation data standard that the team had also built ten years previously. MODES was designed to be easily afforded by middle-scale museums, and within a year of its launch the package was used by up to 100 institutions (Nuttall 2000: 10.7). Developed for the PC, a deliberate decision was made on the number of levels of nesting that would be possible on a record (five), and on the number of different fields allowable in the data structure (254). These were decisions made to make the life of the programmer easier; 254 was, after all, the maximum number of fields permissible in a MODES record because, simply, that is what the processing system of the PC could deal with. With a couple of exceptions, the number was entirely to do with the byte and the number of binary possibilities within 8-bit processing. In other words, with 254 fields the processing power of the computer had limited the number of fields. MODES, in other words, imposed a restriction on the developing standards themselves. In each case (the fields allowed in the UK's new documentation standard, the prescriptive hierarchies of MAGUS, or IBM's dictionary of approved words) the computer system was allowed to shape the museum's notion of (and practice of) standards in documentation. These things were done not just because they were the most intuitive for curators, nor because they were the most efficient, nor indeed because they mirrored existing practice. They were done in this way also because that is the way they needed to be for the computer to process the data.

It is important to note that unlike the 'automation' that was taking place contemporaneously in Washington, DC and New York, the members of the team in Cambridge, in the UK, were at pains to stress that the consultation work for IRGMA was centred on documentation standards and giving priority to the philosophical integrity of curatorial information (Light 2005). IRGMA's standards sub-committee consisted of, on the one hand, curators who looked at subject information headings, and, on the other, computer and information scientists who looked at records with the intention of developing a computer system that could process these headings and the types of information they were likely to contain (Nuttall 2000: 4.1. iii). The logic, in other words, came from the understanding of the types of information that museums had been recording historically and wanted to continue to record and the types of way in which they wanted to give access to that information (Roberts 1984). Any standards that emerged 'were developed to be a reflection of the standards and the ways we felt about information' (Roberts 2005). Crucially, the philosophy of the standard (developed by the IRGMA groups) determined the structure of the manual object cards, which in turn determined the input fields of the software. The cards, in other words, were the first embodiment of the standard, and it was these that shaped the specification for the computer software (GOS) that followed. Likewise, the early work of the Canadian Heritage Information Network (to create an inventory of the scientific and cultural heritage of Canada) was – crucially – not driven by computing. Like IRGMA in the UK, it invited the community of practice to come together to talk about what they recorded about objects, and only then was this synthesised by computer scientists into fields (Sledge 2005).

And yet, even in the UK, where the Cambridge group endeavoured to ensure that the 'cart' of computing did not go before the 'horse' of curating, it seems – even there – that protocols were developed so that information could be expressed not just in a manner more amenable to manual indexing, but also (and determinately) in a form that was processible by a computer.

> The philosophy was clear. People were looking forward and seeing that computers potentially would be a great enabler in trying to solve these problems without necessarily knowing how they would do it. There was a willingness to tackle the informational problems on the assumption that the technology would come along and play its part in the future.
>
> (Light 2005)

Consequently, in the years that followed, there was at least a perception that 'things were prescribed by what you could do with a computer' (Cooper 2005). Perhaps one of the most visible instances of how the twin innovations of automation and standardisation contorted curatorial practice was in the development of the Social History and Industrial Classification (SHIC). Developed over three years specifically for museums, the SHIC was trailed at its launch as 'a comprehensive classification system specifically tailored for curators, which orders, arranges, and collates all information in the field of human history'. Essentially, the intention was that objects could be located within a hierarchical taxonomy and (based upon their location within this 'tree') assigned a numerical indexable code. Within two years 500 copies of the classification had been sold to UK museums, supported by a series of professional seminars, and plans were already under way for an enlarged edition (Vanns 1984). By 1987 the SHIC was a visible international system and was being used in over 350 museums in twenty-two countries (Brears 1987). Seen by some as 'the museums profession's answer to Dewey' (Paine 1982), the system was designed to give compatibility between institutions. However, as Swinney had already pointed out, unlike the sciences, history was collected in an unsystematic way, and there was 'no wide-accepted matrix within which to fit data concerning history objects' (Swinney 1976: 3). In practice, therefore, the differentiating exactitude of the SHIC system was far less adept at capturing and representing some of the more layered and fluid complexities of the object's source community. Despite attempts to extend the system to reflect localised interests not reflected in the code, the homogenising perspective it sometimes inevitably took, to some curators, remained its flaw (Johnstone 1989). In other instances the tyranny of the classifying code met with mixed success. Whereas some institutions were unable to work with some of the generalities of SHIC (Murray and Werner 1987), others contrived ways to make it work; for instance, by 1986 a manual card system at Blaise Museum (in Bristol) had been constructed around the new SHIC system, with different coloured index cards (green for objects, blue for documents, yellow for photographs) being filed according to the system's numerical codes (Ingram 1986). Ultimately SHIC was a success and widely used. Moreover, it never had the pretensions to be more than 'just a filing system', a finding aid, a reference list. The intention of its authors was never to define (quixotically) a universal index (Fleming 2007). And yet, pressing, as it did, social history into the hierarchical classifications in a way that mirrored the approach of the systematic and taxonomic sciences, SHIC exemplified how the new standardising culture (*the cult of the code*) swept through the sector from the mid-1970s onwards. SHIC was history by numbers.

To borrow a phrase from Gere (1999: 51) the 1970s marked a point for many museum sectors across the world when 'a different epistemological structure' was imposed upon collections. This was the episteme of the industrial production of knowledge, of automated process, of computer logic and of the science disciplines that led the march into systematic documentation. Written by the hand of the curator,[7] the day book had belonged to the object-oriented culture of the commonplace book, the diary, and the day-to-day life of the collection – reflecting diversity and change. In contrast, the new codes keyed into the computer and the data bank now represented a system-oriented culture of standardisation and information – valuing rigidity and indexed on points of commonality. More than that, this was Procrustean computing – as hard as the architects and the programmers may have worked to mirror the nuances and priorities of curatorial practice, the result was invariably a screen full of fields into which the museum's collection now had to be made to fit.

From cabinet to computer

To summarise, there was a complex dialogue between the 'programme' of standardisation being developed by the curators, and the 'program' being written on the screens by the information scientists. And yet, in whichever way one views these developments, it is very hard not to conclude that computers were far from benevolent in this move to standardised practice. Computing played a central role in the development of shared standards and systems within museum documentation. In most cases, automation (and the use of computers) was a consequence rather than an impetus for improved approaches to collections management. It was, after all, the desire for improved accessibility for users inside and outside the museum, in the face of growing collections and accountability that drove most of these pioneering documentation projects forward – rather than just technophiliac curiosity.

Even if they were not computer-*led*, these pioneer projects were nonetheless computer-*enabled* and at times computer-*oriented*. It may not be an exaggeration to conclude that computer logic ultimately shaped (rather than just supported) the late twentieth-century systematisation of documentation. However, the implications of such a conclusion would involve a reappraisal of some of our other received readings of museum history and curatorship. It is, after all, frequently assumed that it was following the age of Enlightenment, in the age of positivism, or the 'classical episteme' (as Hooper-Greenhill calls it, as she reaches for the nomenclature of Foucauldian history) that the fluidities and dualities of the Renaissance structures of knowing were trapped and pinned down by new unambiguous scientific taxonomies. According to those versions of events, it is in the eighteenth century and afterwards that knowledge is seen to become a 'pure tabulated relationship of words and things' (Hooper-Greenhill 1992: 192). However, conversely, it could be argued that up to the Victorian period and into the first half of the twentieth century, curatorship was still, for most museums, very varied, polyvalent and personalised; more characteristic in many respects of the systems of ordering and practice that have commonly been applied to earlier (Renaissance) contexts. The documentation processes of these nineteenth- and early twentieth-century museums relied substantially on curatorial knowledge and memory, on personal strategies for organising and making meaning of a sometimes chaotic and miscellaneous collection. In these contexts, documentation could afford in many cases to be run as almost a personal filing system, by the curator, for the curator. In other words, idiosyncratic and localised approaches to ordering the world continued for many years, and was not something that ceased with the birth of the Royal Society. In a sense, the curators of the 1950s still had 'cabinets' – collected and arranged by each individual curator's own rationale.

For these institutions it was perhaps the industrialised, automated, systematised documentation introduced in the 1970s (rather than an abstract and high-level, intellectual shift two hundred years before) that put an end to this practice.[8] In other words, we might argue that in actuality, on the ground, every day in the museum, curatorial practice remained extremely fluid and idiosyncratic right up to the last quarter of the twentieth century. For most museums, it may be more accurate to conclude that the moment of ordering, tabulating and uniformity did not come in the eighteenth or nineteenth century. In reality, it was much later, in the 1970s and 1980s, when the curatorial process became (or at least aspired to become) universally ordered. It was then, and not before, that the multiplicities and varieties of multiple systems of knowledge production aspired to move to something resembling harmonisation and order. The computer-enabled systematisation of documentation in the 1970s was a rationalising discourse, aiming to bring order to the bricolage of earlier twentieth-century curatorial practices. It was perhaps here, therefore, rather than two hundred years before, that the culture of the creative 'cabinet' was finally superseded.

The automated museum: the database as museum metonym

Evidence of the curator's hand may have begun to disappear from the records, replaced by the anonymity and homogeneity of the digitised text of the dataset. New tabulated and taxonomic logic may have been imposed on to the documenting of collections, sometimes like a Procrustean bed. The new standards, terminology control and the factory-like systematisation of data entry may have represented a significant cultural shift for many institutions and individuals. And the slow and expensive route to automated collections management may have created for many museums a 'long tail' of object records that remain (even today) only on a manual paper system, not to mention others that may still have eluded even a baseline inventory. And yet, another reading of the move from the era of the day book to the era of the data bank allows us to see the many new possibilities brought by the coming of automation. This – in contrast to the tensions of the previous discussion – reveals instead an alternative history of compatibility between automation and the museum. In fact, rather than being at odds with the museum's core functions, the computer here emerges as the very embodiment (a metonym even) of what it was to be a museum.

New linkages, fresh perspectives

The records of the Museum of History and Technology of the Smithsonian Institution were considered to have become, over the years, 'incredibly muddled' (Ruffin 1967: 1). Noting how cataloguing was being undertaken 'in a haphazard fashion', one audit concluded that the current systems seemed to 'fail utterly' to accomplish even the most elementary of the purposes of identification, documentation and organisation. 'There are quantities of unidentified objects and partial and confused records', the report explained, 'for which objects cannot be found. It is often impossible to decipher old records even when they can be located' (ibid.: 3). Furthermore, some of the existing filing systems that museums were running were proving clumsy. By the time computing arrived in the 1960s, the 80-column punched card had provided a standard means of interrogating data for the previous fifty years. However, to process information meant literally re-sequencing and moving (and perhaps even handling) the cards (Suszynski 1969: 1). Significantly (if not representatively) to one contemporary, the older more manual version of the punched card system was 'probably the worst modern invention with which museums have been afflicted in recent years' (Whiting 1966: 86). Despite being 'good solid stock' these card systems were not free from wear and tear:

> when several hundred or even several thousand cards are involved, the physical labour of 'rodding' all of the cards is considerable. When the process has to be repeated several times, e.g., to isolate 'Hopi, Women's, Shoes' the task becomes prohibitive.
>
> (ibid.)

It was this awkwardness and this inefficiency that computerisation worked to address. As early as December 1967, international conferences of practitioners and researchers were drawing conclusions on the efficiencies that new computer technology could afford to museums: 'computers have the capacity to handle', one delegate had concluded, 'masses of information' (Smithsonian Institution 1968b). Certainly for museums working with large collections, the difficulty arose from the time needed to locate particular objects or specimens on the shelves in order to read their labels. The case, to some, was very clear:

There are many questions of interest in current biological research which are just not asked due to the difficulty in the correlation of information from these large collections. For example, it is extremely difficult to answer questions such as: 'What specimens exist in a collection, from a specified region, from a certain time period, and are of a certain age?' By present techniques this would require a person to examine each individual specimen label and perhaps also consult the field note of the collector. While as much as 95% of such manipulative clerical work as finding correlations, forming matrices etc. is now done by scientists, a computer-based system could do this more reliably, extensively and rapidly, liberating them for more creative research.

(Kochen et al. 1970: 2–3)

To practitioners such as David Vance (registrar at MOMA and key figure in the US museum automation community) the logic was quite simple:

Like the human mind, the computer can store, sort, compare, and retrieve information according to any criterion, update records regularly, and reproduce them in any of several formats. Unlike the human mind, it can handle vast quantities of data in fractions of a second and can pass its contents intact to future generations.

(1973: 1)

The new speed of indexing and information retrieval from these very large collections of digital records not only had the potential to bring an order and an efficiency to curatorial work, but it could enable, as one slightly breathless piece of promotional literature promised, 'a transition to new patterns of thought' (Smithsonian Institution n.d.). The opening up of research possibilities was also presented (at times) as a key driver on the Museum Computer Network's early visions of a single, central, shared (and most importantly) machine-readable inventory file of museum holdings in the US. Writing in 1969 on the completion of an experimental database – supported by data input via 80-column punched cards – the consortium stressed to its members how:

The data bank being assembled will be a valuable source for locating works of art, for producing checklists of works known or suspected to exist in any given category, or for answering specific inquiries concerning works in public collections. It is designed to accept, store, and retrieve any information or classification, and also to provide a general basis for research. In the beginning, and until it is expanded to include the more detailed or specialized information required by the scholar, the data bank will primarily serve as a starting point for original research.

(IBM and Ellin 1969: 1.2)

In only the second meeting of the consortium (held on 3 March 1967 at the Whitney Museum, New York) the benefits that computing could bring to research were already evident. Even as it formulated what its 'Computer Network Project' might entail, the two dozen practitioners, researchers and technologists present 'generally conceded' that the use of computers by humanities scholars had not been shown 'to constrict or mutate the classical modes of their research'. On the contrary, so it was thought, 'it has been demonstrated that computerisation serves to encourage new, more imaginative levels of inquiry' (Ellin 1967b). The new indexes, linkages and pathways through a collection that the collections database made possible, encouraged new directions for research. Computers will 'require us to rethink some of our assumptions', Hoving surmised as he addressed one group of museum curators and technologists, 're-examine some cherished pre-suppositions, sharpen our perception, cleanse our terminology' (1968: ix).

Initially, the first (1970s) generation of database management systems in the museum tended to tolerate only data models based upon a *hierarchical* logic. It was a 'tree-like' and cascading series of levels and nests that, for instance, provided the underlying structure and conceptual framework for MDA's hugely popular collection management software MODES.[9] However, in time (during the 1980s) the linkages made possible by the next generation of *relational* database management systems allowed for more complex and sometimes more efficient structures to represent collections. Relational data sets allowed discrete flat files of data to be cross-referenced and made dependent upon each other in a freer and less layered way. Rather than holding all data in one large grid or 'tree' of fields, a relational system could allow, for instance, an entirely separate table of donor information to inform all references to that donor in a table of object records, that itself might be connected to another table giving details of institutions to which a museum had lent or was lending items. The single large 'tree' of data could, in other words, be felled and replaced by a series of interflowing pools of information. Freed from the hierarchies of first-generation database management systems, Nottingham City Museums and Galleries, as part of major reconciliation work of their collections, were by 1999 not only building a registry database, but beginning to digitise and link relationally a wealth of paper sources going back to the establishment of the Nottingham Natural History Museum in 1867. Consequently, accession registers became linked to annual reports, committee minutes, financial records, museum and Town Clerk's correspondence, keepers' and taxidermists' records, and local naturalists' society records, linked in turn to a flat file of the museum's past exhibitions, as well as a biographical database of collectors, curators, donors, researchers and vendors (Cooper 2005; 2007). A rich and powerful information resource such as this was made possible not just because of the advent of computing, but specifically because of the flexibility and interconnectedness of relational data modelling that the next generation of database management systems made possible.

As the architectures of databases evolved, so also did entry and query methods. By 1990 the retrieval system for the material held by Cambridge University Museums was combining 'free text' with structured (Boolean) searching techniques – adding the possibility of 'probabilistic' searching wherein terms were 'weighted according to formulae derived from probability theory'. Essentially, this allowed users to ask questions from the Cambridge Database System in a natural language (Macfarlane 1991). Systems such as these represented an inventive step up from the tabulated formalities of previous searching proto-cols, and removed another barrier between curators and their collections data.

This language of searching and describing extended further within the context of Web-based collections. The Web not only allowed collections to become more visible to a wider (on-line) public, but it enabled these publics to be involved in the act of describing and ordering these same collections. The first generation of museum computing was characterised by a strict taxonomy of differentiat-ing expert terms being used inside the museum to slice and dice a collection's records. In contrast the user-driven distributed network technologies of twenty-first-century digital heritage instead empowered users outside the museum to generate and contribute their own 'keyword indexing' (Chun et al. 2006; Chan 2007). The top-down taxonomies familiar to the community of practice within the museum could now be matched and connected to the bottom-up folks-onomies more familiar to the communities of users outside the museum. As they 'tagged' on-line content, users themselves became collectors of informa-tion, and the act of curatorship itself became open and shared – if conditionally. Compellingly, in this new information space museums' on-line users become 'curators of meaning' (Pratty 2006).

Consequently, whereas once the grid-irons of the first data models were per-haps at odds with some disciplines within the museum, the new relational and semantic (and object-oriented) architectures instead emphasised individual mean-ing-making, relativistic terms, layered readings, as well as changing signifiers and descriptions – all of which was much more consistent with (and indeed fed off) modern curatorial practice and museological thought (Cameron 2003). After a generation of fixed standards, terminology control and disciplined automation, computing had begun to reveal a culture of information management where personalised indexes through collections were assembled, where multiple epis-temologies were able (if not encouraged) to sit upon collections, and where the collections themselves (rather than the systems and standards for describing col-lections) were brought to the fore. By as early as 1968, museum directors such as Thomas Hoving, at the Met in New York, were anticipating the 'fresh perspec-tive', as he called it, that museum computing could bring to collections research and management. He foresaw how new technology would help to stimulate 'the intuitive flash, the pyrotechnics that go off in our skulls when a discovery is made, a fact is perceived, a relationship seen' (1968: ix). It may, for most mus-eums, have taken thirty years, but Hoving's visions eventually became a reality.

The museum as database / the database as museum

Just as in the late 1960s and early 1970s when the computer was implicated in the rise of standardised practice and the professionalisation of collections management within the museum, so, today, it is the computer again that is supporting the new documentation of the post-modern moment. As fields of a museum's collections management system are made visible to its publics, and as these publics add their interpretation to the content of that system, and, furthermore, as the fundamental conceptual relationship between the fields of that system are related in a way that both the machine and the user can understand,[10] new forms of curatorship become possible. This is *post-documentation* – the documentation of the semantic, folksonomic, object-oriented information landscape of post-modernity. It is almost as if with the newer more fluid systems and more amenable software of post-documentation, museums are learning to be comfortable with heterogeneity and chaos again. With the age of standardisation and automation behind it (and the flagstones of interoperability in place), collections management today can with confidence (when appropriate) be unpredictable, inconsistent and personalised once again.

However, the implications of this go deeper. The database itself has become profoundly iconic for the museum. It has done so in a way similar to how other 'new technologies', in history, have become iconic to other institutions and ages. This is the concept of a particular technology coming to exemplify (through its form and its impact) both the operations and values of a particular historical or cultural locality. For instance, Erwin Panofsky's study of linear perspective considers the extent to which its regulatory 'systematic space' and privileging of a humanistic eye were powerfully consistent with and defining for the Renaissance cultures that rediscovered this visual technology in the fifteenth and sixteenth centuries (1991: 49). Similarly, albeit within a wider remit on the 'computerization of culture', Manovich took this concept of a technology assuming 'symbolic form' from Panofsky and then applied it to the role of the database in today's information age:

> Indeed, if, after the death of God (Nietzsche), the end of grand Narratives of Enlightenment (Lyotard) and the arrival of the web (Tim Berners-Lee), the world appears to us as an endless and unstructured collection of images, texts, and other data records, it is only appropriate that we will be moved to model it as a database.
>
> (Manovich 1999: 81)

Manovich's assertion is that in its digital granularity, its de-privileging of narrative, its unending editability and lack of completeness, the database stands as the 'symbolic form' of the post-industrial age. The database, in other words, has become a rationalising system for the modern world – more than just a tool, but a system of thought. We think (so the thesis goes) in terms of databases, we conceive information and knowledge in terms of database logic. Manovich's observation is equally relevant to the workings and the status of the museum today. Just as the database might be seen to serve as the synecdoche of modern life, so it has also become embedded within the function and thinking of the modern museum. At present, the museum's notion of 'collection' is not only structured to accommodate the tools of automation, but is imagined (and frequently presented to its publics) as a database. The logic of the database is now embedded within museums' management of their collections. To a great extent the computer-oriented systematisation of documentation has led to an unprecedented fetishising of the museum database. Just as once it was the day book, today it is the database that is the metonym of the museum. It may certainly be true to say that at no other time, perhaps, in the history of the museum has its catalogue been avowed with such high status. The veracity of objects is today, seemingly, gauged by the extent to which they are recorded in the museum's database. 'It is an information scientist's perspective, perhaps', laments Knell, 'which seems to encourage a belief that the thing only comes real when it is captured in a digital form and converted into information' (2003: 137).

Furthermore, Manovich alerts us (if inadvertently) to another implication of the database's new status in modern society. To illustrate his point (that we experience, and expect to experience, aspects of the world through the logic of a database) he uses the example of a CD-ROM and a user searching through a body of digital content as if walking through a 'virtual museum'. It is here that we are reminded not just of how the museum is increasingly being conceived through the language and structure of the database, but how the database itself (as a framed collection of digital objects, through which users can build their own narratives) is being endowed with the qualities traditionally associated with the museum. As various digital lists and on-line collections (mis)appropriate the label and trope 'museum', and as museums, concurrently, offer experiences through the portal of the database, the challenge for users and curators alike is how to differentiate between the two.

Knowing (and caring) about the difference between a collection of digital things that appears like a 'museum', and a museum that is presenting digital things based on its collection, comes down to questions of trust and definitions of authenticity. And, in fact, it is these issues (and their relation to Manovich's principle of new media as a numerical rather than physical entity) that is the basis for our next discussion. If through their long histories museums have been principally about material things (physical visits to physical objects) what possible role could there be for a machine that can only display information, surrogates and simulacra?

4

Recalibrating authenticity

The analogue museum: privileging the material world

In a 1969 report, in their description of how an information system for American museums might be visualised, IBM's Federal Systems Division had made clear the premise that computers worked with code: 'a system of symbols and signs used to represent words or concepts', and that in computer processing, all codes must be translated to a numeric code in order to be interpreted by the machine itself (IBM and Ellin 1969). What IBM were attempting to convey to this new constituency of museum computing professionals was the same key point that Manovich (2001) would later include in his five principles of 'new media'. That is, that digital media are intrinsically *numerical*. Within computers our multi-dimensional, analogue world is distilled to an unambiguous string of 1s and 0s. Aided by its ability to see statements as true or false, to answer logical questions with logical answers of 'yes' or 'no', and to set switches as either 'on' or 'off' within its circuit of semi-conductors, the processing at the very heart of the computer is of numbers. Figuratively speaking, at an 'atomic level' computing is a black and white world of binary oppositions.

And it is here that the principles of computing collide with the principles of the museum. For it was the privileging of complex tangible things that for many centuries defined what a museum was (Hein 2000: 71). Museums traditionally have been the material world in a box, a cabinet of ostensibly *physical* curiosities. Museums were the fundamental point of reference for the system of collecting physical things (Pearce 1995: 387). Textbooks for students spoke of how 'the museum has a unique role as a repository for three-dimensional objects gathered from the natural and man-made environments' (Stone 1984: 127). Similarly, it has been the essential physicality of the objects on display (their size, their distance from the visitor, and the sense of what it might be like to touch them) that has directed readings of some modern museography (Radley 1991: 72–7). Even when we write about appreciation and experience of museum objects, such as art objects, it is to their materiality that we are drawn; 'quality resides in the object', Eitner explains, 'and it endures as long as its physical substance' (1975: 78). Likewise, the Enlightenment inheritance that museums and galleries continued to carry was (crucially) of physical demon-

Figure 4.1 Rodin's *Thinker*, Legion of Honor, San Francisco. Copyright Jon Pratty.

stration and exposition. This is the world, as Macdonald tells us, rendered to a visible and ordered 'instantiation' of scientific and political certainty (1998: 11). Thus, for the arts and sciences alike museums are 'material heaven' (Pearce 1995: 387), they represent 'the triumph of the physical' (Pachter 2002). The types of objects that may have been collected, and the disciplinary frameworks that have interpreted them, may have changed over time and varied across different cultural settings, but the tangibility – the collecting of things of weight and of substance – has endured over centuries.

Therefore, for digital media to accept only a world reduced to its limited array of binary digits was in many quarters anathema. After all, what place could there possibly be in the museum for a machine that could only comprehend the world in numbers – and two numbers at that? One of the first comprehensive manuals of museum computing went straight to the point:

> Storage of information in a computer system requires that the 'natural language' of existing museum records be converted to a set of symbols that can be read and interpreted by the data processing machine.
>
> (Vance 1973: 18)

Perhaps this brusqueness did not acknowledge some of the real anxieties that curators already had over virtual codes. When commenting on the advances of computational technology that he saw around him in late 1960s society, the director of one world-renowned art museum spoke of how 'there seems to be something horrifyingly dehumanizing about numbers themselves' (Hoving 1968: viii).

The library sector had, by this point, already faced some of these questions. The group developing the MARC standard had made it clear that automation was not about changing practice but about offering a system that could do all the things librarians' existing manual systems were able to do, only 'better and faster, and to add new services and features' (Library of Congress 1965: 14). And yet, by November 1965 discussions were confronting the extent to which the computer might require naturalised documentation language to be re-expressed as standardised code:

> For example, it is difficult to search on data as variable as the publisher's name in the imprint statement, yet a system of coding for publishers could be established as a fixed field and would be far more economical for machine searching. This presupposes that some kind of authority code list is maintained for publishers. It is much easier to manipulate a fixed code in the machine compared to manipulating variable alphabetic data and saves computer time because of the ease of matching. This is why the fixed field is used for information which can be formatted. Obviously unique, non-recurring data such as author and title cannot be rigidly formatted. There would be extra intellectual effort involved in maintaining a publisher authority file, and the trade-offs between this effort and the machine time required to manipulate the publisher's name in 'natural' form (not encoded) in the record would have to be analysed.
>
> (Library of Congress 1965: 12)

This fact (that the computer preferred to work in standardised codes than in free text) had a significant bearing on some of the early museum computing discussions at the Smithsonian Institution. In 1965 the Museum of Natural History entered into a contract (funded by the Smithsonian's Office of Systematisation) with the Federal Systems Division of IBM to study the feasibility of the codification of biological names (Squires 1969a: 14). The results of this project indicated that the codification was not required and suggested that biological nomenclature be treated alphanumerically. Nevertheless, it was one of the early warnings that a certain degree of 'translation' might be required for the syntax of computing to work alongside the vocabulary of curatorship. But whereas the specimens at the Smithsonian might, after 'extensive editing' (Creighton and King 1969: 5), have managed to synchronise these two language systems, other practitioners worried about the compatibility of other types of objects in their care. Some quantifiable elements of museum collections and museum work might have allowed themselves to be broken down into digits, but the question was, Hoving suggested, 'can we break down art into numbers?' (1968: viii).

Opposing the 'virtual' to the 'real'

Indeed, it was art, particularly the display of art, that seemed to crystallise a number of the problems curators had with the digitisation of collections. Computers appeared to generate only facsimiles and representations, whereas museums were institutions that prized and prided themselves upon the presentation of the original and something called 'the authentic'. It was on this particular point that a great deal of anxiety came to be placed, and in some cases some quite hysterical polarisation ensued between notions of the 'virtual' and the 'real'. On one side stood *real* objects, genuine and trusted: these were the collections that gave the museum (so the argument went) its core function and role in culture and society. After all, it was the 'real thing' that was the 'essential difference between museums and other information sources' (Lewis 2007). On the other side stood the *virtual* 'objects'; inverted commas now emphasising the shortcomings of these faux assets. 'Immaterial' in every sense, these digital representations appeared to be viewed as secondary and marginalised within the main functions of physical display. Digital media might well provide informational and experiential benefits to visitors, but they could not 'provide the visceral thrill of being in the presence of the original' (Anderson 1997: 21).

This discourse, of 'real' against 'virtual', mirrored the dichotomies that were habitually set up within wider debates in sociology and elsewhere about computer-mediated communication; what Shields has described as a 'dualism which pit the human against the technological, the developed against the underdeveloped, the natural against the artificial' (2000). Such was the bi-polar nature of the debate that two futures for the museum were routinely presented: one in which the museum, confronted with a tide of digitality, would witness the death of the object and the visit; the other in which museums would be a refuge and sanctuary for material things in an increasingly digital world.

Resounding with some of the same 'apocalypticism' that characterised other readings of the impact of digital imaging and digitality on the world (Kember 1998: 1), commentators on museums painted nightmarish scenarios of a museum reduced to simulation:

> Experts say it eventually will be possible to produce perfect copies of works of art, pay a vicarious visit to a museum wearing a virtual reality headset, or summon up a three-dimensional electronic hologram of the Venus de Milo [. . .] Technology will also increasingly move into the museums themselves, even though many curators distrust it. A proposal for a $75 million museum of British history calls for the use of interactive computer technology, large-screen movie projections and live actors to help bring the past alive. The idea, according to one backer, is to 'get away from the idea of using dead objects'.
>
> (James 1995)

As museologists such as Šola described (if somewhat mischievously) how the 'marvel' of the information technology represented a 'Trojan horse' being wheeled into the 'fortress' of the museum (Šola 1997: 147–8), so some museum directors winced at the digital dawns being orchestrated on the horizon by government initiatives.

> One obvious version of the future has been established as an orthodoxy in current government thinking. This is the idea that museums may simply be swept aside by the tide of new technology; that there is no point looking at a pile of old bones if you can study them just as well, if not better, on the worldwide web. This is the doomsday scenario – or, looked at from another point of view, the technophiliacs' dream.
>
> (Saumarez Smith 2000)

The frustration for other critics was less with the technology itself (which could be seen to deepen access and widen participation), but rather with the ways in which the technology was being applied to gallery environments and visiting experiences. Nevertheless, this was a frustration that, again, set up the then familiar dualism between 'real' and 'virtual':

> Collections form the substance at the heart of the museum. The essential experience museums can offer is confrontation with the real thing, the essential insight they can offer is knowledge about these real things. Yet today, the value of the real thing, and the value of knowledge about the real thing, are being undermined.
>
> (Appleton 2001)

In its more extreme form, the debates even foretold the end of the museum visit. With ready Web access to digital surrogates and resources, visitors might simply stop visiting museums. 'In this day and age, when time appears so scarce', Besser speculated, stirring the debate, 'people are less likely to make a special trip to a museum to see an original object if they can see a quite reasonable facsimile at their home workstation – especially if they can "play" with it' (1997: 120). As the Web began to encircle and connect the world, and its presence was being felt in the everyday lives of museum audiences, the idea of continuing to travel to a particular place to gain knowledge began to appear, at least to one commentator, 'endearingly quaint' (Hughes 2007).

As an alternative to this dystopia was a more utopian vision of the museum emerging as a sanctuary from the flatness of modern digital life. In this discourse the museum was fashioned as the bastion of originality within a wilderness of media-driven duplicity and insubstantial virtuality. As digital copies multiplied it would be the original objects that would gain value. Here it was to museums' capacity to be 'oases of originality in a virtual world' that some curators clung (Anderson 1997: 20). This was a future where museums might become 'zoos for the real' and 'sacred spaces for the unmachine-mediated savouring of relics' (Wallace 1995). In this world museums would become 'more and more important', not less and less so (Pachter 2002).

In these first debates as curators reviewed their options, digitality would (it seemed) result in either the end or the heightening of the museum project. Either way – at least initially – the virtual and the real were discussed as if mutually exclusive; a point, as we shall see, that would soon be rectified. Moreover, cutting through all of these worries was the question of trust and museums' responsibility to present the authentic.

Authenticity and trust

Museums were places that the public trusted (Miller 2002: 23). The digital landscape, however, was perceived to be an environment that could be characterised by its 'pervasive deceit' (Lynch 2000: 33). Used as evidence both of the problem and of the potential of reproduced media, a common reference point for a number of theses on this point of authenticity has been Walter Benjamin, specifically his essay on the work of art in the age of mechanical reproduction (Besser 1997; Hazan 2001, 2003; Miller 2002). Benjamin's essay is a complex and highly politicised polemic, a point which is not always acknowledged by scholars and students keen to cherry-pick its evocations on the cultural specificity of 'aura' and 'authenticity'. This essay was written by Benjamin in the late 1930s as fascist powers grew up across Europe (fuelled by mass produced propagandist messages), and only a few years before his flight from Germany and his eventual suicide in 1940. In the essay he builds a link between, on the one hand, the mass-production of images of art objects during the first half of the twentieth century, and, on the other, the aestheticisation of politics by the forces of Fascism. As a counter-response, Benjamin's recommendation is that Communism should politicise art. However, to make this very political commentary on the explosive contemporary events to which he was witness, Benjamin described his understanding of the relationship between art and technology. And it is here that the essay has provided rich pickings for media writers and those interested in intellectualising (and relativising) the notion of the 'authentic'. He presents the art object from ritualistic beginnings, but, once ritual is removed, its purpose becomes 'politics'. At one pole is the cult of the object, at the other its public presentability in exhibition. Benjamin's point is that, at that time, art was moving from one pole to the other – art conceived to be consumed on a mass scale. And here Benjamin holds up the example of film and photography as 'the most serviceable exemplifications of this new function' (Benjamin 1999: 219). Consequently, to him the logical result of Fascism is 'the introduction of aesthetics into political life', to which Communism must respond by politicising art (ibid.: 234). From the outset, Benjamin makes it absolutely clear that the thesis comes from a Marxist context, and is 'completely useless' for the purposes of Fascism, but, instead, is 'useful' for the formulation of revolutionary demands in the politics of art (ibid.: 211).[1]

The key point used by writers on museum computing has been Benjamin's thoughts on authenticity:

> The authenticity of a thing is the essence of all that is transmissible from its beginning, ranging from its substantive duration to its testimony to the history which it has experienced. Since the historical testimony rests on the authenticity, the former, too, is jeopardised by reproduction when substantive duration ceases to matter. And what is really jeopardised when the historical testimony is affected is the authenticity of the object.
>
> (ibid.: 215)

Crucially, it is in the act of reproduction that an object's 'aura' is undermined and withered. This questioning of what was authentic and whether the 'aura' could (or should) be preserved within a digital surrogate appeared to bring into question all that was genuine, trustworthy, reliable and valid about the museum experience. The presence of digital objects prompted practitioners to revisit the very term 'authentic' and what they thought it meant: 'Can we still think of authenticity in the realm of digital objects?' (Steamson 2002: 11). If one's notion of the 'authentic' is defined in terms of something's singular originality and uniqueness, then the fact that 'all digital objects are copies' (Lynch 2000: 41) presents a fundamental problem. Even in the most articulate and informed instances, debate on what authenticity could mean in the case of digital objects came unstuck. For instance, metadata might have a vital role to play in determining provenance of digital objects, and consequently verifying their credentials as 'authentic'. And yet, as Lynch explained, even with the existence of international standards (such as the Dublin Core) the details of exactly how such metadata would work remained, to him at least, uncertain.

> I do not believe we have a clear understanding of (and surely not consensus about) where provenance data should be maintained in the digital environment, or by what agencies. Indeed, it is not clear to what extent the record of provenance exists independently and permanently, as opposed to being assembled when needed from various pools of metadata that may be maintained by various systems in association with the digital objects that they manage.
>
> (2000: 42)

Other questions related to where the valid and genuine digital object might be when the operating system, run application, interface and output device required to realise it might vary from user to user. Furthermore, the effortlessness with which duplications could be made implied the ease of illicit use and piracy (Levenson 1998: 90). More worrying still, the ease of access to these duplications of surrogate images (authorised or otherwise) might erode the status of the original upon which they were based. There was a real concern that the increased access to images may 'lead the general public to confuse the on-screen image with the photograph that it represents' (Besser 1997: 120). The fear was that

Figure 4.2 Turner Prize exhibition 2004, Tate Britain. Copyright 24 Hour Museum.

rather than being just a temporary substitute, eventually the digital image (the surrogate) might supplant the original.

Other digital objects, those that were born digital, pushed curatorship (sometimes intentionally) to the limits of what the authentic could be. From some perspectives museums did not, for instance, have a natural role in distributing Net Art. In this case it was the Web that provided both the format and possibly the function of the museum. Frequently dynamic and ephemeral, Net Art did not fit well into the hierarchy of the traditional art institution. 'While painters and writers often are dependent on galleries and publishers to distribute their work', Vigh explained, 'net art is independent of these institutions' (2002). Disarmingly, the presence of a piece of Net Art could not only subvert the experience of encountering art on-line, but could trouble the notion of where and when art work existed (Cook et al. 2002: 68–9). As if an anomaly, Net Art appeared to demand a reappraisal of ownership, acquisition, procurement, collection, archiving and provenance (ibid.: 71).

How do we trust the digital?

Digital surrogates, objects and models also appeared to raise questions about what could and should be trusted in a museum context. In this respect, the persuasive and, at times, photorealistic environments of three-dimensional models were a good case in point. During the mid-1990s, as museums grappled with what value digitised Web-based images might have, three-dimensional modelling and Computer-Aided Design (CAD) prompted similar questions. Some commentators, for instance, had seen the trend in many applications of 'historical CAD' to reduce potentially illuminating work to 'edu-tainment' (Robson 1996). For instance, the world's first Virtual Heritage conference (held in Bath in 1996) presented models of Pompeii, an ancient Egyptian fortress and Cluny Abbey. The hit of the convention, however, was a virtual reality version of the prehistoric cave paintings of Lascaux in southern France, replete with 'ambient cave sounds and flute playing'.[2] There were a number of sensitive issues that lay within the use of historical CAD. The computer modelling did not accommodate the constant refocusing and recalculating (the 'saccadic' movement) of the eye. Instead it represented a static unblinking interpretation that (arguably) falls short of our normal visual experience. Connected to this is the fact that the pixel representations generated by the computer could only mimic three-dimensional space on a two-dimensional surface. Furthermore, in their beguiling completeness, these digital models ennobled the speculatory, valorised the imaginary and made credible and persuasive what sometimes could (like any history) only be speculated from fragments of evidence. When modelling three-dimensional space one cannot avoid the gaps in our historical knowledge and the sometimes imperceptible ways we fill or subvert them. Consequently, this sort of model building was a process that seemed to foreground the role of the imagination within the work of the historian (Parry 1999). In the case of these virtual reality simulations and animations it was their high verisimilitude (the fact that they looked real when sometimes they were just a hypothesis or a semblance of some space that may or may not have existed) that drew debate.

What worried museums just as much was the way in which digital objects also appeared to jettison many pre-existing processes for long-term storage and preservation. Bits and atoms required fundamentally different strategies for preservation (Lyman and Besser 1998: 18). It was both the persistence of the digital data, but also the means (the software and hardware) to read those data that soon challenged curators, especially as both the coding and the means for extracting that code were relentlessly pushed onwards by technological innovation.

> In the analog world, previous formats persisted over time. Cuneiform tablets, papyrus, and books all exist until someone or something (fires, earthquakes) takes action to destroy them. But the default for digital information is not to survive unless someone takes conscious action to make them persist.
>
> (Besser 2000: 156)

It soon became evident that institutions needed firm and clear strategic thinking in place to plan for the long-term management of digital material – a real challenge for many institutions that had no long-term funding in place to provide for such management (Simpson 2005). To compound the anxiety, not only did digital objects question the indices of authenticity and trust that museums held so dear, but even the institution's central function (of preserving that which was in its care) was also called into question. Challenging 'the sacredness of the original' (Besser 1997: 125), the computer – numerical, digital, insubstantial – appeared to strike at the heart of what it was to be a museum.

Or, at least, this was one version of events.

The informational museum: valuing the virtual

In fact, there was another line of thinking, another trajectory of development, another school of curating, that enabled the *numerical* quality of digital media to become highly compatible with the workings and values of the museum. From another perspective (a perspective that reflected upon the longer history of museums and that saw museums as a constantly adaptive medium), 'virtuality' and the 'informational' were both seen to be entirely consistent with traditions of curatorship. These were the traditions that recognised the museum as a place of make-believe as much as a place of fact, traditions that acknowledged that the primacy of the object meant very little without the knowledge and contextual material that sat around and gave meaning to that object. These were, furthermore, traditions that had previously managed to accommodate the reification of many different (non-material) items from human experience into 'objects' without too much existential disruption to what it was to be a museum. And it is to these traditions – traditions in which digitality found a comfortable fit – that the rest of this chapter will look.

From tangibles, to intangibles . . . to e-tangibles

Despite the worries, dystopian visions and critical questions with which digital media were met, museums have, in fact, steadily accessioned and managed a growing number of digital objects, surrogates, models and resources. Today it is relatively easy to find in the collections and assets of museums (and cultural heritage organisations) a digital sound recording for a local oral history project, or a high resolution digital surrogate of a painting in its collection (MacDowell and Richardson 2005; Roles 1995). We might find a curriculum-based 'learning object' built and made accessible by the museum with a specific formal education context in mind, or perhaps a digital video recording of a ritual performed in a gallery (Kennedy et al. 2006). We might find an official document that exists only in digital form (such as the UK National Archives' class mark PREM 18), or a piece of multimedia art (that might sit in the store on a DVD). We might find a piece of Net Art commissioned by the museum (that might only ever exist in its original and authentic form in multiple iterations on the

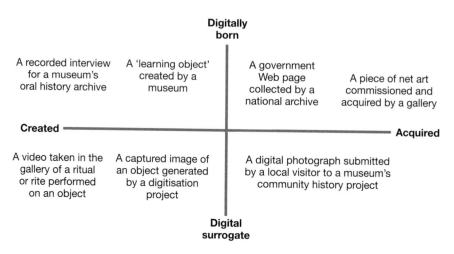

Figure 4.3 The emerging typology of e-tangibles.

Web), or perhaps even a 360-degree virtual model of a real or imaginary space (Fernandes et al. 1998). Today, all of these (and more) have been perceived by museums as items and assets worthy of collection and display. In other words, just as, a quarter of a century ago, museums grew formally to recognise 'intangibles' as valid material to collect and document, alongside their 'tangibles', so, in the past decade, museums have extended their conception of the collectable to accommodate also objects that are grasped through the intervention of a computer. These are museums' new 'e-tangibles'.

The processes and indices of reification have changed through the past century. In the industrial and mechanical age, tied to a legacy of structures and empiricism, where power, knowledge and wealth appeared proximate to physical things, curatorship gave primacy to the materiality of objects. However, in post-industrial curatorship, rather than seeing 'objects' as principally material things, they came to be understood in a wider sense; as discrete, contained units of human experience, identified and extracted in order to help substantiate (to evidence), record or define an individual or collective epistemology (system of knowledge) or ontology (sense of being). In this more circumspect definition the language of 'objects' (an augmentation rather than replacement of the 'material object') is released from the semantic quibbling about 'real' and 'virtual', or 'physical' and 'informational'. Instead 'object' becomes a term more appropriate and responsive to the preoccupations and assumptions of our current cultural condition, that is, an electronic, polyvalent, representational culture, where 'objects' are recognised to be in a state of motion, and may occupy or migrate through different states and media. Moreover, framed as an 'e-tangible', these new objects provide museums with reassuring nomenclature that intentionally aligns them to the existing typologies of objects traditionally collected by the museum. Furthermore, just like intangibles, e-tangibles can be reliant on tangibles (a digital surrogate, for example), or they can be entirely independent of other objects in the collection (such as a piece of digital or Net Art). Likewise an e-tangible may relate to or be the format for an existing intangible (such as a curatorial essay written in HTML about an object), or it may relate only to itself (such as, for example, an on-line or in-gallery game).

What has emerged, therefore, is not only an augmented and more supple definition of 'object', but an understanding of the sometimes complex interdependence (rather than discreteness or opposition) between terms such as tangible, intangible and e-tangible. The more museums used e-tangibles, the more they also learned to differentiate between those that are created by the institution (the captured surrogate, for instance) and those that are acquired (the digital image submitted by a local resident to a community history project). Likewise, museums continued to identify important differences between e-tangibles that were 'born digital' (i.e., there is no parent of which they are a digital manifestation) or a 'digital surrogate' (a copy captured from an original for preservation, representational or research purposes) (Dickins 1998). The further challenge, however, has been that each of the e-tangibles (acquired, created, born digital or surrogate) may be in one of many different digital formats (sound, video, HTML, 3-D) – each of which brings with it its own developmental history, cultural meanings and set of technological considerations. And yet, in this new mind-set (and deprivileging of materiality) such questions are proving no different (and no more or less challenging) than thinking about the different needs and formats between, say, a dress, a geological or a photographic collection. Indeed, we can already see the basis of a more differentiating approach to various types of e-tangibles emerging (Frost 2002; DigiCULT 2002: 50–1).

Defining virtuality

A key to unlocking this new reification, and the acceptance of e-tangibles, has been the reconciling of the dichotomy between the 'real' and the 'virtual' through the use of a new concept – 'virtuality'. As we saw in the previous chapter, some writers on new media had revelled (if sometimes somewhat opaquely and self-indulgently) in the problems that may exist in distinguishing between a 'real' and a 'virtual' world. These were the distinctions between a world that exists and a world that does not – or at lest does not according to some arbitrary rules that we may choose to impose that define 'realness' (Žižek 1996). These were the problems that ensue, as Druckrey puts it, when the 'unrepresentable "real" collides with the unreflected "virtual"' (1996: 19).

However, some curators and critics worked hard to negate and refute these unhelpful oppositions that were proving a barrier to museums engaging confidently with the possibilities (and necessities) of the digital age in which they now found themselves. Lynch, for instance, meticulously showed that digital objects were far from devoid of integrity and provenance and that, in fact, they still interacted with frameworks of authenticity and trust. He argued for digital objects possessing their own sense of integrity (the data not being corrupted) and reminded us that claims made about them could actually be verified. After all, we make a judgement on trusting a digital signature or a watermark in a digital object in much the same way as we make similar judgements ('subjective probability') about the validity and trustworthiness of countless other items in our modern lives (Lynch 2000). Another important, and widely read, contribution came from David Anderson's report, *A Common Wealth: museums in the learning age* (1999). Here, with a less conceptual and more strategic tone, the report included a section on 'The Emerging Cultural Network' within which the potential of new media technologies in the enhancement of education provision were unpacked. Anderson detected (astutely, it turned out) a shift in the 'control of media production' – and with it, control of the learning process from transmitters to receivers, teachers to learners. Moreover, the report identified a movement wherein the visual, interactive, social and experiential dimension of the new media was replacing the provision of textual information as the dominant mode of communication. In the 'Learning Age' digital media would no longer need to be a poor surrogate to the physical museum experience. In fact, new digital media had, rather, a vital role to play. The report concluded:

> It is probable that technology will not undermine but stimulate the public's desire to have a gallery experience; the virtuality offered by new media may balance and complement, rather than erode, the actuality that is to be found in real human relationships and contact with authentic objects in museums.
>
> (ibid.)

Through a careful choice of language, specifically in this one term 'virtuality', Anderson had managed to capture a set of principles that allowed the museum to see and work with digital media, not as a threat, but as an opportunity. Unlike the connotations of incompleteness and speculation that the word 'virtual' brought with it, the term 'virtuality' carried instead a positive set of meanings for the museum.

> Virtuality comes from the Latin *virtus*, which has several meanings, including excellence, strength, power, and (in its plural form) mighty works. The word describes a modus of participation and potentiality. In this sense, virtual objects can be seen as illuminating the potential meanings of art and other objects [. . .] Thus, virtuality should be understood as a complex cultural interpretation of objects that forces us to rethink the tangible and intangible imprints of our cultural history.
>
> (Miller 2002: 22–3)

Unlike the disorientations and subversions of the 'virtual' world, 'virtuality' was in contrast a safe space, an arena in which museums could learn to explore 'the "thingness" or artefactuality of the works in their care' (Trant 1998: 117). Not only did the virtual need the real (its hardware, its inspiration, its users), but the real was now seen to be full of the interpretations and representation common to the virtual. For the museum, the virtual could now complement the real.

Indeed, with respect to technologies such as virtual reality (technologies, we recall from our previous discussion, that raise questions of trust), the new discourse of virtuality allowed for a more confident acceptance of what the media could offer and represent. Virtual reality technologies would continue to be used by museums as tools for 'reconstructing' past or inaccessible built or natural environments (Parry and Gogan 2005). However, as well as a 'model', virtual reality could equally (perhaps more creatively) provide a space into which visitors could assemble or explore ideas. Rather than identifying a known space, virtual reality could present the user with a 'knowledge space', a sort of three-dimensional mind-map within which to think. The Smithsonian Without Walls 'Revealing Things' project, launched in March 1998, provided perhaps a glimpse of what could be possible. The goal of the on-line 'exhibition' was to

> convey to the visitor that everyday objects are more than the sum of their function and use; everyday objects are important signifiers of cultural and personal meaning. Ideally, after experiencing Revealing Things, visitors will begin to interpret the messages and meanings that everyday objects communicate, and ultimately will gain an increased awareness of the objects that surround them [. . .] In a museum, objects can be in only one place at one time. In Revealing Things, objects are dynamically positioned depending on the preference of the user.
>
> (Tinkler and Freedman 1998)

Using Java-based technology, the Web site generated three-dimensional 'maps' that diagrammed the connections between objects which the user had searched for and selected. Its 'reconstruction of the complex network of meaning that surrounds every object in the collection' was an example of virtual-reality-type technology being used, not for a reconstruction or for a metaphorical 'gallery' space, but for a think space; a three-dimensional space for ideas and thought to be arranged within (ibid.). The Smithsonian project demonstrated what could be gained not just from using virtual reality as a 'blank landscape' on which to build familiar building shapes, but as an analogue of mental space, a frame of reference within which to pull together and organise a collection of ideas, objects and experiences. This certainly becomes an attractive train of thought when we also think about some of our modern discourses on knowledge. Modern philosophy (and, indeed, modern museological thinking) continues to re-emphasise constructive, discursive, fluid meanings of objects, characterised by the way they resist meta-narratives, explore coexisting realities, layer concurrent discourses, centre the 'I'/eye, and constantly interplay and reconfigure the signifying world (Hooper-Greenhill 1994, 1992: 204–15). These are the tenets (the defining characteristics) of the linguistic, cultural, pedagogical milieu of our contemporary state – frequently gathered up under the umbra of something called 'post-structuralism'. But, however much we may agree or disagree with the fetishising that goes on about this critical theory, it is, nevertheless, hard to ignore the connections between these characteristics and the characteristics of virtual reality technology. For virtual space is, likewise, dynamic and fluid in the way it interconnects elements within its structure. And, as with all hypermedia, virtual reality space revels in layered meanings, and coexisting discourses. Moreover, unlike other formats and media, it celebrates and centres the eye of the user; the connectivity between objects (i.e. 'meaning') is assembled entirely for the individual. In this way, virtual reality might be seen as a perfect analogue for the post-modern condition. In virtual reality everything is reduced to representation. Nothing has an accessible history. Everything is configured for and revolves around the individual. Looking/reading is interactive, and, therefore, an act of production and creation. It is a self-oriented world of surfaces and contemporaneous moments. In a sense, it is the very essence of post-modernity.

The space of virtual reality also appears consistent with the new spatial discourses of the modern museum. We can detect, for instance, in the past generation or so shifts and changes within the ways museum spaces are routinely conceived, constructed and used. Today we are familiar with creative attempts to subvert, re-imagine and re-configure many of the qualities of classical space (the proportioned façade, the symmetrical plan, rooms arranged linearly *en filade*) by something more malleable and visitor centred. Similarly, in the museum of the new century we are used to exhibition content that is not necessarily fixed, but can be affected and changed by the visitor. Likewise, we recognise (and encourage) in today's museum an active dialogue (whether physical or intellectual) between the visitor and the museum, with the visitor's capacity to imagine, and the visitor's imagination being acknowledged and used. And, again, in contrast to its classical forebears, museum space today strives to be physically and intellectually inclusive, relevant and welcoming, reducing the number of material and cultural barriers, complementing linear narratives with highly entropic spaces that do not privilege one single pathway. Consequently, the twenty-first-century museum visitor is understood to be engaged and immersed within the experience, rather than a passive spectator or acquiescing recipient of it. With both the physical forms themselves (the architecture) and our conception of them (the discourse) transformed, we witness a movement from a museum space that is prescribed, authored, physical, closed, linear and distant, to a space that instead tends to be something more dynamic, discursive, imagined, open, radial and immersive. A movement, we might say, from *hard* space to *soft* space. Therefore, as the paragon of soft space, virtual reality (and the space of virtuality) becomes a compelling medium to use in today's museum.

The role of the 'unreal' in the museum

Virtual reality also provides for museums a liminal space, a space somewhere between the tangible and the imaginary. This is a threshold, indeed, upon which museums have always thrived. In fact if we look back at the history of museum

Figure 4.4 Replica biplane at Bristol's City Museum and Art Gallery. Copyright Jon Pratty.

display and visiting, we quickly see that, as well as being fortresses of the genuine and the original, museums have also, importantly, been performative spaces; a fact that is crucial to understanding how virtuality came to be accommodated in the museum. The acts of collection and documentation in the museum have always been selective, creative and culturally specific (Pearce 1995; Šola 1997). They are, consequently, a performance of sorts, something authored, and something ultimately subjective. Even some of the items museums have attempted to collect (such as the photographic negative or the mass-produced commercial product) have made curators and visitors alike ponder where the 'original' object might reside (Besser 1997: 118). Likewise, the disciplines of conservation and restoration have continued to pose their own set of dilemmas on how an object might remain 'authentic'. Furthermore, be it in the pressing of prints, the incising of engravings, or the casting of statuary, even the art object itself is forever entwined within a complex culture of re-production in which the notions of the 'original' and 'genuine' are not always clear (Miller 2002: 26). Evoking the sensation of watching other forms of media, Anderson reminds us of how even the act of looking at a framed painting in a gallery can invariably be 'through a glass screen' (1997: 21). Moreover, by using models and dioramas in their displays museums had, of course, always walked a careful line between fact

Figure 4.5 Perspectival illusory effects in an exhibition blurring the real and the imaginary. Copyright the author.

and make-believe. Immersive environments in the museum were by no means the prerogative of the modern 'virtual' age. Pearce explains, for instance, that as far back as 1810 visitors to 'showman' William Bullock's museum in Picca-dilly were witness to an illusory spectacle (the like of which London had never seen) of a natural setting of animals, including artificial trees and mock veg-etation (2007). In fact, two centuries earlier, at the start of the seventeenth century we find entertainments at the English court creating even more spectacular effects among their sometimes didactic and instructive narratives. These court masques (spatial expositions of the royal wisdom) were one of a number of precursor festivals and exhibitory events that would feed into the varied histories of the modern museum. Within these entertainments (a mix of dance, music, poetry and visual spectacle) the normal rules of reality were suspended by something more studied, fantastic and affected. As they presented their histories and allegories through the latest mechanical devices and perspectival technologies, the grand expository spaces in which these Renaissance court shows took place attempted temporarily to transport their audience away from the trappings of the everyday. It was these traditions (of liminality[3] and instructive other-worldliness) that the museum would inherit (Strong 1995). And it was these traditions that would forever keep performance, theatricality and (in a sense) 'virtuality' as a defining characteristic of the museum.

Consider for instance the way the British Museum's exhibition *Mummy: the inside story* was trailed:

> Ancient Egyptian mummies, jealously guarding their secrets, are a constant source of fascination and mystery. As a reflection of this enduring interest the British Museum has undertaken a unique project that will unlock the secrets of a 3,000 year old mummy and forever alter our understanding of ancient Egyptian civilisation. The result of this project is an extraordinary new Virtual Reality experience which has been sponsored by BP. The British Museum has carefully selected one of its most remarkable mummies, that of Nesperennub, a priest from the temple of Khons who lived in 800 BC to undergo the first ever 'virtual unwrapping'. Using leading edge computer technology and state-of-the-art medical scanning techniques, the British Museum will reveal the mysteries of Nesperennub's mummy non-invasively, without opening the case and disturbing the carefully arranged wrappings and amulets. In what is a world first, the Museum has teamed up with computer specialists Silicon Graphics (SGI), to take visitors on a unique journey of discovery, exploring the lives of ancient Egyptians, and allowing visitors to see beneath the wrapping of the mummy. Visitors to the British Museum's special exhibitions gallery will enter an introductory area where they will learn about the world of ancient Egypt, the practice of mummification, and how 3D technology can reveal the secrets of an unopened mummy-case. A spectacular twenty-minute Virtual Reality experience will then be shown in a specially designed immersive theatre which is equipped with a twelve-metre curved screen and stereo projection equipment. Wearing 3D glasses, visitors will experience a virtual tour of the mummy's body, discover how it was preserved 3,000 years ago and what special objects were placed in its wrappings. The experience will feature computer generated models and historical reconstructions showing how Nesperennub would have lived. The final area of the exhibition will feature Nesperennub's mummy displayed in its spectacular painted coffin alongside examples of the fascinating artefacts featured in the 3D

projection. Explanatory panels and labels will tell the stories from the hieroglyphs and inscriptions on the mummy's beautifully decorated case and
coffin.

(British Museum 2004)

Here virtual reality technology is presented as a tool, a 'technique' for finding
out more. And yet, it is also conveyed as part (if perhaps an extension) of the
usual display devices and interpretive media that a museum might use – and has
always sought to use. The spaces and experiences presented here (the introductory area, the theatre, the final physical reconstruction) are consistent with the
other 'displays' and 'models' that we might encounter in a museum. These, in
other words, are presented as familiar curatorial tools of display. Furthermore,
the language here is of inspiration ('first ever', 'will be revealed', 'unique journey of discovery'), education ('will learn about', 'fascinating', 'explanatory')
and entertainment ('spectacular'). Consequently, rather than 'dumbing-down',
the message here is designed to assure us (and perhaps the museum) that this
'experience' is entirely consistent with the institution's usual mission. The virtual mummy is, in other words, as credible and as real as anything else the
museum might offer.

The masquing hall, Bullock's London museum, the dioramas of the nineteenth
century and the reconstructions and simulations of the modern gallery experience, are all part of the same tradition of spectacle within museums, a tradition
of illusion and the suspension of disbelief. Hence, curators and visitors have
been used to negotiating questions of trust and validity even before the advent
of digital technology and so-called 'digital objects'. Whether in noticing that
the trees in Piccadilly were not real, or that the mummy on the screen is only
a picture, museums' staff and audiences have colluded over many centuries to develop a subtle visual literacy that has always managed to distinguish
the authentic. Intangibility, virtuality and simulacra are all part of what a
museum has been and continues to be. In its 'otherness', therefore, digitality
has a powerful (and entirely compatible) part to play in such a project. In short,
virtuality is another instantiation of the mimesis that museums have always
enjoyed: 'a reflection upon the virtual is what guides our understanding of the
real' (Lefebvre 1991: 219).

Objectifying information

However, there was another factor that facilitated the acceptance of digital
objects (numerical new media) into the museum. Not only was digitality consistent with pre-existing modes of spectacle and mimesis, but it was also
concordant to museums' long-established reverence for the informational. As
much as museums had prized and collected objects, so they had prized and collected the information that gave meaning and context to those objects. The
object and the information about that object have been forever fused, part of
the same whole in museum curatorship – one rarely existing without the other.

This is perhaps exemplified best in the humble museum label. For some four hundred years museums have used textual labels in their displays, labels that are fixed both in terms of format and of content. Textual commentary and interpretation on the material collections of a museum (the 'emblematic approach') is entrenched in curatorial practice and visitor expectation. And yet, today, the text label lives. In fact, writing text labels is for most museums still the orthodoxy. Reflexively, curatorial practice still presupposes the existence of text labels in exhibitions. Text books and seminal studies remind students and curators alike of how '[w]ords make us think, and our thoughts conjure up pictures in our minds', and how, consequently, it is through the mental pictures like these (which we find in a museum's text) that we 'discover the world around us' (Ekarv 1994). 'The exhibit that tells its story successfully', McKay (1982) prescribes, 'does so through the effective organization of label information and historic materials.' Understanding the relationships of labels to one another, it is said, is one of the keys to good exhibit work. Consequently, when Hirschi and Screven (1996) think about the education benefits visitors receive from attending a museum, it is, for them, through the information contained specifically in the labels that 'any true understanding of the exhibits' can be gained. The principle that every object in an exhibit should have some form of identification appears to be engrained in best practice, and embedded in curatorial culture; '[i]f it is important enough to show the public,' so the thinking goes, 'it's important enough to have a label' (DeRoux 1998a).[4]

Indeed, many museums remain uncomfortable with the idea of displaying objects without labels. It was this assumption, after all, that helped define the Henry Moore Institute's exhibition in 2001–2, 'Unidentified Museum Objects: Curiosities from the British Museum'. Curators James Putnam and Stephen Feeke filled the small space of 'Gallery 4' at the institute (in Leeds, UK) with a number of objects ('UMOs') from the British Museum's collection that had evaded classification and whose function and provenance were shrouded in doubt. However, it was the capricious absence of text labels (and, consequently, the un-tethering of meaning and the removal of the voice of the authoritative museum) that served mischievously to unsettle and provoke the visitor. The curatorial joke, the intellectual exercise, could only work if text labels were understood – by museum and visitor alike – to be an essential part of what an exhibition should be. The 'missing' labels, therefore, brought not just the objects, but the whole idea of an exhibition into question.

Even in the hypermedia moment, the emblematic coupling of text-and-image, text-and-object, has been resilient. At times, the frames of reference for building digital content in museums are, it seems, defined by the established practice of 'label writing'. Aspects of the presentation of mobile multimedia are likened to 'the titles of written labels', and the mobile text itself functions 'like interpretive labels' (Katz et al. 2006). Similarly, the semiotics of 'labels' has remained (sometimes predictably so) part of museums' design of digital interactive applications (Speroni et al. 2006). And, certainly, if we turn to an example such as the targeting and depth of information provided by the 'Smart Web Exhibit' (by the Carnegie Mellon University Libraries, the School of Computer Science at Carnegie Mellon University and the Carnegie Museum of Natural History) we see at play perhaps an augmentation (rather than a jettisoning) of the traditional label. For the curatorial approach here is still, essentially emblematic (Callery and Thibadeau 2000). Object labelling remains present in the habits of thumbnailing that characterise our presentation of on-line catalogues (Trant et al., 2000), the textual descriptions that structure our digital resources (Addis et al. 2005), the metadata that encode our on-line image databases (Bennett and Jones 2001), and the alternative text that tags our accessible 'captioned images' (Bowen et al. 2001). Even the current phenomenon of social tagging in the context of museum collections is described by its leading exponents as a form of 'labeling' (Chun et al. 2006). Evidently, the formats may change, interfaces may vary, the content may be more dynamic, but in each of these cases the culture of the museum 'label' is sustained.

There are (at least) two cultural streams that flow into the emergence of the museum label, in the European tradition: the culture of the *emblem*, and the culture of *classifying*. One tradition is from the world of pageantry, poetics and display, the other from the world of natural philosophy and cataloguing.

In terms of the former, it is with reference to Valeriano's *Hieroglyphica* that D. J. Gordon (see Orgel 1980) helps us to understand a European Renaissance moment where text and image became conjoined within (and to) museum culture. Through emblems and *impresa*, it was in the sixteenth century that a 'combination of picture and motto or legend' (ibid.: 16) was fuelled by a great vogue for hieroglyphs. Although the meaning of these emblems was at times deliberately 'elitist, abstruse, exclusive' (ibid.: 18), the goal was both to convey and to embody a 'hidden wisdom'. For the Elizabethans, Gordon explains, there was 'an area of ambiguity, powerful in its application, about the relationship between name and thing, representation and object – even name and person' (ibid.: 21). Consequently, as the early seventeenth-century natural philosopher Francis Bacon had explained in his famous *Advancement of Learning* (1605), 'Emblem reduceth conceits intellectual to images sensible, which strike the memory more' (Yates 1966). Therefore, the early museums' and cabinets' use of an emblematic presentation of images and objects (with interpretive and instructive text) would have been recognisable within (and consistent with) the rest of the cultural landscape of the late Renaissance and Baroque in Europe – a landscape where this marriage of image/object with text was understood to be an act of eloquence and wisdom. Crucially, the place we would recognise today as 'museum' comes into focus for the modern eye at just this time, and consequently, it is not surprising to find an emblematic tradition at the core of the museum's *modus operandi* – both then and today.

However, flowing into this early modern impulse to caption image with text came another discourse – more systematic, but just as complex and just as laden with meaning. As the magic, resemblances, interpretations and dualities of the medieval and Renaissance worlds became outmoded (at least for those individuals influencing political and intellectual life) by the reason and systematic rigour of new scientific projects of measurement and order, so the museum became a place of 'overarching explanatory narratives' (Pearce 1995: 371), where 'the establishment of records, of filing systems for them, the drawing up of catalogues, indexes, and inventories, worked as a way of introducing an order between all things' (Hooper-Greenhill 1992: 137). Crucially, it was from this moment (at the end of the seventeenth century) that museums such as the Aldrovandi in Bologna and the Plater museum in Basle were among the first institutions to incorporate text labels into their exhibitions (Murray 1904). Here, their text labels became an embodiment of this 'classified time' (Hooper-Greenhill 1992: 137) and the instructive agenda that the Enlightenment museum held at its core. A museum had a collection, but giving order and meaning to this collection were its labels.

With this rich heritage behind it, and with exhibition texts understood (by some) to be a 'central component of a museum's communication agenda' (Ravelli 2006: 3), practitioners today continue to reflect upon the form, function and content of labels. Analysis has varied from practical approaches on use of tone and style (Kentley and Negus 1996), to more empirical measuring and testing of text label legibility and readability. Equally, the conception of label text has varied from approaches that have advocated 'concrete' structures and condensed writing, to others that have emphasised the importance of rhythm in the construction of gallery text; 'you can concentrate text', says Ekarv (1994), 'to an almost poetic level'. Guidelines on writing text labels have at times been prescriptive (McKay 1982; DeRoux 1998a), stipulating typeface size and style, line length, leading, avoidance of overprinting, use of one idea or natural phrase per line, use of active verbs, avoidance of subordinate clauses, and so on (Gilmore and Sabine 1994). At other times, less regulatory, critical linguistic analysis has been applied (Coxall 1991).

Unsurprisingly, however, the text label has not remained insulated from modern museological criticism. Whereas a writer like Coxall might fear how a curator's text on a label might unconsciously perpetuate a stereotype or myth through its choice of language, Gurian's concern instead is rather for the myth of the text label itself (as medium) – and the assumptions it makes about visitor experience and learning. For Gurian (1991), the perpetuity of the text label in the modern museum is symptomatic of more lasting, and what she sees as more worrying, curatorial suppositions about the needs of a 'civilised person' within an exhibition.

And so it is that the modest text label (at least in its traditional, printed, static form, authored and given context by the museum) remains both iconic of what a museum is, and a symbol of what a museum should strive not to be. Moreover, for our discussions here on the informational nature of museums, it reminds us of an inherent non-materiality of the museum. To try and conceive 'museum' without information is to try and imagine 'object' without record.

> In terms of product, museums are (at the most fundamental level) concerned with information; and, by extension, with the knowledge shaped

from informational entities, and ultimately the wisdom acquired from extensive and experience-enriched knowledge.

(Macdonald and Alsford 1991: 306)

Moreover, to conceive 'museum object' (that is an object that has been selected and collected from another external, localised everyday context and placed within the frame of the museum), is fundamentally to conceive, by definition, a molecule of interconnecting pieces of information.

> The object is not the centre of the Universe. The sun does not go around the earth [. . .] the object is one of many equal components: materials, techniques, places of manufacture, geography, events, are all equal with the object name.
>
> (Sledge 2005)

The manual index card systems of the twentieth century (the information management tools that pre-dated the coming of standardisation and automation) poignantly represented, perhaps, the value that museums bestowed upon information. With their locked front doors and locked drawers, thought was being captured and then organised according to a personal rationale of the collector-curator. Rather than objects (and material culture), it was information and records that were being contained and ordered. It was now information about the collections that was being framed and prized in their own 'cabinets' – just as the objects themselves had once been. For generations, students of curatorship have been reminded of this point: 'the fundamental role of the museum in assembling objects and maintaining them within a specific intellectual environment emphasises that museum are storehouses of knowledge as well as storehouses of objects' (Cannon-Brookes 1984: 116). Consequently, the Smithsonian's initial grant application for federal funds to support its research and development into an automated information retrieval systems was aware of the complexity of information that surrounded an object: 'A specimen may be thought of as the kernel about which information accretes in successively more abstract (less specimen directed) layers' (1967). Therefore, today – as ever – the museum collects information, as much as it collects material things. Computers' ability to process, store and distribute information has proven, therefore, to be entirely compatible with this function.

However, the difference today may be in the value that is attributed to this information. In an ICOM conference keynote address, professor of sociology, Manuel Castells (2001: 5) reminded his audience of museum professionals of a fact they probably already knew: 'Much of our imaginary and our political and social practices', he explained, 'are conditioned and organised by and through the electronic communications system.' To Castells, the community of practitioners gathered to hear him were living within not just an information society (a society that super-produces and privileges the currency of information) but an informational society (a society that is also characterised by the way it focuses on the means by which information is produced and exchanged). That is, as much as modern society obsesses about having information (and attributing value and power to it), so equally it values (some might say fetishises) the systems by which this information is distributed. The notion of an 'information society' may have its roots back in the Second World War, and the invention of artificial intelligence, and may as a term and a concept have been in currency for some expert communities as early as the 1960s (Mattelart 2003: 2). However, it has been with the widespread adoption of digital technology – particularly distributed network technology and hypermedia – that the idea of the age defined by its preoccupation with generating and exchanging information has entered the popular imagination. In a single generation, technology has 'freed information from being a rigid, static, paper-bound, labour-intensive, difficult-to-communicate commodity accessible only to the select few into a plastic, dynamic, infinitely malleable, multimedia, available-to-all, ubiquitously present feature of our daily lives' (Abbott 1999: 138). In such an environment – an environment where information has a currency and proximity to power once associated with material possessions – the museum as both a rich repository and an active collector of information acquires both greater resonance and greater significance.

From the object-centred to the experience-centred museum

As the cultures of modernity increasingly came to venerate information (and value credible information) information technology became correspondingly more embedded in museum work. However, digitality also helped to support a realignment of museography that was taking place, from object-centred to experience-centred design (Hooper-Greenhill 2000; Witcomb 2003). Today, as Montaner notes, the 'positivist and classificatory culture of the post-Enlightenment' has (in the main) been supplanted by a more interactive and experiential learning ethos (1990: 18). 'Beyond the cult of the valuable object', Montaner observes

> the predominant element in these museums, much more than the object in itself, is the discourse – the logical sequence, the syllogistic chain, the reasoning process which each individual display and the overall script of the exhibition as a whole seek to expound.
>
> (1990: 21)

Therefore, rather than threatening the museum, another reading of the past forty years of museum computing sees digitality and virtuality (and the 'e-tangible') synchronising with existing curatorial discourses that had valued information, liminality and mimesis. A machine that processed data, that could provide an alternative representational space and that could generate simulacra, was highly compatible with practices already present in both curatorship and the visiting experience. Simply put, before computing came along, museums had already been performing many of the functions of computers.

81

5

Rescripting the visit

The museum as framed experience: event and circumscription

In the previous two chapters we have looked at how both the *automated* and the *numerical* qualities of digital media played against the workings and discourse of the museum. In each case we have seen points of fundamental incompatibility: the numerical reductionism in an environment that privileged materialism; and the emphasis on systematisation and standardisation on curatorial practices that were localised and idiosyncratic. Working alongside these histories, however, we have also highlighted the points at which the concept of the museum and the functionality of the computer synchronised, specifically in terms of the role of simulation and display within each, and of how both worked to store, index and connect data. In this chapter we shall take the third of Manovich's principles of new media – *modularity* and its composition as discrete blocks of content which can be reordered or dispersed. Here, as in previous and subsequent chapters, we will resist building a single narrative, working instead to draw out the contrasting stories of compatibility and incompatibility. We shall begin by considering how the modular nature of digital media (networkable and fragmentary) did not sit well – at least at first – against the singularity privileged by museums. As we shall see, new media's ability to disaggregate had awkward implications for museums – particularly in terms of the ideas of the museum 'visit' and the museum as 'venue'.

'Bringing a multitude into one': the museum and spatial architectonics

Until very recently, museums across the centuries have had a tendency to arrange something approaching absolute knowledge, within something approaching a single, absolute space. Hence, museums have been part of a powerful culture of systematically constructing knowledge through space. This is a culture (particularly in the European tradition) of seeing the shape and arrangement and content of buildings and landscapes as a framework for arranging ideas. One of the best-known demonstrations of this reading of space as mental analogue is Gaston Bachelard's *La Poétique de l'espace*. Written in 1957, this is a lyrical and mesmerising account of the *house* as a site of human reverie and memory. Reading poetry as the experience of a series of separate ('isolated') images, that exemplify our relations with the world, Bachelard used the familiarities of building space to co-ordinate his own 'phenomenology of the poetic imagination' (1994: xxiv; Jones 1991: 12–13). Positioning the house image as 'the topography of our intimate being' Bachelard drew upon Jung to present the structures of the built environment as 'a sort of picture of our mental structure' (1994: xxxvi). In Jung, Bachelard sees the grounds for 'taking the house as a *tool for analysis* of the human soul' (ibid.: xxxvii). To Bachelard, houses are 'psychological diagrams that guide writers and poets in their analysis of intimacy' (ibid.: 38).

> In the poetic house, therefore, we pause at various intimate stations (the cellar, the wardrobe, the garret), at each site contemplating (topoanalytically) the ontological power of the poetic image to retrieve through 'resonance' and 'reverberation' our (the reader's) memory of such a space.
>
> (Ibid.: xxii)

La Poétique de l'espace is, in other words, the 'self' as architecture. Of course, to modern criticism this concern with archetypes fails to give due consideration and weight to changing cultural conditions and differences of reading that should make generalisation at the level of the poetic image difficult, if not impossible (Langston 1982: 403). (In our current post-structuralist and post-colonial condition, we would tend to resist such universals, especially those that impose cultural assumptions.) And yet, the use of physical spaces such as Bachelard's poetic house to delineate, denote, embody or evoke a specific shape of knowledge (a mental architecture) remains an enduring trait of our modern Western cultures. Bachelard (and *La Poétique de l'espace*) remind us of the close, enduring associations that exist between space and knowledge.

At the moment when many of the first museums of early modernity were being formed, the scholar Sir Henry Wotton explained how buildings could stand as important loci, with

> Every Mans proper Mansion House and Home, being the Theater of his Hospitality, the Seat of Self-fruition, the Comfortablest part of his own Life, the Noblest of his Sons Inheritance, a kind of private Princedome; Nay, to the Possessors thereof, an Epitomie of the whole world.
>
> (1968: 82)

This Renaissance culture in which Wotton lived (and in which museums as we know them today were born) was a culture that expressed its thought through shape. Moreover, the pattern that perhaps most characteristically shaped the thought of the Renaissance mind was that drawn from the built environment – from building. The Renaissance, more perhaps than any other time before or since, was a period within which physical space (particularly physical *building* space) carried profound, analogous associations with the abstract mental realm. Spirituality was one such realm within which analogies between mind and building were frequently made. To present the church or indeed faith as a physical building in this way would prove to be far from an uncommon device in the sixteenth and seventeenth centuries. With plentiful biblical themes and verses on building, sermons on the church 'built on the rock of Christian Doctrine' were commonplace (Barrell 1624). In a sermon, for instance, preached in the chapel of the Free School in Shrewsbury (at its consecration by the Bishop of Coventry and Lichfield on 10 September 1617) Sampson Price had urged his congregation to conceive the Temple of Heaven as they would a 'material Temple'; 'Here we are in Gods chamber of Presence', he had pressed, 'that we may be brought into his presence and chamber of joy, whence we shall never be shut out' (1618: 25). Similarly, back in 1590, when Richard Alison had dedicated his treatise on Brownism to the queen's privy councillor, Sir Thomas Henedge, urging him to continue 'furthering the Lordes building', the author's sense was as much to the concept as it was to the physicality of the church as architectural project (1590: dedicatory epistle). Moreover, this was an architectural project – as a printed sermon of 1624 explained – within which the archbishop of Canterbury was 'Master-builder', and Christ 'that greatest, and chiefest Architect'. At least this was the scheme of things according to Robert Barrell, who in 1624 presented 'the art of Spiritual Architecture', a doctrine on 'how to build up thy self to be an house or temple for the Lord' (1624). Later, within his *Architectural Consolation* William Gilbert promised the reader that he would 'keep close the Metaphor of Building' (1640: 5). And, sure enough, Gilbert kept to his word. Built according to 'Christian proportion', with the promises of God's Word 'the grounds', the words themselves 'the materials', he drafts a design of spiritual consolation within which the Holy Ghost acts as 'Head-worker' (ibid.: 18, 6, 16 and 7).

As much as physical building space served as a metonym of the macrocosm of the universe, so knowledge of this universe came to be expressed in the shape of buildings. For instance, in his book entitled *The Castle of Knowledge*, geometrician Robert Record had (in 1556) conceived the whole of knowledge itself as a building, fully illustrated as an emblematic image on the treatise's opening page. Likewise, the compendium of choice histories of great princes, collated by one William Painter (clerk to Queen Elizabeth I), was presented under the title *The Palace of Pleasure*. The author made clear in his dedicatory epistle that he thought he had chosen this title 'fitly', for 'like as the outward show of Princes Palaces be pleasant at the view and sight of each mans eye [in] our Palace here, there be at large recorded the Princely parts and glorious gifts of renowned wits represented'. In effect, it was in the architectural form of an archetypal palace that Painter saw an appropriate imaginary space within which he could 'dutifully exhibit' his collected thoughts (1556: dedicatory epistle). A similar approach had been adopted by the inventor Hugh Platt when he produced a short reference book on 'Husbandry, Distillation and Molding'. In an attempt to 'disclose and manifest, even those secret and hidden magisteries [. . .] which I had long since entered in a case of marble', Platt fashioned his exposition as *The Jewell House of Art and Nature* (1594: dedicatory epistle). Likewise, the manual of spelling and arithmetic (dedicated to King James I) arranged in 'brief and compendious Tables' was positioned by its author, John Evans, as a *Palace of Profitable Pleasure* (1621). Stansby (the printer of Evans's book) two years later printed a sermon which went on to explicate these building tropes fully. *The Kings Tower and Triumphant Arch of London* contained a passage wherein its author, Samuel Purchas, presented the whole world as a 'magnificent house', where heaven is 'the roof', the moon and stars 'night-Lamps', its regions 'rooms', the earth is 'the floor', its surface 'an embroidered carpet', the sea 'a mote', and the woods, sands and other partitions of countries are 'walls' (1623: 26–7). Thoroughly and systematically, Purchas conceived the world as if it was a 'common hall'. As with Painter's and Evans's 'Palaces', Platt's 'Jewel House', and Record's 'Castle', Purchas's world (reduced to the image of a house) is part of the wider early modern culture that comfortably realised both the site and content of knowledge as recognisable building spaces. In each of these cases (and many more besides across England and Europe at this time) mental spaces were finding resemblances in the shape of building. Knowledge was being exhibited in (and through) space. It is in these schemas that we begin to see the origins of museum exhibition and display.

One reason why Renaissance culture arranged and presented knowledge as physical building space was to do with memory – or mnemonics. From Cicero to Giordano Bruno, artificial memory was a cognitive method that dated back through the Middle Ages and beyond. The English edition of one such treatise on mnemonics (published in 1562) showed how it was the ordered spaces of imaginary buildings that provide the 'true proportion' and 'degree' to remedy confused thoughts. The reader is instructed to

> take or choose a great and empty house, to which you must not go often but seldom, [. . .] and set the first place which at the door. Let the second place be twelve or fifteen foot distant from that. Let the third place be distant from the second even as many as twelve foot and there may be perchance another corner [. . .] And if you will have any more places, go out of the chamber, & so mark or note the other chambers proportionally.
> (Bergomatis 1562: Chapter VIII)

In effect, an individual uses the shape of a building (or a series of buildings) as a structure within which to arrange and store the thoughts to be remembered. (A list of tasks arranged along a familiar route or journey; a set of objects remembered by arranging them around an imaginary house.) In short, buildings serve here as an absolute space, a frame to contain and structure information and ideas. The use of these 'knowledge architectures' (Cubitt 1998: 13) brought 'a multitude into one' (Bergomatis 1562: Chapter VI). This was a cognitive method that had a prodigious history back to antiquity (Yates 1966: 1–2, 26). By the time the first English museums (of the Tradescants) were beginning to welcome in the public, full mnemotechnic manuals were circulating in English society, including diagrams of rooms set out as memory places, and providing readers with fully developed personal strategies for organising thought and knowledge.

And, again, here is where this history feeds into the history of museums. For it is through these traditions (architectural and mnemonic) that we find the preconditions and precursors which became the modern museum exhibition – where ideas and knowledge are arranged within the confined walls of an absolute building space, and where physical space becomes an analogue of mental space. To see the modern museum (as Hetherington does) as a 'spatial relation that is principally involved in a process of ordering' is to locate museums within a particular spatial culture and tradition that was prevalent at the time of their inception (1996: 155). The origins of this tradition were within the memory architectures and macrocosmic buildings of the Renaissance.

The modern museum can be read as knowledge made spatial. For instance, within their study of the Natural History Museum, London (designed by Alfred Waterhouse and first opened to the public in 1881), Peponis and Hedin (1982) have offered important observations on its spatial organisation, especially the connections with the transmission of scientific knowledge. In their work, the space of the Natural History Museum's original Bird Gallery is shown to correspond to 'the table of classification on which immutable beings find their correct position' (in other words, the theory of Natural History prior to Darwin's theory of evolution).[1] The expository space is connected to the 'underlying governing rules of knowledge'. In short, the museum space is categoric, as the tabular classifications of nineteenth-century science were categoric. What, therefore, Peponis and Hedin show so powerfully is how the layout of physical space can become part of the reproduction of forms of enunciation and transmission of thought. In the nineteenth-century museum, as in the space of the sixteenth-century house of thought, we see space 'utterly enmeshed in the organisation of knowledge' (1982: 25, 21).

At a very fundamental level, therefore, museums are involved with what we could usefully call 'spatial architectonics' – the systematic construction of knowledge through space. In one sense museums are a medium that – enduringly – uses physical, tangible, three-dimensional space to present certain formations of thought. And, it seems, this owes a great deal to the early modern and classical moment that saw their nascency. For it was in the Renaissance (in Europe at least) that the singularity of a building space (whether real or imaginary) came, habitually, to denote the shape of knowledge. Whatever way they may change (whether as ecomuseum or on-line resource), museums today forever inherit and belong to this classical tradition – the tradition that entwined architectures of thought with the architecture of buildings; that created mental formations in the shape of buildings, and physical buildings formed by mental shapes.

The museum as hyperspace

For much of their existence, therefore, museums were condensed and consciously framed spatial demonstrations of knowledge. Hence they could serve as a microcosm of the world. If collections (and the act of collecting) were, as Mac-

Figure 5.1 The traditional exhibition space as a cabinet and microcosm. Copyright the author.

donald has argued, a 'way of maintaining some degree of control over the natural world' and 'an attempt to manage the empirical explosion of materials that wider dissemination of ancient texts, increased travel, voyages of discovery, and more systematic forms of communication and exchange had produced', then the so-called 'cabinets of curiosity' were, in turn, a strategy to organise and contain these collections within physical space (1998: 6). The world in microcosm, as captured in Renaissance cabinets, was just part of the myriad histories that fed into what we today recognise as the modern museum. And like the modern museum, these material arrangements of thought generated their own shape of space.

The imperial palace of Rudolf II, in Prague, had been significantly reworked to accommodate the shape of his magnificent collections (Kaufman 1988: 17). Rudolf's project was part of the same tradition that, in the previous century, had borne Piero de' Medici's *studiolo* – a contrived compact spectacle of manuscript books, gems and precious objects, formed as a testimony to the patron-collector's acquired wealth and learning (Jardine 1997: 183). On a less sumptuous scale (but following the same architectonic programme) the 'store' of Robert Cecil's former gardener John Tradescant the elder was – in the 1630s – co-ordinated in London into a singular exhibition space, known as 'The Ark'. In the words of the younger John Tradescant this was a collection of diverse 'rarities and curiosities', indexed by a 'catalogue' (conceived by its author as a 'view of the whole') and displayed for visitors to see for a payment of sixpence.

As Francis Bacon observed, these cabinets (essential commodities of the learned gentleman) were 'in small compass a model of the universal nature made private'.[2] In each of their co-ordinated taxonomies, mapped on to physical space, the architectures of knowledge contrived by early modern individuals such as the Medici family, the Emperor Rudolf and the Tradescants, advertised conspicuous connections between the orderings of the mind and the orderings of the physical world. Their cabinets represented another architectonic space, where a systematic structuring of knowledge was exhibited by the arrangement of material culture within a three-dimensional spatial medium (Pearce 1995: 371–2).

The dominant tradition in museums was to offer a circumscribed view of the world. In this respect museums connected to the programmes of 'pansophy' (universal, state-sanctioned acts of educational reform) pursued by men such as Samuel Hartlib and Comenius from the 1630s onwards; in Hartlib's case, the dream was of a great new public library in London, built on the foundations of the collections confiscated after England's civil wars in the middle of the seventeenth century (Greengrass 1993: 47). Indeed, from Marlowe's *Dr Faustus*, to Flaubert's *Bouvard et Pécuchet*, and from the 'pansophy' of Samuel Hartlib to Sartre's *Nausea*, the written culture of recent (European) history is punctuated with fables of obsessive projects to structure and contain knowledge – in many cases all knowledge. Museum discourse has frequently been flavoured with this rhetoric and this ambition. The ideal of a common catalogue of all collections had been in the background of UK museums from the inception of the Museums Association in 1889; one of the items on the agenda of its inaugural meeting related to the creation of an index of all provincial museum collections (Lewis 1965: 21; 1967: 88). Even at the nascent period for museum computing at the end of the 1960s, practitioners wondered whether the new technology 'might make possible for the first time in history a truly encyclopaedic, integrated, unified body of knowledge about man' (Hoving 1968: xi). Consider, for instance, the language of the Smithsonian in 1967:

> The collections are the substance of man's knowledge, the objects forming a three-dimensional library basic to the educational process and, as such, may be borrowed, visited and examined by students and professionals in the continuing process of expanding our knowledge of our environment, our world, our universe.
>
> (Smithsonian Institution 1967: 3)

In *La Production de l'espace*, Lefebvre describes a type of (what he calls) 'monumental' social space – a space that 'constituted a collective mirror' and offered members of a society an image of their membership, while implying a supercoding that tended towards 'the all-embracing presence of the totality' (1991: 225). In their aspirations to be universal mnemonic and framed microcosm, museums were for many centuries a monumental space.

For Lefebvre, however, museums would also be considered a hyperspace – a space in which the modes of spatial production were focused and intensified.

Museums, after all, were outside of the everyday. They were part of the world, but at the same time removed from the world. The world was around them, and yet they contained the world. Moreover, according to Lefebvre's philosophy, a museum would be a place where the different realms of space (lived space, representational space, and spatial logic) would form an intense dialectic (*trialectic*) producing an extraordinary space within any given society.

The central 'problematic' of Lefebvre's *La Production de l'espace* is 'space' itself. Lefebvre's objective is to establish and understand the 'paradigm' of space. Instead of analysing things in space, his subject is, rather, space itself, with a view to 'uncovering the social relationships embedded within it' (1991: 211 and 89). The kernel of his thesis (what he calls his 'critique of space') is a repulsion of the concept of space as an *a priori* condition of life (ibid.: 92, 85). Far from being a pre-existing void, Lefebvrean space – 'literally filled with ideologies' – is highly politicised. Consequently, in addition to being a means of production, social space (as a political, ideological construct) is – in Lefebvre's words – 'also a means of control, and hence of domination, of power' (ibid.: 26). Lefebvre articulates these ideas in a powerful – if sometimes quite overwhelming – way. From notions of inside and outside, symmetry and mirror images, to ideas of body space, gesture and sleep, Lefebvre takes the reader on a journey through the sometimes cluttered terrains of his thought, pausing (sometimes without warning) to take stock of what we have already seen, or to direct us towards a new vista of exploration, whether it be of Cubism, pollution or modern motorways.[3] This sense of Lefebvre sharing the act of charting a way through his own dense thesis is reinforced by the typesetting and formatting conventions that he uses for his text (such as indentations and bullet points). Each is a mental note, an *aide-memoire*, a summary. Similarly, his urgent use of italics at critical moments seems as much a signal to himself as to the reader that an important station has been reached. But perhaps the most characteristic aspect of the book is the use of short, sometimes even fragmentary, gobbets of writing. Indeed, one of the last pages describes sugar, coffee and a square of cloth – as if to give away a daily street-side routine that produced the essays that together make up *La Production de l'espace*.[4] In these ways (bullets and gobbets) Lefebvre seems at pains to provide simplicity wherever he can. (Frequently, he sets himself a question that he then distils to an emphatic 'Yes!' or 'No!') Part of this self-conscious plainness may be explained by his obvious suspicion of what he saw as the opaqueness and fetishised abstractions of modern critical theory. And yet, it is, in fact, theory that provides the spine for Lefebvre's work. For it is difficult to avoid the firm trunk of Marxism that stands at the core of his thinking. Lefebvre was a Marxist, and Marxism informs much of the thought of *La Production de l'espace*. He writes about following Marx's 'plan' (in *Capital*) 'in dealing with space' (1991: 100). His linear, incremental, progressive conception of historical time is shaped (to a great extent) by Marxist historiography (ibid.: 199–200). Even his rhetorical style (continually built from thesis, antithesis and synthesis) is shaped by a Marxist dialectic. Moreover, this inherent Marxism was allowed to form Lefebvre's thesis into a political document. For as much as *La Production de l'espace* may be read as a private engagement with spatial discourse (a lexicon to help us – as well as Lefebvre himself – articulate a history of space), it is at its centre (and, perhaps, primarily) an explosive public call for revolution against modes of capitalist production from a Paris still crackling with the events of 1968. His closing remarks make the point explicitly:

> This book has been informed from beginning to end by a *project*, though this may at times have been discernible only by reading between the lines. I refer to the project of a different society, a different mode of production, where social practice would be governed by different conceptual determinations.
>
> (1991: 419)

The 'project' that is the kernel of *La Production de l'espace* (apart from grappling with the 'orientations' of spatial production itself) is Lefebvre's 'revolution of space' against the 'phallus' and Capitalism of the modern state, against its violent domination, its betrayal of the body, and its dislocation of the mental from the physical realm. His engagement with space (however useful to us) is a means to an end – an end concerned with social change. 'To change life', he fires from the page 'we must first change space' (ibid.: 190).

The essence of Lefebvrean space, therefore, is a continual (and, more importantly, a historically specific) interplay between three different realms. The first of these is what Lefebvre calls *l'espace perçu* – the 'material space' or 'spatial practice' as perceived in the everyday world. The emphasis here is very much on visual perception. In contrast, the second realm (*l'espace conçu*) is the expert 'representation of space'. This, to Lefebvre, is the language, logic, techniques and knowledge of space. It is in this realm that the production of space gains its context of codes, theories, and 'conceptual depictions'.[5] *L'espace conçu* is, consequently, the space of 'social engineers', of quantified movement, and of the ordered isotropy. The third and final spatial realm is *l'espace vécu* – the essence of 'space as it might be, fully lived'. This is the realm of the ideal, of imagination, of categories of social thought and the spatiality that provides meaning to all aspects of life. It is, in a sense, the space within which we allow ourselves to think. In other words, the three realms are: discourses that see space; discourses about space; and the spaces within our discourses. They are: the space we see around us; our language and logic that we use to describe and understand it; and the spatiality inherent within this understanding. In short: the space perceived, the space conceived, and the spatiality of living.

Lefebvre's key point is that at each historical moment, and within each cultural situation, the state of each of these three elements may shift and change; at different times and in different contexts each realm may (or may not) be latent, perhaps ideological and sometimes (but not always) physical. It is the characteristics that each of the three realms has in each historical and cultural locality that distinguish that culture's mode of spatial production. The modern museum belongs, therefore, to a strong dialectic between the realms of 'material

Figure 5.2 An unambiguous threshold at the entrance to the Natural History Museum, London. Copyright the author.

space' and 'imagined space', organised and articulated through the assumptions amassed within the realm of *l'espace conçu*. Consequently, by using the predication, nomenclature and methodology of Lefebvre, a vision of museums emerges in which they are seen to be unique, separate, absolute spaces within which formations of social thought are given physical form in a focused, contained, structured and condensed way. We begin to see them as sites at which ideas are made topographical, thought made tangible. Moreover, we see them as unique arenas (unlike much of the social space around) in which the dialectic (the interaction) between each of the realms of space is very intense, and very conspicuous. Museums, in a sense, are the result of a very strong and very augmented spatial dialectic. They are (for want of a better word) *hyper*-space.

To summarise, therefore: for many centuries museums were influenced by some very specific European traditions of mnemonics and spatial philosophy. Consequently, they had grown to be highly singular, framed places. They were part of the world, but at the same time removed from it. The world surrounded them, but they too tried to encapsulate the world. As mnemonic, microcosm and hyperspace, the museum was a place (a circumscribed venue), and it was a space (a type of environment). To be anything other was for it no longer to be a museum. Consequently, the 'visit event' had traditionally been a framed experience, both in space and in time. A museum was something you went to, with a threshold that marked its separation from the everyday and that demarcated where these new forms of spatial production would begin. The problem was that the modularity of the computer was highly distributive and frameless. When network technology presented itself to the museum it appeared to contradict these defining tenets and deep-rooted cultural principles that for centuries had framed the museum as a specific, physical, microcosmic site. The advent of computer technology – or more specifically networked hypermedia – challenged the very notion not just of *what* a museum visit was, but also of *when* and *how* a museum visit could occur.

The challenge presented by distributed network media

Its inventor has called it 'a single, global information space' (Berners-Lee and Fischetti: 1999: 5). One of its leading patrons sees it as the device that 'will draw us together' (Gates et al. 1996: 314). The business world sees within it the ability to make commerce faster, cheaper and easier, whereas some social commentators view it, suspiciously, as part of a larger 'instrument of exploitation' and oppression (Cubitt 1998: 2). To others it is, variously: 'a networked consciousness' (Costigan 1999: xx); a tool for personal, community and gender empowerment (Alshejni 1999: 216); a repository of 'richness and diversity' (DfEE 1997: 4); and, in the words of one museum educationalist, it is considered to be part of 'a new world of human experience and behaviour' (Anderson 1999: 21). All this about a medium which, to many of those who use it each day, can sometimes seem somewhat banal. And yet, whatever our perspective, it is difficult to avoid the fact that since the mid-1990s a new form of mass communication has arrived. It is a computer-mediated communication that has reshaped many of the world's information exchanges. It is, of course, the World Wide Web.

Even before the Web had been invented, discussions in museum computing had envisaged a distributive network of museum resources.

> Only when the curator, the academic scholar, the registrar, and the exhibit designer, for example, have at ready access data banks in machine-readable form of museum holdings, bibliographies, and photo collections throughout the country – if not the world – will the 'museum without walls',[6] to borrow a phrase, become a reality.
>
> (Bowles 1968: xix)

As early as 1969 the Computing Centre at the University of Oklahoma had a system for the recovery of museum specimen records, called GIPSY (General Information Processing System). The data bank of records could be accessed via the telephone. At the time it was understood to be the first functional system for museum collection data retrieval that was completely accessible from any-where within the United States (Smithsonian Institution 1969b). The idea of a data bank came and went over the two decades that followed, but by 1993 – as the software for accessing the Web took a significant leap forward – regional museum services such as that at Nottingham (UK) were already cherishing 'the dream of a detailed on-line public-access database' (Cooper 1993: 12). Pro-active organisations such as the Canadian Heritage Information Network were, by 1994, immediately engaged with the potential of the Web for the museum community, with a CHIN home page, using Mosaic, directing users to infor-mation about the group, its services and products. 1994 was indeed the year when at least twenty 'pioneer' museums (mostly institutions with large budgets) were on-line around the world (Bearman and Trant 2006). The Virtual Library museums page (an on-line directory of museum Web sites originally started as a personal project by Jonathan Bowen in the UK, before its ownership moved to ICOM) had by August 1994 received 3,459 visits (Bowen 1997: 14). With heightened interest from a number of museums, the perspective of CHIN at least was that by the summer of 1995 'the Internet has engulfed us' (CHIN 1995).[7] In December 1995 a policy statement adopted by the executive council of ICOM announced that museums should be active contributors of informa-tion to the Internet about their programmes and collections in order to fully play their role in the service of society. In the same year a national conference, organised by the MDA in the UK, focused principally on museums' relation-ship with the Internet. By 1996 manuals on how museums could make the most of the Web were readily available (Gordon 1996). In 1997 the influential *Mus-eums and the Web* conference began its annual meetings, drawing around 400 practitioners together from around the world to reflect upon how each of them was making use of the new networked hypermedia. By 1998 museums' use of the Web had even reached a stage at which first histories and reflective sur-veys were being published internationally (Bearman and Trant 1999). And so,

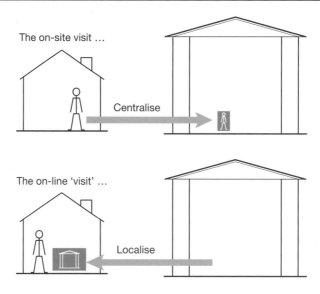

The on-site visit …

Centralise

The on-line 'visit' …

Localise

Figure 5.3 Centralised visiting to on-site museums and localised dissemination to on-line users.

by 1999, just five years on from the first attempts by the sector to confront the potential of this new technology, commentators were suggesting that it was already possible to see ways in which museums were being rethought in light of the Web's existence (Gere 1999: 60). As in many other parts of society, the impact of the Web on museum work was fast and widespread, and in a manner without precedent.

And yet the Web posed several problems for the museum. Its networked (modular) nature ran counter to the cultures of the microcosmic, the singular space and the physical visit that had been built over several centuries. First, there was the question of the visit. 'Visiting' had meant *being there*. A museum's business had been to attract visitors to its physical galleries. Visiting a museum's Web site was, therefore, thought by some to be a poor substitute, with any value given to a Web site 'visit' (compared with a *real* visit) merely an accident of language within the parlance of the new Web medium. Moreover, the traditional visit event involved the visitor (along with other visitors) congregating in the museum – having a social experience with the physical collections and sensations of the tangible exhibit. These were the spatial architectonics that had made museums what they were. Disruptively, the notion of a Web 'visit' turned this dynamic on its head. The museum would no longer be a centralised venue, with a threshold distinguishing its special liminal space from the outside world, but would instead be a broadcaster and publisher distributing packages of content to myriad localised and varied contexts. It would, in other words, be the museum that was doing the visiting. This was an entirely different proposition and appeared to go against the engrained protocols of curatorship and display.

Furthermore, if a museum did go on-line (and begin visiting its audience) it was likely to have very little control of (not to say, very little idea about) the exact circumstances, place and location of that visitor. In the gallery the museum knew exactly where the visitor was, and could manage most aspects of that visitor's experience. However, on-line, the visitors could have been anywhere. Were they at home, at work, at school? What assumptions could be made about the resources they had at their disposal, or whether there was anyone else with them? What time of day was it where they were? And did that matter? In other words, the centralised, shared and (largely) controlled experience of the on-site museum visit was, with the coming of the Internet, augmented by an array of more localised and potentially more individualised and unpredictable on-line experiences (Parry and Arbach 2005). The sense of the unknown was compounded by the fact that for many years of Web development, there was a lack of substantial and robust evidence on who exactly was visiting museum Web sites and what their motive for doing so was. Data were somewhat derivative from each other and drawn from small samples (Reynolds 1997; Futers 1997; Chadwick and Boverie 1999) or related to very specific types of services, resources or museum settings (Semper et al. 2000; Goldman and Wadman 2002). In fact, after the first pioneers made their hopeful way on to the Web, museums would have to wait almost a decade before they could obtain data that gave a rich and evidenced view of the motives and habits of their on-line users (Grant 2003; 24 Hour Museum 2003).

Another challenge to the entrenched notion of the circumscribed, site-specific museum was the way the Web appeared to scatter all that the institution had worked so hard to aggregate and frame. The modularity of networked hypermedia appeared to break down into individually discoverable chunks of data, the collections that museums were meant to bring together as a meaningful whole. As the Web (its users and its technologies) developed, so, unsettlingly, emerged the notion of a museum literally turned 'inside out' (Pratty 2006). Their modular nature made computers very good at grinding material down into atoms of digital content that could escape from the museum's traditional 'frame'. Whereas museums had traditionally sought to build a microcosm under one roof, and bring a multitude into one, computers, in contrast, appeared to shatter both this once-contained collection and this once-framed experience into a million globally dispersed fragments. The Web promised a museum 'without walls, with no sense of place, without any analogy to the three-dimensional institutional world of culture' (ibid.).

For many institutions (which may have taken a hundred years to develop their missions, organisational structures, documentation, exhibition philosophies), it would be difficult, when confronted with the exponential growth of the Web, to reshape and redistribute themselves to accommodate this new workflow and this new ontology. For many museums it would require not so much for them to adapt as fundamentally to re-sequence their DNA. For them, in a very fundamental way, the modularity of the distributed network was incompatible with the singularity that had for centuries defined the museum.

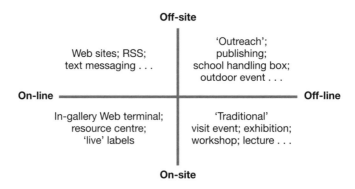

Figure 5.4 The evolution of modes and spaces of museum visiting.

The de-centred museum: from 'outreach' to 'in-reach'

Established practices of mobile and distance learning

However, there were other discourses and traditions also at play – and ones which were far more amenable to what the Web was offering. If museums looked hard enough at their histories, they could see that there had, in fact, been other cultures and other forms of practice that had – before the advent of the Web – already begun to disrupt the singularity of the circumscribed on-site museum. Huhtamo, for instance, has argued that pre-existing exhibition designs and interactive media (such as Futurism's and Dadaism's activation of the viewer, or the way other artists explored the use of art installations in domestic settings) were 'anticipations' of the sorts of approaches that museums could and did take to building their new 'virtual museums' (2002). More obviously, however, we can see that the idea of an off-site experience, of distance learning, of publication, of communities of visitors (and Friends) existing and interacting around and outside the museum building, were (just like the tradition of the 'microcosm') also all part of the museum's past. But unlike the microcosm, these were traditions of practice that had meant museums were, in many respects, already equipped to address on-line users – even, perhaps, to cope with Pratty's 'inside out museum' (2006).

Thirty-five years before most museums were reaching out with the Web, Leeds City Art Galleries had (in 1961) established a picture loan scheme based on its Print Room and Arts Library (Foster 1984: 74). In the 1970s there were travelling units already taking museum objects and exhibitions to the people. Sheffield City museum mounted travelling exhibitions in showcases located in branch libraries and hospitals (ibid.). Vans from the Visvesvaraya Industrial and Technological Museum in Bangalore were travelling into rural areas (Devaraj Urs 1974). Likewise, there had been object boxes in schools, and reminiscence and handling sessions in other institutions, as well as, of course, catalogues and other means of dissemination, enquiry services, not to mention

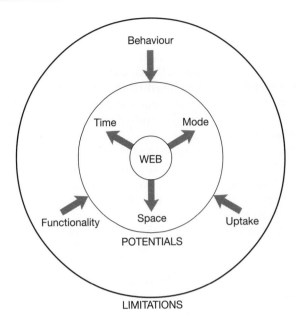

Figure 5.5 The potentials and limitations of the Web for museums.

multiple-site museums, museum 'outposts', and ecomuseums and integrated heritage management scenarios encompassing a geographically wide and complex area. The point was that well before they embraced the Web medium, museums had already managed relationships and supported learning with audiences at a distance and away from their physical galleries. Many of the skills and much of the apparatus required to publish, reach out and broaden participation were already in place in the museum. It did not take institutions very long, therefore, to associate the role and function of their new Web sites (which started to appear from the mid-1990s) with these previous attempts to offer visitors museum experiences outside the four-walled venue. The Web became just another of the multiple channels that museums were already building. Computing and the Web synchronised with these types of audience relationships, these patterns of work, and these visions of what a museum could be. New media became part of a wider *rescripting* of the traditional visit 'event', where a museum experience could not only happen at a distance, but could also perhaps be fleeting or unexpected.

The new modes of address

Like any of these other 'out-reach' programmes and projects (each with their own risk, resource implications, or curatorial choices) the Web was not without its limitations. First, the Web was not (and continues not to be) universally used and totally pervasive within society (Abungu 2002; Shneiderman

2000). This century, systematic and statistically significant research[8] has helped to generate a much higher resolution image of the complexities (as well as the imbalances) within Web usage. Access to connections, speed of connection, IT literacy, motivation and awareness all still determine that large proportions of modern society remain disenfranchised from, or simply choose not to participate in, the network community. As much as the Web empowers, so too has it the potential to deepen social divides and emphasise class structures at both a national and an international level (Cubitt 1998: ix). Even as uptake of the Web began to increase apace within the museum sector, critics aired concerns over the exclusivity of the medium, about the extent to which the museum remained 'in the hands of and largely the preserve of the, for want of a better phrase, bourgeois intelligentsia' (Gere 1997: 65). Plainly put, to use the Web medium is not to reach out to the entire community. Second, the Web is only as good as the technology that is driving it – the software that is coding it, the hardware that allows us to use it, and the connections that permit us to download it. Both the explosion in social computing and the rapid uptakes in broadband connectivity are testimony to how the functionality, appeal and content of the Web are ultimately driven (and limited) by the software and the hardware upon which the medium sits. Third, museums have begun to see how not everyone uses the Web in the same way, and how these patterns of usage and communication are culturally specific and in a constant state of change. So far audience research on on-line museum visitors is, compared with other parts of museum visitor studies, relatively poor. Through the use of on-line software, museums have become better at generating key types of data: how many unique visits the museum's Web site has; through which sites these visitors access the museum's site; and the length of time visitors stay on the site, and which pages they access. However, the challenge remains for museums to explore (and keep pace with) how the on-line museum culturally fits into the everyday lives of its users and potential users.

Pushing out at (and perhaps outweighing) these limitations remain the potentials of the Web for museums. Even by 1995 some commentators were in little doubt that the advent of new media presented museums with the opportunity to develop new ways of communication which allow the visitor to explore collections 'at their own pace and to their own requirements' (Fahy 1995: 82). Specifically, the Web can be seen to offer a new space, time and mode of experience for museum audiences. Most obviously, unbound by opening times (ironically the information that would most frequently adorn the first museum Web sites), users can choose to 'visit' the museum at whatever time suits them best and stay as long as they choose. (Indeed, the fact that the UK's first national virtual museum was styled in 1999 'The 24 Hour Museum' was tacit acknowledgement of this point (Stiff 1999).) In Web-time, consequently, both the repeat and the unplanned visit become potentially easier.

Second, the distributive nature of the Web allowed it to overcome and overarch boundaries and distances that ordinarily would punctuate and obfuscate the day-to-day physical landscape. It was as Benjamin had seen with mechan-

Figure 5.6 Tower observation floor, De Young Museum, San Francisco. Copyright Jon Pratty.

ical reproduction, the Web could put a copy of the original 'into situations which would be out of reach for the original itself' (1999). Like other reproduction technologies, the Web enabled the original 'to meet the beholder halfway' (ibid.: 215). The Web's provision for a more geographically spread constituency went without saying. More enthralling perhaps was its ability to relocate the museum in a way that might remove social and cultural obstructions that would preclude a visit, even for its local community. Consider, for instance, the example of the Royal Ulster Constabulary Museum, in Northern Ireland. Here the staff became 'aware that there were very specific barriers that severely restricted the nature of its audiences', located as it was then within the RUC headquarters in a high-security complex (Sandell and Dodd 1998). With what was then a deeply divided sectarian community, both religious and political sensitivities restricted access by particular audience segments to the museum. Consequently, faced with this, the museum chose to develop a Web resource to foster wider access to its collections across the whole of the community. It was only by drawing upon these alternative modes of address, and media of communication, that a bridge could be built – across the political divide to another audience. It is for just these sorts of encounters that Gere (appropriating a term from anthropologist James Clifford) sees the Web as a 'contact zone': 'the space in which peoples geographically and historically separated come into contact with each other and establish ongoing relations' (1997: 62).

Indeed, it was the nature of these relations that characterised the third key potential of the Web medium for museums. The Web allowed museums an entirely different (and unique) mode of address through which to connect to and build relationships with existing and new audiences. At a very basic level this meant supporting 'experiences that are not possible in the physical setting of the museum' (Bandelli 1999). Equally, it could mean accepting that the Web may provide an environment that is less excluding and more familiar to certain audience groups, as in the case of a project in Birmingham (UK) that used the cult(ure) of mobile phone ring tones as a hook and way of the museum connecting to a group of local children at risk of exclusion (Parry 2001a). Here the Web simply provided a more relevant, accessible, suitable means of interaction. However, what both these points speak to is the fact that the Web appeared to recodify acts of social engagement. It is van Dijk who helps perhaps to see more clearly how these operators of interaction came to be rebuilt. Van Dijk identifies a series of models of communication each of which can be related to existing or older media (1999). *Allocation* (the simultaneous distribution of information to an audience of local units by a centre) is not changed and, if anything, is eroded by new media. *Consultation* (the selection of information by local units, which – unlike allocation – decide upon the subject matter, time and speed) is enhanced by new media. The opportunities for *registration* (the collection of information by a centre which determines the subject matter, time and speed of information sent by a number of local units) are also increased by new media. Van Dijk argues that a fundamental change had taken place in the pattern of *conversation* (the exchange of information by two or more local units, addressing a shared medium (instead of a centre) and determining the subject matter, time and speed of information and communication themselves). Of much greater significance, however, was the way the new networked digital media environment appeared to agglomerate each and all of these different modes of communication. The 'network society' drew the operators of *allocation, consultation, registration* and *conversation* into a single medium – an integrated network. It is for this reason that the new networked media represented a 'communications revolution' (ibid.: 12–15). And it was in this way that, during the 1990s, the Web presented to museums an entirely unique communication model. It was a model in which the museum could, at different times in different contexts, be both at the centre and at the periphery of communication, it could initiate or it could respond, it could both authorise and request, and it could address a multitude or connect to a single user. Consequently, with its functional ability to support both inter-personal and mass communication, the new networked media could effectively sustain whole communities of 'network users'. Therefore, really, the Web offered the museum (and its audiences) a medium rather than a product, a set of tools rather than a specific experience. The on-line museum was not just a repository, but more a community of activity, dialogue, exchange and creation, comprising public and private spaces, formal and informal interactions, shaped by the community themselves, and (perhaps) complemented by on-site, or face-to-face experiences.

When museums first began to build their sites in the mid-1990s, the information architectures on these new on-line spaces invariably aped the physical and institutional architectures of the on-site space (Trant 1998: 108). However, in time, as Battro has noted, the virtual museum has ceased to be a simple reflection of the real one; it has developed a life of its own (1999). The Web has moved beyond what a frustrated Bandelli once called 'just graphic representations of existing spaces' (Bandelli 1999). And – enthrallingly – it is the *modularity* of digital media (the very same modularity that had appeared to threaten the sanctity of the 'visit event' and which appeared to dissolve the cohesion and integrity of the framed 'collection') that has reshaped and relocated the museum. Drawing on the existing practices of out-reach and publication, the Web has allowed the notion of the visit to be re-scripted further, and more channels to be opened through which a museum can build a relationship with its widening audience (Rellie 2004). What was once unthinkable (a de-centred space, with distant visitors and atomised distributed collections) is now becoming what the 'multi-channel museum' aspires to be.

6

Rewriting the narrative

The museum as cultural freezer: fixity and authorship

This movement from outreach to 'in-reach' (Parry 2001a) identified in the previous chapter marks a significant change. Rather than being approached by the museum, audiences instead have the means (through digital network hypermedia) to initiate and create, collect and interpret in their own time and space, on their own terms. It amounts to nothing less than a realignment of the axes of curatorship. This shifting in the curatorial landscape is made possible not just by the *modular* nature of new media (which allows digital content to be broken down and moved), but also because of what Manovich calls its *variability*. New media are variable in as much as, unlike the fixed text of the printed word, the final cut of a film, or the live broadcast of a television transmission, their content remains, instead, open to further editing and authorship. With no finalised moment of imprint or publication, digital content is forever an unfinished project, open to further amendment or reconstitution. This *variable* quality of new media provides us with the next (our fourth) principle through which to understand the relationship between museum and computer. Much like Manovich's other principles that we have investigated thus far, the impact of this function proves, likewise, to be double-edged – both a challenge and an opportunity for the museum. For *variability* interferes with the authorship and authority of the curator, and yet allows new narratives to be told and new voices to be heard.

The museum as controlled environment

The orthodoxy has been for museums to value stability, to act as cultural freezers into which societies drop and trap elements of their world and experience, preserving them as best they can – a 'controlled environment' both intellectually and physically. It is then from this 'control' that museums assume their position of authority, and it is the verifiability and credibility that this authority then brings with it that has traditionally given museums their unique edifying position in society (Hooper-Greenhill 2000; Sandell 2007: 134–5). Underpinning this position of authority and authorship were a series of documentation systems that privileged their unique role as arbiter on 'their' collections. The most important of the documentation tools within the pre-automated, pre-systematised museum was the accession register. Large, leather-bound volumes, written with suitable ink, the accession registers aspired to record everything that was in the museum collection – if an object was 'acquired' then an entry was made in the register. Invariably registers contained descriptive but usually semi-structured information about individual items acquired by the museum. A linear ledger, with records added to the bottom of the list, usually as a one-off entry, the register represented a way of formally recording objects in the collection. However, before the introduction of documentation standards in the 1970s, the composition and use of registers was not consistent within the sector. For instance, in the UK, a small regional museum such as Leicester was using its registers in a very 'free text' and not standardised way, perhaps entering sketches as well as words, in an approach that evolved over time and which varied from curator to curator (Marshall 2005; Stiff 2005). The presence of a register did not always guarantee continuity. When, for instance, the Smithsonian's Museum of History and Technology opened in 1964, it was estimated that there were around seven different numbering systems in operation – with each division in the institution approaching cataloguing in a different way (Ruffin 1967: 4). Contrastingly, there had always been an element of centralisation in the record keeping in museums like the Victoria and Albert Museum – which had a centrally administered accessions register since it was established in the 1850s. However, in 1909 the V&A divided into smaller collections, each with its own keeper. The use of accession registers continued, but from that point the records management was more compartmentalised – a situation that continued up to the late 1980s. From 1909 forward, therefore, there was no standardisation within the museum, with each of those departments essentially acting independently in the way it managed and recorded its acquisitions, loans and correspondence (Lloyd-Baynes 2005).

Despite the lack of consensus and conformity between institutions on the content of their registers (before the coming of the new standards in information management), the register was, nevertheless, for some museums the only formal and complete document it had detailing the collection. Remembering her early career in this pre-automated pre-standardised professional culture in the mid-1960s, Susan Pearce attributes high value to these registers:

> These were very holy. They were sacred texts. They counted as the sacred books without question. You did not carry anything else when you were carrying them in case they got damaged. And they lived in their special reliquary.
>
> (2005)

In time registers would also come to be held in high regard as the tool for auditors to demonstrate accountability (Roberts 2005). Equally important, however, but perhaps not as revered, were the museum 'day books'. Usually somewhat unassuming, hard-bound books with horizontally ruled pages, these tended to be carried around by curators all day. These were personalised and journal-like notebooks, somewhere between research diary and log book, an instant and immediate form of recording (ibid.; Lewis 2007). They were part commonplace book (attached to that early modern tradition of collecting thoughts and happenings), and part lab book (attached to a scientific tradition of day-to-day recording of work and results). The reality for many museums was that the day book was what kept a daily account of what was coming in and going out – in a sense every object that passed through the curator's hands would be entered into the day book (Marshall 2005). However, day books might also record noteworthy correspondence or the arrival in the museum of an important visitor (Philips 2005). Although the presence of day books was something of a mainstay in the museum sector for many decades, there was a lack of consistency and considerable variability in their use both within and between institutions. Both the quality and the level of maintenance of day books could vary considerably. During the early 1970s a British city museum service such as that in Leicester was providing all curatorial staff in all departments with detailed written instructions on their 'routine' for using day books. The museum's *Staff Regulations* contained a section on 'Accessioning, Cataloguing and Loans' that instructed how, on receipt of any specimen or group of specimens offered for sale, gift, loan or bequest, the curator was to make an entry in the day book. Following a series of numbers assigned to each department, curators were directed to detail: the date of receipt; the day book number; a brief description for identification only; the name and full postal address of donor, vendor, lender or enquirer; the accession number (if accepted) and the date of return to owner (if rejected) (Lewis 2007). In contrast, at the same time, the use of day books in city museums such as Exeter and Liverpool was remembered to be somewhat more 'freeform' (Pearce 2005). And yet, in other museums, such as Nottingham, the day book historically had an important role to play. In the early years at Nottingham a considerable amount of the museum's collection on display was on loan from the South Kensington Museum and from private collectors. Also at this time, the museum's curator was actively and productively acquiring some very large and generous acquisitions. Consequently, there was a substantial turnaround of objects coming in and out of the museum each year. Unsurprisingly, therefore, a day book system was instituted in Nottingham, on the opening of its Castle Museum, in 1878 and ran (as bound ledgers) for approximately a hundred years after that date – when in 1972 they were replaced by day book 'slips', pieces of paper that were eventually stapled together into annual volumes (Cooper 2005). The result, at the end of the nineteenth century, for a museum with a single curator trying to keep up with all of this complex documentation, as well as the day-to-day running of the museum, was that an entry in the day book became very important. However, because of this workload, entries were also frequently somewhat brief. Consequently, the Nottingham day books sometimes carry only a limited amount of information. In 1977 (coincidently the year the MDA was established, heralding a new era of standards in museum documentation in the UK) Nottingham, after a hundred years of day book use, ceased using this mainstay of museum information management. Within a decade, the neighbouring museum service in Leicestershire had also stopped using its day books – and, in fact, some curators saw the practice as frowned upon (Marshall 2005). However, just as Leicester was closing its day books, a museum such as that in Docklands, London, established in the early 1980s, was, in the absence of a formal catalogue, still reliant on its day books as the only record of its warehouse collection (Murray and Werner 1987).

Alongside the register and the day book was the curator's head; 'it was', to quote one registrar, 'all being held together by curatorial knowledge' (Cooper 2005). In the nineteenth century and until the 1960s museum documentation processes relied substantially on curatorial memory (Lloyd-Baynes 2005; Roberts 2005; Seal 2005). Many curators up to the period before the Second World War had spent a lifetime in museums, and 'an enormous amount of knowledge was never recorded' (Lewis 2007). The reality was, certainly in the UK at least, that guidelines and standards took some time to find ways of capturing all of this valuable knowledge about collections that remained in the heads of curators. In 1994 the first iteration of SPECTRUM (the UK museums documentation standard) had to a great extent been a deliberate rejection of the MDA's original 1970s data standard (Stiff 2005). As well as introducing 'procedure', SPECTRUM was there to be applied appropriately to an institution. It was a reaction to a fixed idea of how data ought to be structured, presenting instead the units of documentation, the basic concepts, that a museum should observe in its system – rather than the structure and shape of that system. The greater challenge, however, was how to capture some of the more ephemeral information that was slipping between the fields of the database and the input boxes of the record cards. 'SPECTRUM Knowledge', therefore, was released as MDA's attempt to recognise and then suggest processes whereby the information trapped in filing cabinets and knowledge tucked away in curators' heads could be recorded and rendered accessible. If something of an add-on to the UK documentation standard, 'SPECTRUM Knowledge' nevertheless represented the modern attempt to recapture and revalue this critical missing link from museum information management. It was an important admission that the data models and documentation standards thus far had missed something rather important: the other complex knowledge that surrounds the objects and collections. Moreover, it was another salutary reminder of the individual control that curators had over the collections in their care.

Exemplifying this control were the highly personalised card index systems that curators used to access their collections. The card index was, up to the moment of automation at the end of the 1960s, the *state of the art*. The manual index cards were usually housed in a wooden drawer or series of drawers in a cabinet, skewered and fixed by a metal rod, cross-referencing the museum's collection by one or more themes – such as artist or donor. But an index card could only ever be part of one series, one particular interpretation and ordering of the collection. To see a collection in a different way, to index it according to other criteria, meant copying out the object's index card again and building another parallel series. A museum such as the Ashmolean, in Oxford, that had between 1939 and 1940 had most of its collection catalogued, and that had a record card entry 'for about 99% of the existing collections' was perhaps the exception rather than the norm in the museum world (Mowat and Edwards 1989). By the mid-1970s, the Sedgwick Museum in Cambridge had several cross-referencing manual indexes that were 'diligently kept up to date' (Light 2005). At the Natural History Museum, Smithsonian Institution, the Division of Marine Invertebrates had (atypically for the museum) compiled since the start of the twentieth century 'a remarkable' file of 125,000 specimens (and basic associated data), which could be searched via this manual index of cards (Manning 1969: 673). The practices in such departments, consequently, could be thorough and systematic:

> A cataloguer would compile the data necessary for each entry, hand enter it into a ledger catalog, hand-write the label, type two copies of a specimen data card (one copy was to be filed in the species files, the other to be filed in a geographic file), and type a neck-label for the jar.
>
> (ibid.: 674)

But, outside larger national museums and some university museums, such uses of card indexes were far from widespread. Typically, a medium-sized regional UK museum service such as Nottingham did not begin work on a card index for its natural history collections until the 1950s – when some records were indexed in species name order, and some attempts were made to build a classified index. However, the Nottingham natural history card index was never finished and, evidently, rarely used (Cooper 2005). Even at the Victoria and Albert Museum in London, after the formal accession entry and the entry into what the museum called the 'central inventory' (a central brief description by museum number), there was no centralised co-ordination of indexing. It was, therefore, up to individual collections, or individual curators, to create, for example, artist indexes. Individual curators, consequently, might have an object category index on cards sitting on their desk – structured in a way that might be unique to their department, or, perhaps, just to them (Lloyd-Baynes 2005; Seal 2005). The experience of many curators was of index systems and cards that were 'mostly handwritten and often missing' (Marshall 2005). Moreover, individual curators would often keep files that were more-or-less adequate for their own research (Chenhall and Homulos 1978: 43), and, significantly, might speak of 'their' card catalogue (Ruffin 1967: 6).

The museum, in other words, was not a place of standard practice and rigid protocols, either within institutions or across institutions, but rather a complex environment where an ecology of different curatorial processes, indexes, rationales could coexist and evolve. Before their more familiar modern roles as interpreters and facilitators, it was not by chance that museum curators in places such as the UK were titled 'keepers'. Frequently possessive and protective of their collections, and with the exhibition space being an extension (a physical manifestation) of their understanding of the collection, curators' identities and self-esteem were powerfully wrapped up in their relationship with their collections. 'It was deeply personal', Pearce (2005) recalls: 'one was one's collection in a work sense – the quality of the objects that you were responsible for was also the index of your personal prestige'. Poignantly, looking back on mid-twentieth-century methods of documentation, we see registers filled in according to localised systems of authority, curators literally carrying knowledge on their person in the form of day books, and card systems built to fit personally ascribed indexes of value. There were the technologies of a relentless individualism within the profession. The information management processes of the pre-standardised, pre-automated museum grew out from (and preserved) an unchallengeable authority of the curator. The curators were, in every sense, the authors of their collections. And as author and authority, the tradition was that once a record ('their' record) had been entered, it remained largely inviolate (Seal 2005). It was a culture of fixity. Unfortunately, digital media were proving to be the antithesis of all of this.

The liquidity of digital media

Over the past four decades digital technology has moved increasingly towards greater levels of connectivity, mobility and personalisation. On this trajectory, the fixed, tethered, stand-alone computer terminals of the modernist age have, within the post-industrial age, given way to user-driven, ambient, wireless, 'intelligent' media. The ascetic expert with the hermetic in-situ mainframe database has, today, been eclipsed by lay user-producers generating distributed and multiple inter-relating networks of diverse and dynamic multimedia content through pervasive everyday technology.

In particular, it has been this dynamic content, this liquidity, of new media that has appeared (inviting addition and amendment), that seems to have been at odds with notions of fixity or closed authorship in the museum. It was this openness that Manovich was at pains to stress:

> The open nature of the web as medium (web pages are computer files which can always be edited) means that web sites never have to be complete; and they rarely are. The sites always grow. New links are being added to what is already there. It is as easy to add new elements to the end of a list as it is to insert them anywhere in it. All this further contributes to the anti-narrative logic of the web. If new elements are being added over time, the result is a collection, not a story. Indeed, how can one keep a coherent narrative or any other development trajectory through the material if it keeps changing?
>
> (1999: 82)

In contrast to the highly personalised, closed narratives and fixed records of the traditional manual curatorial systems, therefore, digital media appeared somewhat unsettling (Žižek 1996: 291). Rather than being inviolate, authorship in the digital world was a continuing process. Consequently (and, again, in contrast to the highly 'authored' curatorial systems) the verifiability of digital writing became problematised. On the digital network all users could suddenly become authors. The instantaneous, user-generated content of the Web, and

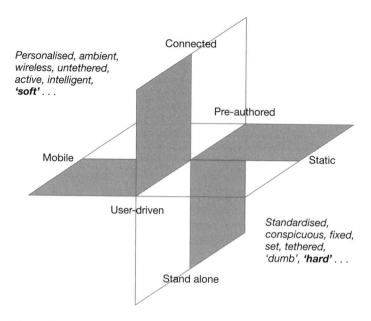

Figure 6.1 The technology cube.

the new social software, suddenly gave all visitors a microphone, the opportunity to rewrite the script, to reposition the camera, and to rearrange the props. On such a stage, where data can be manipulated quickly, authority can speedily come into question (Gere 1999: 48). Much like in the Renaissance, with the move from manuscript to print, the Web frustrated many content providers with the rapid and seemingly unrelenting way it (like moveable type almost five hundred years before) had democratised the modes of textual production and the channels of communication. Lisa Jardine reminds us of the ways in which, soon after the arrival of the printing press in Europe in the early modern period, the new technology was soon taken over by individuals wishing to make money – sometimes with very different standards to what had come before through manuscript production. She retells the frustration of Erasmus, who in 1526, 'in the midst of preparing the sixth edition of his Adages, his best-selling encyclopaedic volume of proverbial sayings [. . .] broke off from the project to describe the way the new technology of print had been commandeered by unscrupulous entrepreneurs'. With the new mass production of print widespread and accessible, it was the 'innumerable crowd of printers', to Erasmus, that now threw 'all into confusion' (Jardine 1997: 228).

This, in a sense, is what Trant saw when she asked: 'When authors are creators and anyone can be a publisher, what is the place and role of cultural heritage institutions?' (1998: 108). Other commentators, such as Besser, captured perhaps best of all the anxieties that some curators now felt:

And when members or the general public have (from their own home) access to a wealth of digitised images and scholarly information, many will begin to make their own links and juxtapositions among these images. This may further erode the authority of the curator as the leading figure who places images within a context. A possible result may be an erosion of high culture in general, with the curator's role becoming somewhat akin to that of a film critic.

(Besser 1997)

The amplification of the cacophony of voices that digital media allowed for, the potential loss of editorial control that they appeared to encourage, and the increased mutability of content that they seemed to support, were all at odds with the clarity and authority of the curator's prized authorship. The *variability* of new media (epitomised in the un-moderated user-generated content of the Internet) seemed to sit as counterpoint to some entrenched practices of curatorial authority and control.

The personal museum: variability and localisation

However, elsewhere, the museum had already been prepared to let go of both its authorship and its authority. 'People's shows', community galleries, visitor books, comment boards, gallery tours, participatory workshops, as well as Friends' Societies, focus groups and visitor evaluation, had all given museum audiences the opportunity to participate and to express themselves in the museum and to make their views and responses known. We might trace this museography back, as indeed Bennett (1998) does, to the nineteenth century and the liberal reformers who began to place greater emphasis on incorporating principles of auto-intelligibility into museum displays. It is here that the visitor gains an independence – 'increasingly self-directing and self-managing' (ibid.: 31). In this curatorship (the curatorship of social responsibility and, later, the new museology) museums see themselves in a new place, 'in the total social environment [. . .] more outward looking, seeking to serve their public' (Council for Museums and Galleries in Scotland: 1977). For those practitioners and institutions that sought to diversify the voices heard within a more responsive and relevant museum, new media (and the Web in particular) provided a powerful tool where non-visitors could be reached, multiple narratives could be layered, and where interpretation (to remind ourselves of Manovich's lexicon) was as *variable* as the medium itself.

Consequently, the 'opening up' and 'reaching out' and 'letting go' that accompanied the Web medium (particularly in its later incarnation, so-called 'Web 2.0'), could be seen, in fact, to be highly consistent with some of these emergent practices, projects and philosophies in the museum. In this way, the liquidity of digital media connected to the discourse and aspirations of the new 'personal museum' – a place where authorship and authority could be shared rather than made the preserve of the curator alone. Consider, for instance, the way Chun

109

Figure 6.2 Visitors post their thoughts on a gallery wall. Copyright the author.

et al., describing the process of social tagging on the Web, connect the fluidities and variability of digital authorship with the new social circumspection of the museum:

> Tagging lets us temper our authored voice and create an additional means of access to art in the public's voice. For museums, including these alternative perspectives signals an important shift to a greater awareness of our place in a diverse community, and the assertion of a goal to promote social engagement with our audiences.
>
> (2006)

Far from being disruptive, here it is the liquidity of new media that allows the museum to realise its new social role.

Figure 6.3 Opportunities to have a voice at the Science Museum, London. Copyright the author.

From label to LIVE!Label

A good demonstration of this new shared authorship and openness to 'let go' and 'leave open' has been some of the work that has taken place on one of the icons of fixed interpretation, authorship and authority of the curator – that is, the text label. The label – fused (sometimes literally) to the object – still encapsulates how the museum used to author its inviolate content. The 'LIVE!Label' project run by the University of Leicester attempted to mirror the same principles as those exploring social tagging on-line. It, too, worked to temper the voice of the curator-author in an exhibit's labels, to turn the label into a space for other voices to be heard. However, it tried to do so in a way that would connect the iconic fixity of the gallery environment to the new authoring possibilities of the Web. LIVE!Labels represents the ways digital media are allowing the narratives of the museum to become more fluid, more responsive and more polyvocal.

Helpfully, DeRoux (1998b) reminds us that 'museum label-making techniques change and evolve with the times, and with new technology'. So, rather than sweeping labels aside, what if we acknowledged (and preserved) the embedded and informed practices of label writing and the intrinsic and historic part that labels play in the imagining and building of exhibitions – but, at the same time, also explored the implications of simply making the labels *digital*? Rather than using the full functionality of digital media (the reflex temptation whenever computers are introduced to the gallery floor), what if the label was not a touchscreen, and not the tip of a multimedia iceberg of archival material, but was simply and cleanly *just a label* – but a label (crucially) that could be updated by the curator (or perhaps even the visitor) locally or remotely via the Web? What if the label the visitor looked at (at first glance the same as any other) was in fact 'broadcasting' the very latest interpretations of its object? What if the labels in that exhibit could change (like some of our Web sites) at particular times of the day, or in response to certain planned or unplanned events? What if the labels in the exhibit could be changed, as easily as changing the stylesheet of a Web site, to tune its content to the needs of a particular visiting group, moment, or occasion? ('The exhibit this week is curated by . . .', 'Here are the labels your school class sent to us . . .', 'Why not try our lunchtime trail . . .?'). What happens, in short, when the new editorial practices of on-line publishing developed by museums over the past ten years, are allowed to reflect back on to the on-site exhibit?

This was the premise of the 'LIVE!Labels' (L!Ls) project – a collaboration between the Digital Heritage Research Group within the University of Leicester's Department of Museum Studies and Simulacra, a specialist producer of technology-enabled learning resources and tools for the museum and education sectors.

The objective of the project was to design and then test a prototype of L!Ls. Research into existing practice and consultation with practitioners (including a day-long 'concept workshop' attended by a range of museum practitioners and representatives from the collaborating organisations) helped to determine a series of design principles. L!Ls needed to: easily reconfigure labelling layouts; accept changes in display media; limit the impact on existing IT installations; allow for remote updating – for large or distributed sites; support the automatic/timed updating of labels; easily integrate user-generated content via phones, hand-helds, or Web sites; easily integrate third-party content such as RSS feeds; and (ultimately) offer a museum reduced costs over printed labels.

The front-end evaluation and market research also revealed, first, that L!Ls needed, wherever possible, to build upon existing curatorial practice. The challenge for curators (especially in an accountable era where public funded museums, in the UK at least, are under great pressure, with limited resources, to demonstrate their 'value') is to continue to build exhibits that are relevant, fresh, inclusive and engaging. Introducing a tool or technology that disrupted or was incongruous to established practice was thought, therefore, to be undesirable – however innovative that technology might be.

Second, it was agreed that L!Ls needed to provide a solution that was powerful but 'polite'. Historically, when digital media have been used within a gallery setting, they have invariably been in the form of multimedia interactives, games, simulations, Web terminals and searchable databases, frequently contained in 'kiosks' and installations that are at best discrete from (and at worst incongruous to) their gallery settings. The museum sector is keen to utilise the power of digital media but in a fashion that is sympathetic to (and ambient with) the unique environment of the gallery setting, and in a way that does not distance and over-mediate the object on display, or alienate less computer-literate segments of the visiting public.

Third, the L!Ls needed to exploit the growing resource of the on-line museum, as well as the *convergence* between the on-line and on-site channels. As more and more museums realign their missions and strategies to embed digital media activity and provision into their core functions, and as more museums become immersed in the promise of the digital age, there is as much talk of 'broadcast' as there is about 'outreach', of 'channel' as much as 'exhibition', and of 'user' as much as 'visitor'. Curatorial resource is being invested into developing day-to-day new interpretive content for museum Web sites. L!Ls (in some respects an object's own updatable Web page that sits next to it in the gallery) is one way this productivity can begin to have an effect not just on the on-line but on the on-site museum as well.

A matrix of different 'triggers' (*events*) and 'generators' (*authors*) was formed to capture and to begin to rationalise the myriad ways in which L!Ls could be used. Content, it was thought, may be *generated* by curators, by visitors (submitted on-site or on-line) or by an approved third party. The uploading of this content to the label would then either be: time-driven (triggered to the time of day/week); visit-driven (triggered by the type of visitor); event-driven (triggered in response to a planned event, programme or 'guest curation'); or news-driven (responding to unplanned events or new research).

Across this grid of 'triggers' and 'generators' it was also thought that content was likely to be in four key forms: *contextual* – using the label's editable quality to provide new or changing interpretations of the object ('This week scientists discovered that objects like this are . . .'); *promotional* – using the label's editable quality to bring to the visitor's attention other events or services provided by the museum ('To find out more about this object why not go and see the next showing of . . .'); *directional* – using the label's editable quality to highlight connections to other objects and displays in the museum's changing provision, or to build a thematic 'trail' ('Another one of these objects is currently now on display in the . . .'); or *responsive* – using the label's editable quality to allow a voice for visitors in the gallery ('A 10-year-old visitor who saw this object yesterday said it reminded them of . . .'). To provide the best possible initial glimpse of the potential and functionality of L!Ls, it was agreed that the testing and evaluation of the prototype would ideally be distributed across a combination of these generators, triggers and forms.

Over a seven-month period, the collaborators worked to build, demonstrate and evaluate a prototype of an editable, wireless, in-gallery digital label system that used a Web-based authoring tool. To deliver this concept – of a gallery label which can be remotely updated – the collaborators built a number of slim LCD 'labels' (in two sizes: 6.4" diagonal; and 10.4" diagonal) with in-built wireless capability, that connected to a simple Web-based content administration system.

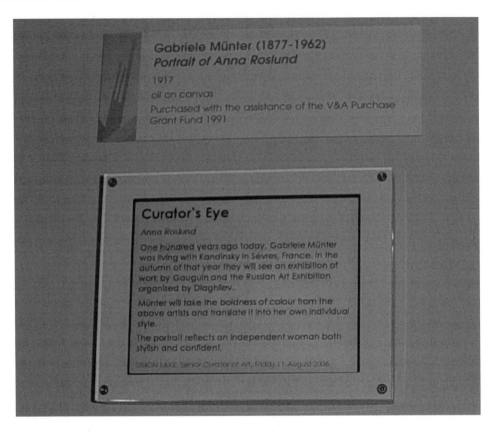

Figure 6.4 A 'LIVE!Label' at New Walk Museum and Art Gallery, Leicester. Copyright the author.

This administration system enabled curators to author label text, select font and background colours or images, and set the times at which specific labels would be shown. Content was then sent via the Internet and a wireless connection to each of the L!Ls.

L!Ls were installed in three galleries, at two different institutions, in a period of testing that ran in total for nine weeks. The galleries were chosen to present a range of subject disciplines (art, natural history and science/technology), but also a range of typical gallery environments ('white cube'; cabinet and pedestal gallery; highly immersive discovery space). Significantly, the partner museums were also chosen for their differences in institutional organisation and governance: New Walk Museum and Art Gallery (Leicester) is a local authority museum run and resourced via a city museums service; the National Space Centre (Leicester) is a not-for-profit education charity; and the Natural History Museum in London (which provided ongoing consultation through the project) is a national museum funded directly from the central UK government.

In the German Expressionist exhibit at New Walk Museum and Art Gallery, the senior curator of art was able to use the labels as a way of capturing his latest thoughts and observations on the works on display. Under the title of 'Curator's Eye' the LIVE!Labels sat alongside the permanent catalogue and labels, and over three weeks were approached, effectively, as in-gallery blog for two of the paintings. 'I looked at this picture again today, and it reminded me of something I saw last week when . . .' Updated labels were dated and the curator's name was given.

In the Dinosaur Gallery at the same institution, another member of the curatorial staff invited younger visitors to 'Be a Dinosaur Curator for a day'. Over a three-week period visitors could write on a postcard what they wanted to see on the LIVE!Labels around the main dinosaur exhibit. The curator could then email them to say that their label had been chosen to be on display in the gallery – they would be the 'curator for the day'. The Web-based L!L authoring system, linked to the wireless labels, made it relatively straightforward for the curator to embed visitor-generated content into the exhibit.

At the National Space Centre (NSC), Leicester, Head of Space Communication, Kevin Yates, used the LIVE!Labels to give visitors the very latest information (updated daily over a three-week period) on the number of Near Earth Objects (NEOs) in space – and how many of them (that day) were classified as 'hazardous'. These were data that the NSC was already recording each day, but was not making available to visitors in the NEO exhibit. During the trial, one member of staff was even able to update the label in his exhibit from his home, via the Web, one Saturday morning.

Curators were interviewed before and after the trial on their expectations and reflections of the L!Ls (both hardware and software). They were also observed in using the system, and were encouraged to use a 'diary' to record instances when the labels were changed along with any other observations. Furthermore, across a twenty-day period, 763 visitors were observed (and interaction with the L!Ls coded) in the three gallery locations. From this observed group, 149 visitors were interviewed. (The visitor observation and interviews were circumscribed to a non-probability sampling and as a consequence its results should not be considered representative of the potential population of the three museums that participated in this study. The feedback obtained from the visitors relied on the availability of the subjects.)

Half of the 763 visitors did not look at the labels. Only around 20 per cent of the total number of visitors to the galleries actually read the labels. And of this group, only around 1 in 5 visitors saw them as in some way 'live'. Very few visitors noticed that the labels were dated. For around three-quarters of visitors who read the labels, they had no change or a positive change on their experience. Only one visitor out of the 149 who read the L!Ls thought they changed their experience in a negative way. And only two visitors out of this same group saw them as a 'distraction'. Around a third of visitors touched the L!Ls. Visitors at the NSC (a vivid and, at times, loud 'discovery' space with a number of other digital and non-digital in-gallery interactives) were much more expectant of interactivity than those at the German Expressionist gallery at New Walk; at the NSC visitors were seven times more likely to touch the screen. Contrastingly, visitors were more likely to describe the labels as 'digital' or 'different' in the German Expressionist gallery than at the NSC.

Although there was abundant evidence to suggest that the L!L prototypes were not distracting nor out of place in the gallery (but rather in the majority of cases were a positive addition to the exhibition space) there was, nevertheless, an equal amount of evidence to suggest that visitors did not notice that the labels (at least as they were used in the trial) contained potentially 'live' information. And yet, around a quarter of visitors commented positively upon the informational role of the L!Ls. In fact, when asked, most visitors commented upon the content and clarity of the information rather than its 'liveness'.

LIVE!Labels would appear to bring into focus a series of questions about narrative, text, and authorship in a gallery context. The consultation and front-end evaluation undertaken to develop the design specification of the prototype, and the results of the live testing, both strongly indicated the following: that curators were not explicitly claiming authorship and ownership of their textual content in exhibitions; that (perhaps in an attempt to speak to myriad learning styles, intelligences, experiences, knowledge levels and modes of visiting) there was a reticence over using a single, consistent curatorial voice; and that many museums have still to resolve how authorship, authority and narrativity function in a hypermedia context. It is here perhaps that we remember Walsh's comments on the writing of text labels in exhibitions:

> The typical interpretive art museum label, for example, is the work of a committee of educators, editors, scholars, and administrators who not infrequently disagree. Even the simple line "attributed to" can, in a museum label, conceal fierce behind-the-scenes debates over the nature of the art object it purports to describe.
>
> (1997)

Unlike the committee work and conflict Walsh describes, it was assumed (mistakenly perhaps) with L!Ls that curators could potentially change their in-gallery content with the same speed, frequency and confidence as they appeared to be able to when updating their on-line Web content. Instead (from the perspective of this research at least) it appeared that curators viewed their in-gallery and on-line content differently. One unintended outcome of this research and development into L!Ls was the revealing of this disparity between an on-line provision that was thought to be active and responsive, and on-site (in-gallery) provision that was perceived to be largely and traditionally rigid and unmoved by events and visitors.

7

Reorganising production

Manovich's – and our – last principle of new media (*transcoding*) relates to the way digital technology is both formed and, at the same time, informed by the culture in which it is based. A culture designs technology and allows it to develop. Consequently, the assumptions and ideologies of that culture remain embedded within it. And yet that culture can in turn be affected by the presence of the technology, either directly or indirectly, tangibly or intangibly. The result is that both the technology and the culture are codified (given meaning) by the presence and influence of the other.

It is an interesting exercise to take the concept of transcoding and (as we have done with the automated, numerical, modular and variable qualities of new media) also use this as a lens through which to look at the dialectic between museums and computers over the past forty years. In this context, our concern here will largely be with the concept of 'change', specifically the extent to which the institution of the museum resisted or allowed technology to shape its organisation and vision. Did museums, in other words, resist or pursue change in the face of technological innovation – and, more importantly, why?

The risk-averse museum: rhetoric and resource

For very many reasons (as we shall see) museums remained, for many years, institutionally ill-equipped and indisposed to deal with the influence of digital technology. Partly this was out of their control, but partly this was an informed choice.

Risk

For a great deal of time computers represented a risk, in strategic terms, for the museum. From the early days the rhetoric surrounding museum computing promised a great deal. Museums were told that 'the information storage and retrieval capabilities and potentialities of computers far exceed the rather limited capacities of the human brain' (Bowles 1968: xvii). Some practitioners were fizzing with excitement at the vistas that were opening up. When discussing positions that were opening up in the newly formed Museum Computer

Network, David Vance (from the Museum of Modern Art) had enthused, in a letter to the group's director, on the MCN's 'unlimited potential growth'. Evidently inspired by what he saw the Network already achieving, just within its first year, Vance thought becoming the second professional member of staff within the organisation would be 'like joining MOMA in the '30s – literally the chance of a lifetime . . . I don't anticipate any comparable opportunity in museum work' (Vance 1968). Such was the fervour that many advocates in the sector were feeling about 'the brave new electronic world' that lay ahead (Ellin 1969). Surrounded by such rhetoric, it was unsurprising perhaps to find (as the 1979 ACS study into museum computer projects had) that it was common for museums to have unrealistic expectations of what a museum might be able to do (Sarasan 1981).

And yet, for many years there simply were not enough successes and bodies of strong evidence to support a major resource commitment by a museum to computing. 'It is of the very nature of our Project', mused Everett Ellin (1967c) in a briefing note to colleagues at the outset of the Museum Computer Network, 'that many significant factors defy knowledge or predication with any degree of certainty until the Network is well under way.' Back in the late 1960s, at the dawn of automation and museum computing, practitioners were more than aware, understandably, of the 'substantial risks' of funding projects that were taking professionals and institutions into new territories. In the early 1970s, as projects such as the National Inventory Program began in Canada, it was still, to some, 'not really apparent whether this type of technology would be adequate, or even appropriate for the heritage community' (CHIN 1992).

> I am working at my desk in 1980 and a salesman knocks at my door, sits down, and is so excited about a convention he has just been at. He tells me that in 1990 you will have a box on your desk and it will hold the equivalent of your current mainframe. And my reaction was: why would I want that?
>
> (Sledge 2005)

The reality for curators like Sledge, and the reality for most museums, was that whereas word processing might have had an impact day-to-day for the average curator, the possibilities of computing were still unimaginable and undemonstrable. For the vast majority of museums computing was still something of a myth; 'for the very largest University Institutions it was myth into the mid-1970s, and for those small collections it was myth into the 1980s' (Bearman 2007). It was unsurprising, perhaps, that when the West Midlands Museum Service in the UK surveyed its member institutions (70 in all), it found that, despite 'rapid growth of computer usage in the museum community since 1986', by the end of 1992, 59 per cent still did not have computers (Holm 1993: 6). A quarter of a century after IRGMA, SELGEM and the MCN, only 6 per cent of museums in this typical regional museum community had computerised 90 per cent or more of their collections. The plain truth was that it took some twenty-five years before most museums could begin to see the benefits of data entry and automation. For many years new media technology and production were expensive and specialised with an unproven return on investment both in terms of institutional resource and visitor experience. Computers were – in strategic terms – a risk to most museums.

The technology also remained unreliable. As early as 1985 the Smithsonian was dealing with security issues. In a seven-week period that year a computer located in the institution's Museum Support Center was subject to more than two hundred unauthorised accesses or attempted accesses through the telephone system (Bridge 1985). Essentially, the Smithsonian was being hacked. The first stand-alone computers distributed in the mid-1970s to ten museums in Canada as part of its National Inventory Program, were 'rather large boxes that were difficult to use and [. . .] not very reliable' (CHIN 1992). Similarly, owing to the over-complexity of the systems being instigated (a replacement to its FAMULUS system), the Ashmolean Museum, Oxford had witnessed a 'failed experiment' with computer-based records management in the early 1980s (Moffett 1989b). At the British Museum, around the same time, a full-time Information Retrieval Group had been working on an inventory in the Ethnology, Egyptian and Oriental Departments. Data entry, from documents, was being processed on the Research Laboratory's Hewlett-Packard using the MDA's GOS package. However, by April 1987 the team reported that the batch-working was causing problems and the machine was overloaded (Allden 1987). Even when enjoying the advantages of campus life (and the proximity of leading-edge technology, specialist staff and enthusiastic researchers of which many university museums had taken advantage), an institution such as the Sedgwick Museum in Cambridge was nonetheless 'beset by a variety of problems' in the development of its Oracle system in the mid-1990s (Philips 1995: 3). One report from the registrar at Leicester (UK) details the climate of unreliability that plagued some of these important and visible first attempts to automate.

> 15 old terminals were being used almost exclusively for data entry, although their age was causing line problems to the mainframe. However, they then suffered a flood so all the terminals are being replaced with some Wang PCs (plus one Amstrad) linked to the mainframe. The rate of data entry is still slow despite having an excellent MSC team, the curators are slowing things down by insisting on very long records. [. . .] They are having some difficulty in getting programs written to meet museum specifications.
>
> (Marshall 1987)

Even a service such as Tyne and Wear Museums (UK) that, by 1991, was making productive use of the City Council's Computing Service, was experiencing difficulties with on-line retrieval. Eventually, it was concluded that the city's ICL mainframe could not cope with the complex nature of museum data and the interrogations required (Marshall 1992). It was not atypical, therefore, for a local authority museum service such as this to find that the failing computer system was 'damaging the computer's credibility with staff' (Marshall 1986).[1]

Time

The discourse of museum computing in the early 1970s was far from enticing for most museums. The Cambridge team who were at the heart of the UK's development of new computer-oriented standards were most clear on the realities of this work:

> Firstly computer programming is time consuming [. . .] Secondly the need for programming is continuous, not a once-for-all cost. Programs need to be maintained like any other equipment and given major overhauls when old computers are replaced.
>
> (Cutbill 1971b: 2)

Many museums drastically underestimated how long it would take and how much it would cost to put a network in place, especially if they were trying to operate in buildings that were often inflexible in terms of their structures (Roberts 2005). In 1980 the National Museum of American History suspended its inventory survey in order to reassess its approach. In its work from 14 February 1979 to 27 April 1980 it had already amassed a backlog of 176,454 objects. By 1986, Bristol Museum reported that it had made 'no attempt' to compile full data relating to its natural history collections as it was considered 'very time consuming' and, consequently, 'unjustifiable' (Copp 1986). In the mid-1980s, the National Army Museum expected to add in the region of 10,000–15,000 records a year from their collection of 2.1 million items (Elliot 1986), illustrating that the size of the task for many museums had become dauntingly clear. Over ten years after the original recommendation for the system to be built, an active and pioneering museum service such as Leicestershire had, by 1990, only 110,000 records entered into its object catalogue system, with over a million records still to be transferred from card indexes (MCG 1990). Even with the help of 'teams of graduate cataloguers' funded under a Manpower Services Commission job creation scheme, it took Tyne and Wear Museums Service (UK) eleven years (from 1977 to 1988) to complete around 170,000 MDA record cards, with less than half of this number inputted into its GOS database system. By the autumn of 1991 a backlog of over 35,262 record cards was still to be transferred over to the museum's collections management software (Marshall 1992). At best, data entry remained a problem as curators and keepers were not always willing or able to complete the work (Moffett 1992a). At worst, a lot of the early computer systems were seen to be an extra burden in data entry and cataloguing – 'a new pain in the neck' (Marshall 2005). In short, to the community involved in museum computing during the period of automation, setting up computer systems could often seem to be 'more trouble than they are worth' (Moffett 1989a: 10).

Cost and sustainability

In collections management the commitment needed for the move to automation and digitisation was something that required a long-term priority and investment by the institution – something that was not feasible for many. By the end of the 1960s, when the early automation and standardisation projects had begun, the library sector had already squared up to the realities of the cost of such development. In his foreword to the proceedings of the third MARC conference, L. Quincy Mumford (the Librarian of Congress) was very clear about how the '[d]ecisions to convert current or retrospective catalog records to machine-readable form may eventually involve the library community in multi-million dollar expenditure' (Library of Congress 1966: 1). For museums, even as the first cases for automation began to be made, the spectre of cost began to materialise. Pioneers such as Everett Ellin (at the Guggenheim Museum) marking out the early territories of museum computing, could already see that it was only 'scientists and businessmen' who could 'well afford to pay for this expensive hardware' (Ellin 1967a: 1). Equally, the promise of time-shared computing was, by 1967, already identified as having excellent potential for a large museum that could afford a central processor, but Soper and Perring were quick also to acknowledge that it was unlikely 'that these facilities are going to be available in the near or even distant future to small museums, especially those outside North America and a few countries in Western Europe' (1967: 13). Delegates who had convened in Mexico in December 1967 to consider the potential that computers had for managing large collections of information, such as were held in museums, were equally quick to spot the financial constraints on such development; representatives from smaller museums, in particular, had 'repeatedly pointed out that it *cannot* be practical for the institutions, because their budgets will never be large enough' (Smithsonian Institution 1968b). Within a year, museum directors were already commenting upon 'the high and spiraling costs of maintenance of upkeep' that were apparent (Hoving 1968: xi). Chenhall and Homulos would later comment that the 'cost of creating and controlling the large numbers of cards or sheets of paper necessary to document systematically the collections in a major museum' was at this point in the late 1960s, simply 'an economic impossibility' (1978: 43). Members of the Information Retrieval Group of the UK Museums Association were adamant that in terms of data collection and its conversion to machine processable form, the largest single issue was cost (Cutbill 1971c).

In the late 1970s and early 1980s all of the few systems available to museums were potentially very expensive. It was only in the later 1980s that costs began to fall significantly: 'At last', reported Anthony Fletcher from the US to his colleagues in the UK, 'it appears that there are now solution systems based on a PC or mini, for any museum' (Fletcher 1987). And yet, for a typical British local authority institution such as the Natural History Museum at Wollaton Hall, Nottingham, the purchase of in-house hardware, even at this time, was still seen to be several years away (Walley 1986). Those responsible for computing at Luton Museum Service (UK) were adamant that the institution simply did 'not have the money to throw at bespoke software which may or may not meet user needs' (McCall 1993: 7). In 1995 a working group had been set up at the British Museum to plan for the computerised resource that would, five years later, materialise as the COMPASS project in the Round Reading Room. And

121

Figure 7.1 COMPASS terminals in the Round Reading Room of the British Museum, London. Copyright the author.

yet, even in those early discussions, the museum had thought that a multi-media project on this scale would require far more resources than the institution, at that time, could spare (McCutcheon 1995).

The issue that has continued to loom largest of all over these matters is *sustainability*. A sustainable model for entering, capturing or managing digital resources was not immediately apparent. Indeed, it has remained unapparent. By 2000 Smith was describing a series of possible models that museums might want to follow, including the partnership and co-operation, one-off charging (used by the British Museum and the National Portrait Gallery, London), or ongoing licensing (as in the form of an images library) (2000: section 5). However, three years later, having surveyed thirty-three North American-based digital cultural heritage initiatives, Zorich found the majority still searching for the status of sustainability. Despite a great deal of experimentation they appeared still to 'lack proven, sustainable business models' (2003: 26).

Skills and training

Likewise, the skills required from practitioners were not always made clear and the contracts associated with new media roles not always permanent. Even at the first meetings of museum practitioners regarding automation and data processing, the skills deficit had been tabled. In the UK, in 1967, during the Sheffield colloquium that first explored the size of the challenge and potential of machine-assisted information retrieval, it had been estimated that the shortage of computer personnel was likely to continue for the next ten years at least (Hislop 1967: 96). There was a shift from the late 1960s to the late 1970s from museum computing being a specialist interest area to one which could involve all curatorial staff (Chere and Polyakov 1978). And yet, an American study from that period also had revealed a lack of familiarity with technology in many museums, more pronounced than in the commercial world (Sarasan 1981). By the end of the 1970s, discussions at an ICOM level were already exploring how this skills deficit could be breached. On one side was the option of retraining the entire workforce in computer operation, on the other to retune computers more sympathetically into museum practice (Chere and Polyakov 1978: 1). In the late 1980s some museums made a point of hiring programmers who would work hard to build more 'user-friendly' interfaces for curatorial staff (Marshall 1989). The issue of training and skills continued to be 'disastrous' in many cases during the 1990s, when underqualified IT specialists were attempting without organisational power to introduce quite complicated and expensive changes, and were out of their depth (Roberts 2005). Consequently, many museums had many false starts. And yet, the skills deficit continued for at least another ten years. Within a major study of the training requirements of the UK cultural heritage sector in 2000, Information and Communication Technology (ICT) emerged as the single largest area of identified skills needs – specifically with respect to managing Web sites (Adegoroye et al. 2000). Indeed this was a conclusion that other high-profile studies had reached (Smith 2000).

The plain truth was that over thirty years after the point had been made at the Sheffield colloquium, the UK sector (like so many other professions around the world) was still in urgent need of a training strategy to cover both the capabilities and the applications of computer technology. The sector may now have been calling the technology the 'new media', but the problem was old; in terms of computing, the museum sector was simply underskilled.

Language and jargon

Significantly, one of the first full reports available to the museum sector on the potential and realisation of computer-based information systems was prefaced by a 25-page glossary of over 140 different technical terms: from 'attribute-value language' to 'direct access storage', and from 'operational system' to 'real-time operator' (IBM and Ellin 1969). Likewise, to make the most of Chenhall's compendious guide to museum computing, a reader was best served by becoming familiar with the thirty-page 'extensive glossary' of computer terms (1988). *Computers in the Museum* was, as its opening page explained, 'intended to help museum personnel understand the use of computers in the museum environment' (Vance 1973). To the novice and newcomer, however, the confidence of the technophile versed in the verbiage of the new information science would have been, to say the least, a little daunting:

> For the purposes of explanation, the statements describing the subject of a museum record will be referred to here as 'segments'. Each segment can be thought of as comprising three 'terms', which we can designate as A, B, and C, such that A represents (names) anything that can be defined, C represents anything else that can be defined, and B represents the relationship that is asserted to hold between A and C.
>
> (Vance 1973: 21)

Is it any wonder that, looking back, some curators remember the technology as being 'very hard to understand' and the tools 'difficult to use' (Marshall 2005)? And is it any wonder that museum directors at the time aired their concerns: 'Can we train the people to do the job', one asked, 'and will there be anyone qualified to judge the results?' (Hoving 1968: xii). In the mid-1980s the Manchester Museum reported a 'reluctance to refer to the Manual provided' for the terminals that had then just appeared on their desks (Pettitt 1986). Similarly, a study by the Association of Systematics Collections (ASC) revealed that, by 1979, practitioners (understandably we might say) often used the term 'programmer' indiscriminately to refer to anyone affiliated with computers, rather than differentiating between programmers, systems programmers, systems analysts, systems designers and computer operators. 'Without knowing what level of computer specialist is needed in a particular situation', one account of the results concluded, 'the wrong type of person may be hired for a job' (Sarasan 1981). The acronyms and technical verbiage applied an excluding sheen to computing – 'they helped to perpetuate the computer mystique' (Williams 1987: 3).

Indeed, the reviewer of one piece of collections management software in 1992 shared with colleagues his frustration at the 'araucarian complexity' of the system in front of him, complaining that the written documentation that came with the system was 'voluminous and poor – unless in computing terms you happen to be on a par with Alan Turing' (McCall 1992: 6). Although references to the 'occult knowledge' required to run this system at first appear flippant and exaggerated, they nonetheless speak of a frustration that many curators felt for over fifteen years about the 'cryptic' discourse surrounding museum computing (ibid.). 'So much that is written about computers is full of jargon that reading can be painfully difficult' lamented the reviewer of one (atypically) clear guide to museum computing (McLaren 1988). Even those close to the process of auto-mation and computerisation saw the sometimes dense, sometimes evangelical language of reform as 'abstract propaganda' (Chere and Polyakov 1978: 4).

Factory culture

There were also more complex questions related to how computing was per-ceived. The migration from manual (paper-based) to automated collections man-agement had demanded an enormous input of time as well as data. As early as the summer of 1968 the Smithsonian (through its HEW-funded pilot project) had identified a number of practical human resource issues related to automation and standardisation. First, that it was more efficient to separate the tasks of data preparation and of data input. And second that, provided adequate supervision was given, both roles do not have, as the Smithsonian put it, high 'educational requirements' (Squires 1969a: 16). When, therefore, in 1978 the Smithsonian was mandated by the United States Congress to undertake a comprehensive inventory of its buildings, the National Museum of American History (NMAH) used SELGEM with its own in-house system MIRDS (the Museum Information Retrieval and Documentation System). Consequently, between 1979 and 1983 all resources that had been applied to collections information were redirected to producing a complete baseline inventory of its sixteen million objects (National Museum of American History 1987: vii). The shelf survey that followed involved the hiring of a number of (lower paid) 'keyers', with Raelene Worthington as the National Museum of American History's first full-time data entry person. The UK was then experiencing a time of considerable job creation work that gave much impetus for some museums to input data in machine-readable form (Lewis 2007). Riding on this 'job creation bonanza' (Holm 1993: 1), curators such as Charles Pettitt at the Manchester Museum, for instance, worked with large teams of clerks entering significant amounts of data into the new systems.

However, a culture did exist, evidently, in some museums that only a special-ist could enter the data (Lewis 2007). After all, invariably, it was not curators who were creating and entering the information. A systems diagram from this time, representing the computerisation of object information at the NMAH, was appended with a note describing the 'current flow' of tasks, information and responsibility:

By creating a pool of data entry editors and coding clerks for all object preparation, consistency of category usage, data format, and training of personnel is assured. In addition, divisional staff and shelf inventory personnel do not have to be in command of all aspects of the preparation of data for computer entry, in order to begin such. Familiarity is necessary to begin; increasing knowledge will be gained through involvement.

(Spiess 1981)

One member of the data entry team noted how at one meeting the deputy director of the museum had asked them to take tours of the other divisions in the organisation 'so that we may feel that we are part of the entire museum' (Computer Services Center 1981a). And yet, even though communication was encouraged between the keyers and the curators, the minutes and memoranda from the museum at this time substantiate a somewhat split culture – the perception appears to have been of information being built by an outside group – in the case of the NMAH the shelf survey office. The deputy director of the museum wrote to all staff:

in a specialist project of this sort, which has an impact throughout the Museum, all staff involved need to make a special effort to work with each other and resolve difficulties as quickly and efficiently as possible.

(Evelyn 1980)

Deeply proprietorial, there was a profound sense of ownership not just over the collections themselves but over the information and records that surrounded those objects (Schaefer-Jacobs 2005). Matters were not helped by the production-line protocols and culture that pervaded these types of projects. It was a culture and way of working new to the museum, and evidently at odds with the usual environment of the 'creative cabinet'. As well as giving routine reports on the percentage of records entered and checked from each collection, staff meeting minutes record a focus on 'time-keeping' of the data entry clerks, and when lunch breaks and smoking breaks should be taken (Computer Services Center 1982b). What also emerges is a team under pressure to hit targets: 'In order to get everything completed on time, compromises are being made. We will no longer strive for perfection in all our work', one comment reads. 'We should not worry about inconsistencies among different divisions, only within each division' (Computer Services Center 1982a). Another reads:

If a keyer has any trouble with a control group, they should make a note of the particular problem(s), attach them to the group and return it to the bottom drawer of the file for reediting [. . .] Do not stop to ask the editor a question.

(Computer Services Center 1981b)

In April 1989 Plymouth City Museum and Art Gallery (UK) had embarked on its own Collections Inventory Project. Its objective was to have every item in the collection identified and located by the end of 1991, and for all data to be transferred to a new information management system. Such was the high priority given to the project that by mid-1991 all exhibition and enquiry work by curators was suspended; 'instead, they spend their time cataloguing objects by completing data entry forms' (Marshall 1991a). Curators kept detailed accounts of the number of records created each day which were then compared against targets.

Therefore, for those museums that were resourced and driven enough to begin a process of computerisation from the 1970s (and, indeed, even for those that did not, but rather watched carefully from the sidelines), the coming of 'automation' could be seen to require a not insignificant shift in institutional culture and change in curatorial practice. In many instances this was a change and shift too far. For some the systematic, standardised, uniform process of automating museum collections would always have 'a disturbing, unsettling effect' (Hoving 1968: vi). Curators were being confronted with a different vocabulary, different processes and different sets of values. As well as new termlists and typologies for conceiving collections, this was a new realm of the 'object processing facility', of the 'data entry section', of 'keyers', of 'automation'. This was a different world.

Furthermore, even if the (very) long-term end might have been understood to be beneficial, it was still perceived by many as a 'disruption' (Sarasan 1981) and a 'diversion' of the usual work of the curator (Lewis 2005). Also, in the UK, the experience of the former registrar in Leicestershire (a museum which, compared to many regional museums, was at the cutting edge in its embracement of automation and information retrieval technologies), was that the culture that surrounded the computer was itself problematic:

> 1986 in Leicestershire had a team of clerks producing initial entries. The initial intention had been that rather than the curators sitting at a machine and doing data entry – which was considered to be very menial at the time – the curator would fill out a form that would be copy-typed by a data entry clerk. Bear in mind that at that time, in the mid-1980s, the only people to have computers on their desks, were clerks and secretaries linked up to a word-processing machine. It was not a status to have a computer – it was quite the reverse.
>
> (Marshall 2005)

Moreover, for some practitioners at least, rather than being the lithe creative tools and powerful multimedia communication instruments we appreciate today, computers at this time were still popularly viewed as methodical machines for automating processes. This industrial operation – the factory culture – could be damaging to the profile of computing. Writing on the state of documentation in the 1990s, one practitioner reflected back on the results of this industrialised work of a decade earlier as often 'disastrous' (Holm 1993: 1). Rather than being presented as an agile, intuitive and empowering tool on the desk of the curator, computers were, for many years, for many curators, rather clumsy, industrial-looking things.

This was something of a contrast to the reactions computers would provoke a decade or two later, when, rather than being seen as dull and menial it was, conversely, their gaudy gimmickry that would elicit accusations of galleries being turned into 'funhouses' through their presence (Appleton 2001). One reviewer of the (then) innovative 'Mirco Gallery' at the National Gallery (London) warned against such systems becoming 'simply gimmicks' as they were aped by other museums (Fahy 1991).

Resisting technology-led innovation

There may have been an informality and capriciousness to Thomas Hoving's description of the museum's use of computers as akin to being 'mugged', as he addressed delegates, as the director of the Metropolitan Museum of Art, at the closing dinner of the 1968 New York conference on these new developments. However, there was a serious point being made here. His speech (entitled 'Museums, computers and the future') made it clear that this conference had been 'a turning point' but, more significantly, that the rise of computing was 'inevitable'. And that the evolution ('compressed into revolution') that he and his fellow delegates were witnessing was 'largely machine-dictated'; 'it becomes machine-inflicted, relentless, irrevocable' (ibid.: viii). It is a concern that Knell still detects some thirty-five years later:

> A revolution is at hand. The future of museums is, so it seems from these European developments, beginning to be shaped by the visionary apparatus of technocrats; by computer scientists who have, in the recent tradition of museum operation, been servants of the museum mission. The opportunities provided by technology have developed so rapidly and become so pervasive that these workers are beginning to emerge from their backroom documentation projects to join up with academic researchers from leading university computer science departments, in order to construct a roadmap that will take museums into the future.
>
> (Knell 2003: 132)

'The question is', pondered Philippe de Montebello, director of the Metropolitan Museum in New York, in 1994, 'whether we control the technology, or it controls us' (James 1995).

Non-adaptive institutional structures

Computerisation and reorganisation came early to some museums. The first of five key recommendations made by a computer services study group at the Smithsonian in July 1975 was that a panel should be established to assist in the long-term planning of computer resource distribution in the institution. Planning, it concluded, was the 'single most obvious need for improvement' for the organisation; 'computer use has reached a level important enough', it explained, 'to warrant strengthening in the planning and budgeting process' (Office of

Computer Services 1975: 5). It was as early as 1979 that a joint report by staff at the museum and the County Council made the recommendation that Leicestershire's museums establish a central object catalogue system written in-house, in COBOL, on the Council's 'Sperry' mainframe computer (MCG 1990). For an institution such as the Museum of London, computing has been part of its running since its opening in the 1970s (Metcalfe 1987) and by 1987 all objects received into the museum were accessioned by computer. In 1987 Phil Philips's team at the National Museums on Merseyside (UK) had already reported on a three-year plan for the phased introduction of computers throughout the museum. And, led by the director and including departmental heads, the Royal Botanic Gardens, Kew, had by 1989 established a formal Computer Policy Committee to direct strategy and priorities (Loader 1989).

During the 1980s and 1990s, with a constant increase in accountability and managerialism, British museums experienced a number of changes to their organisational structure – not least a lengthening of the hierarchy and the widening of the horizontal specialising (Roberts 1997).[2] Although this reformation resulted in organisational complexity and demands on new skills sets for staff, it also provided opportunities for the incorporation of computing. As well as the development of documentation and registration as specialised roles (and consequently both the quality and perceived value of these functions), larger museums developed specialist IT units. For instance, during this time the British Museum had established its Collections Documentation Management Section, whose seventeen staff had responsibility for rolling out the computerisation of the records of the collections. And yet, there did not appear to be an ideal fit between the function and activity of this group and the assumptions being made by the rest of the museum:

> we are often uncomfortably caught between central management's wishes for short inventory records and the curators' desire for fully comprehensive records compiled from all available sources of information. We attempt to maintain a balance between the two extremes, but it is not always easy, particularly as various views on this issue continue to chop and change.
>
> (McCutcheon 1993: 2)

The institutional structures of many museums for many years remained rigid in the face of the digital revolution that confronted them. Indeed, when the Association of Systematics Collections had undertaken its survey in 1979 of computer-assisted collections management projects,[3] it was concluded that not only were museums experiencing problems in managing projects, but that these problems were less to do with hardware and software and more based upon inherent weaknesses in the procedures used to initiate and manage these projects (Sarasan 1981). Typically, when as part of local authority restructuring the City of Liverpool Museum became part of Merseyside County Museums in 1974, no provision was made for the new documentation. The organogram (the organisational chart) for the institution was deeply hierarchical, and divided at assistant-director level between academic work (antiquities, botany, decorative art, geology, social and industrial history and so on) in the museum on the one hand and museum services (conservation, design, educational services and technical support) on the other, with a third administrative arm. All of the cataloguing and documentation activity was taking place within the curatorial and academic staff within this structure. Crucially, there was no specialist at all. Consequently, the 'idea' of automation and computerisation was largely promoted from outside the curatorial teams (Lewis 2007; Philips 2005). Even as the drive to computerise became widespread across the museum sector, some observers saw (with, of course, exceptions) problems with where digital media and their personnel sat within many organisations:

> the right people are currently in the wrong places. That is those who know about the potential of Information Technology and how it could be used in museums are not in the positions to realise that potential ... [T]he existing generation of administrators and planners were learning their skills before computer technology became widely available.
>
> (Moffett 1989a)

The commercial sector had, however, already seen this intransigence some twenty years before. Corresponding with the executive director of the Museum Computer Network, IBM's director for Advertising and Promotional Services (Charles Hollister) had in a candid moment offered a glimpse of some of the opposition he had already met: 'Resistance to change, I am sorry to say, seems to be a characteristic of all human institutions. My scepticism in this respect may be unscientific, but has a strong empirical foundation – namely, I have never found one exception to it' (Hollister 1968).

Essentially, in terms of their workflow, personnel and resource allocation, many museums remained ostensibly nineteenth-century-shaped organisations amid a millennium world of new media. Justified by an anxiety over technology-led innovation, these enduring (and in many cases outmoded) institutional structures rendered many museums dysfunctional for the demands of the era of digital management and production. Internal tensions and the need to make the case for digital cultural heritage to the senior management, all set against a backdrop of increasing competition and uncertain market needs, curtailed the development of a number of projects (Poole 2007; Zorich 2003: 28–32). Across the sector as a whole, museums adapted very little and when they did it was not always clear to what extent new media were an integrated activity of the museum and to what extent they were a marginalised endeavour. New departments, divisions and units to accommodate and manage new digital productivity may have been created, such as the 'Information Technology Strategy Group' set up in Glasgow Museums in the early 1990s (Eccles 1993), but many museums continued to struggle with managing this institutional change, identifying the new skill sets required by their workforce, negotiating the changing landscape of in-house and out-sourced production, and (perhaps most importantly) building financial models to make all of this sustainable.

It is perhaps here, therefore, when we hold up Manovich's critical lens that yet another fissure is exposed between museum and computer. The *transcoded* quality of new media relates to the reciprocity that exists between society and technology, with each affected and coded by the other. However, crucially, in the case of museums and computers over the past forty years, this was not always an active or indeed positive synergy – computers invariably caused a disruption (or so it seemed) to the 'real' work of the museum.

The media museum: systemic computing

The MDA's Microcomputer Advisory Group had, by the summer of 1983, identified twenty-eight UK museums that had acquired computers. Their results showed an uptake of computing building from early adopters (such as the Ulster Museum in 1978), with museums spending anything from £600 for an Epson HX-20 (at the Museum of London) to £30,000 for a Star Auditor (at Ironbridge Gorge Museum in Telford). In almost every case the new technology was being used for managing collections information (Roberts and Light 1984).

In spite of all the barriers (risk, time, cost, no sustainable models, wrongly shaped organisations, the fear of technology-led innovation) computers did find their way into museums. Much of the reason for this was to do with increased collaboration, the emergence of standards, advisory groups, strategy, communities of practice, confidence and, of course, funding.

The growth of collaboration

As we saw in Chapter 2, the early museum automation projects of the mid-1960s were in part indebted to the curiosity of individual curators, and were in part an extension of institutional research and development. However, this was a practice that continued for many years. For instance, sharing their practice with colleagues in September 1986, staff described computing developments at the Bristol Museum as 'primarily user-driven rather than the result of museum policy' (Copp 1986). Likewise, it had been by purchasing his own 'microcomputer' that Jim Chimonides (1986) at the British Museum (Natural History) was able to plan a loan system and a type index.

In time, however, agreed standards and frameworks of support did emerge. Just as the work to automate the bird and fossil collections of the Smithsonian Institution National Museum of Natural History generated, in time, a wider *de facto* data management standard for many museums across the United States, so likewise the experimental work of geology curators at the Sedgwick Museum at the University of Cambridge contributed in time to the UK museum sector's first computer-oriented data model for managing and inputting collections records. By 1989, some institutions, such as those involved in botanical collections, were already using ratified standards on the exchange of computer-held collections data. The Royal Botanic Gardens, Kew, for example, was at this time active in establishing an International Transfer format for Botanic Garden Plan Records, the DELTA system for the storage of descriptive information, the Minimum Function Nomenclature and the Plant Existence Categorisation Scheme (Loader 1989). During the 1990s initiatives such as the Consortium for the Computer Interchange of Museum Information (CIMI) and the Aquarelle Project (funded by the EU) both explored the difficulties of achieving on-line access to cultural heritage information held in multiple databases independent of hardware and software used to store the data or search for them (Dawson 1998). Central to their work were the identification and practical application of international standards for digital data – such as the opaquely named 'Z39.50'.

The establishment, in March 1972, of the Museum Data Bank Coordinating Committee (MDBCC) marked a significant step towards the emergence of new levels of co-ordination between organisations. Based at the University of Arkansas Museum, in Fayetteville, and headed by Robert Chenhall, the committee brought together representatives from a number of the pioneering projects of US museum automation – including the Museum Computer Network, the University of Oklahoma and the Smithsonian Institution. Its objective was to maintain basic data compatibility among (and promote data interchange between) the several systems that were flowering at this time (Vance 1978: 51). From November 1974 a number of, at times, quite challenging and technical 'Research Reports' from the committee were published. The 1970s also saw the formation of the Canadian Heritage Information Network (CHIN) in Canada, following the Canadian cabinet mandate for the compilation of an inventory of collections in the National Museums of Canada (Spiess 1986). In 1982 the National Inventory Program became the Canadian Heritage Information Network, and by 1990 CHIN had established its Technology Assessment Centre – working with the museum community and industry to develop technical standards and guidelines, and help to promote the development of technology and applications needed by museums (CHIN 1992).

In 1977 the MDA (Museum Documentation Association) was established in the UK. This represented an evolution of (although, as a limited company, independent from) the decade of work established by the Information Retrieval Group of the Museums Association. MDA's original 'articles of incorporation' made clear that its purpose was 'to promote the development of museums and similar organisations as sources of information by all appropriate methods'. It would do this by researching and developing methods of documenting collections, managing these and other sources of data, and retrieving information from them; by providing training facilities in such methods; and by advising and assisting museums and similar organisations on particular problems (Nuttall 2000). Consequently, at its inception the MDA was one of the few bodies in the world concerned with the documentation of museum collections on a multidisciplinary basis. Rather than trying to form a national inventory of museum holdings in the UK (the rhetoric that shaped the inception of its predecessor, IRGMA, back in 1967), the MDA's aim was in fact to help improve the quality of museum documentation. Similarly, the MDA was not established to direct cataloguing at a national level, nor to impose some uniform scheme of computerisation. Instead its aim was to exploit and develop techniques in handling museum data for the benefits of museums.[4] At the MDA the team continued to adapt the GOS operating system: specifically designed cataloguing/indexing software for museum information. And in May 1987 it launched the MODES collections management software package. Through organisations such as the MDA and CHIN, the sector gained the support network and advisory services that it needed to make the informed choices about museum computing at a time when (as we have already seen) the evidence for success was minimal and barriers to success were many.

The emergence of communities of practice

As important as these formal agencies were the more informal communities of practice that grew up as a critical mass of practitioners began to struggle with the same problems, ask the same questions and seek appropriate answers. As early as June 1969 a conference had been organised at the American Museum of Natural History to discuss the computer-based exchange between universities and museums (Smithsonian Institution 1969a). In September 1967 the first edition of *MUDPIE* ('Museum and University Data, Program, and Information Exchange') appeared. Established by James Peters, the occasional newsletter represented an attempt to keep a community of practitioners informed of the latest developments of 'time-shared computing' in museums and universities. A conference, described by those who attended it as 'momentous' and 'historically critical' (Metropolitan Museum of Art 1968: v), took place at the Metropolitan Museum of Art, New York, between 15 and 17 April 1968, and was supported by a grant from the IBM Corporation. The printed proceedings record some twenty-seven delegates. However, only a third of these were museum practitioners (mostly from the Met), evenly split between curatorial staff and senior management and administrators, including the head of education, the registrar, the chief librarian, and the director – Thomas Hoving. There were slightly more participants from the US higher education sector. Representatives came from the Massachusetts Institute of Technology, Columbia University, Stamford University, as well as the Universities of Illinois, Oklahoma, Toronto and Arizona State. These scholars appear to have come from 'traditional' academic disciplines, including anthropology and sociology. But more than half represented technical departments, specifically electrical engineering and computer science, as well as a computer-based education research laboratory. The remaining five delegates came from industry – and mostly from IBM. It was, perhaps, an indication of how early this event came in the synergy between digital technology and curatorship, that there were only two delegates whose title formally located them at the crossroads of curatorship and computing: Everett Ellin (the director of the newly established Museum Computer Network); and Jack Heller (one of the MCN's founder members but then also director of the Institute for Computer Research in the Humanities, at New York University at University Heights).

MUDPIE and the Met conference were clear indications of how quickly communities of practice emerged within museum computing. Wenger et al. define 'communities of practice' as groups of people who share a concern, a set of problems, or a passion about a topic, and who deepen their knowledge and expertise in this area by interacting on an ongoing basis (2002: 4). Individuals in these communities do not necessarily work together in the same organisation, but do 'find value in their interactions' (ibid.). As a group they may not be entirely homogenous, but they will share information, help each other to solve problems, discuss their shared aspirations and needs. Their focus, Wenger et al. suggest, may be on developing something tangible and specific (such as a standard or a particular tool), but it might, equally, be just a 'tacit understanding that they share' (ibid.: 5). Moreover, communities of practice provide for their members stability and a 'social fabric of learning' (ibid.: 28). Successful communities of practice have a co-ordinator, core members (providing leadership), and an active group around that core. However, they are also characterised by a periphery, where a large proportion of the community resides (ibid.: 56). A key facility of communities of practice is that they allow for migration between the periphery, the 'active' zone and the core. Successful communities, Wenger et al. say, are also able to combine familiarity and excitement, as well as a rhythm to their patterns of work (ibid.: 62).

Through their passionate leadership, regular newsletters, conferences, Web-based resources, groups such as the Museum Computer Network in the US and the Museums Computer Group in the UK, fit this model of a 'community of practice' extremely well. Many of the successes in museum computing over the past forty years in these two countries have been related to the confidence and knowledge that practitioners have been able to acquire through their participation in these types of community. The MCN was established in 1967 under the impetus of the Metropolitan Museum of Art and the Museum of Modern Art in New York, and benefited from funding from New York State Council on the Arts, and the Old Dominion Foundation (totalling $50,500). It began as a 'regional effort' (IBM and Ellin 1969). The group soon realised that its efforts had national application. Nine leading art museums in other parts of the United States were then asked to join the consortium. As momentum was generated, the original fifteen member institutions had, in a year, grown to include the Institute of Fine Arts in Chicago and the National Gallery in Washington, DC (Hoving 1968: x). The MCN was not a community of practice (initially) but a project – it became a community of practice, something akin to a curators' group, later. An indication of the confidence that strong communities of practice can bring to their members came at the 15th Annual Meeting of the MCN, held at the Boston Museum of Science in October 1987. The then president, Ron Kley, emphasised how the intention of the network was to improve the status of computing and documentation in the museum world. For Kley, and for practitioners like Anthony Fletcher who attended the event, this was about visibility and integrity: 'Our status is indeed improving' wrote Fletcher (1987), in his report back to the UK 'sister' organisation (the MCG) on the event. Moreover, the ongoing activity of these groups has contributed significantly to the establishment of museum computing as an 'identifiable and credible' area of practice and research (Parry 2005).

Strategy and funding

With 'digitisation becoming the new watchword for access and preservation' (Knell 2003: 133), by early 1998 major government funding bodies, such as the Heritage Lottery Fund in the UK, had received lengthy and detailed rec-ommendations on where and how they could offer financial support to develop Information and Communication Technology in the heritage sector. Visualis-ing 'a heritage rich information society', the HLF policy fused an important link between digital media (particularly networked hypermedia), heritage information and tangible public benefits. The emphasis was on producing resources that were freely available for educational purposes, emphasising the use of national and international standards, and giving preference to collabora-tive projects. There would not be support for the development of infrastructure, nor Web sites that did not form part of a consistent and coherent information service. The funding would not support research and development, nor, sig-nificantly, the conversion of existing catalogues except where 'value is clearly added' (Economou and Ross 1998). Although the strategic link between them was not always apparent, and although the tail was allowed to wag the dog for some institutions, in the years that followed (in the UK at least) a procession of funding streams became available to museums. Over £50 million of the NOF Digitisation project supported the government's policy for social inclusion, by supporting heritage partnerships to create digital content. Between 1999 and 2001 the IT Challenge Fund 1999–2001 supported eleven collaborative pro-jects that made innovative use of ICT. The £15 million of the Designation Challenge Fund provided significant support for those museums attempting to provide on-line access to collections and collections information. This was followed in 2002 by the Culture Online project from the Department of Cul-ture, Media and Sport (DCMS), which invested £13 million to improve access to arts and culture through digital media. To this was added a further £50 mil-lion of investment as part of the Curriculum Online project that helped schools to buy digital content – including content based on museum resources. More-over, through the 1990s the levels of strategic co-ordination and co-operation had, in countries such as the UK, helped also to generate services such as the Scottish Cultural Resources Access Network (SCRAN), Cornucopia and the People's Network Discover Service, all of which provided (or, at least, aspired to provide) the Google-like simplicity of a one-stop search engine that mines an interoperable series of datasets of cultural content. And on 12 May 1999 the UK even gained its own virtual national museum – the 24 Hour Museum, an independent charity funded by the DCMS, the first virtual national museum in the world. These kinds of services could only exist once practitioners from a number of institutions were able to inform their vision, articulate their case, synchronise their strategies, co-ordinate their resources, and make their data interoperable. Although not perfect (many museums are still unclear on what the next round of funding might be for them, and the sustainable model still remains elusive), museum computing finally, after some forty years, has built some of the resources that Everett Ellin visualised back in 1968 – visions with which our stories began in Chapter 1.

The emergence of the 'media museum'

'The Museum' became a cultural phenomenon just as likely to be experienced on-line as on-site. Its collections were just as likely to be managed and understood through automated computers as manually on paper, its objects at times digital as well as physical. And its narratives and interpretations were increasingly authored by its visitors and not just its curators. They communicated through a number of different channels, and they did not see physical object and physical display as the only modes of communication. This was the new 'media museum'. And so, just as once the filing cabinet, the display case and the register had each been 'new', and had each in time come to represent (in an iconic way) 'museum', so too computers will become a defining (innate) part of what it is to be a museum. And as the 'media museum' (with its digital files, user-driven functions, and distributed network presence) acquires more and more the properties of the computer, so it will become more and more difficult to see where the museum stops and where the computer begins.

8

Computers and compatibility

On 13 June 1894, J. W. Clark, historian of library classification, delivered a paper at the University of Cambridge as that year's prestigious Rede Lecturer. Through a meticulous piece of scholarly work, Clark placed the university libraries that surrounded him and his audience into the context of a sweeping story of civilisation. From Sir Christopher Wren to St Benedict, and from Sir Robert Cotton (who contributed one of the foundation collections of the British Library), to Bishop Alexander of Jerusalem, this was nineteenth-century narrative history at its most introspective and self-congratulatory. It was, however, his comments on the current state of archiving and librarianship that resonate for the history of museum collections and new technology. Clark concluded that 'common sense urges that mechanical ingenuity, which has gone so much in other directions, should be employed in making the acquisition of knowledge less cumbrous and less tedious'. His recommendation, therefore, was a simple one: 'that as we travel by steam, so we should also read by steam, and be helped in our studies by the varied resources of modern invention'. In short, writing at the twilight of the Victorian age of expansion and mechanisation, Clark saw his culture's new technologies as having a role (a significant role) in the organisation of cultural heritage. To him, it was 'the varied resources of modern invention' that had an active and unavoidable part to play in the future of memory institutions. I doubt he could have guessed how true his words would prove to be.

Museums have always been associated with technology. After all, in one sense, they are themselves a technology of sorts; a medium, a physical form of communication. Indeed, over the centuries, our museums, libraries and archives have found their beginnings and shaped their changing roles at the same time as they also found new ways to present, process and protect their objects and ideas. Communication technology continues to inform and support the purpose and practice of the museum world, from the cabinet of curiosity to the illusory diorama, and from the glass-fronted display case to the hands-on interactive, and from the punched card catalogue to the database management system. In short, the histories of museums and the histories of their mediating technologies are inextricably linked. To tell a story of museums is to tell a story (also) of the technologies they contain.

137

Through this book we can trace a story of incompatibility between *numerical*, *automated*, *modular*, *variable*, and *transcoded* computers and a modern museum that instead (and in contrast) privileged the material world; that carried the traditions of the 'creative cabinet' and the idea of the museum as a framed experience; that emphasised fixity and stability and the authorship and authority of the curator; and that held on to institutional structures that resisted being re-shaped by a modish technology. What we learn from this story (I admit, an intentionally astigmatic story) is how beneath the practical and pragmatic issues related to time, money and skills, lie perhaps some more profound discontinuities between how a museum and a computer both function. It is these deeper fault lines, under the surface, well below the rubble and froth of the day-to-day politics of the museum, that perhaps reveal more fundamental reasons as to why museums and computers have taken two generations to find their 'fit'.

It was this same incompatibility that was detected on one of those very first occasions that museum practitioners gathered to discuss computing. The host of the meeting described one unfortunate, but telling, reaction by a colleague:

> An old friend of mine, someone with impeccable credentials in traditional aesthetics, wandered out of curiosity into the [...] auditorium yesterday, got an earful of such things as data banks, input, output, printout, software, hardware, and interface, and rushed in to tell me that I was selling out to the barbarians. He saw himself and me and museums as Rome in the first century, clutching the glories of the past to its bosom, dewy-eyed with nostalgia for the old days, uncertain of the present, fearful of the future, listening to the horrible rattling of the city gates, the incoherent din outside the walls of barbaric tribes who had descended with raw, brutal vitality from the northern wastes. And I was accused of being one of those who betrayed by opening the gates to hordes from Armonk and Poughkeepsie. I think what set him off was a paper on the Analysis of Quantified Data in Numismatic Studies which described the great Sultan Saladin as a 'test variable'.[1]
>
> (Hoving 1968: vi)

We should, of course, note quickly that there is likely to be a certain degree of artistic licence at play here, as the wit and repartee of an accomplished speaker plays to the convivial atmosphere of a conference dinner audience. And yet, in a sense, Hoving was right. It was exactly this misapprehension, this reticence, this resistance to change (this *shock of the new*), which he saw in his colleague's reaction, that was to characterise and determine the faltering starts of museum computing for the next forty years.

However, there has been another narrative in this book. This has been the *history of compatibility*. In contrast to our first story, this is one where museums have adapted and have experimented in order to assimilate new media, not just into their practice but into their very definition and sense of purpose. This is a story not of disconnect and tension, but instead of circumspection and reinvention. Unlike our first story, here our narrative has been driven by institutions willing to embrace change – rather than resisting change. For this is a story of how today's museums have not just become (or at least are becoming) more accommodating and tolerant of computers, but have had their role, function and provision re-evaluated and reshaped – let us say *recoded* – by this new technology. In this story the *numerical, automated, modular, variable* and *transcoded* nature of new media (revealed to us by Manovich) is seen to have influenced some important modern reworkings and rethinkings not only of museums' notion of 'object' and 'visit', but also of their relationship with their collections as well as their construction of their own authority. The 'incompatibility error' that may or may not have stood between museum and computer has (in this version of events) been largely repaired. Consequently, from the perspective of this particular history, what we see around us and ahead of us is: the *information museum* (recalibrating authenticity); the *automated museum* (disaggregating the collection); the *multi-channel museum* (rescripting the visit); the *personal museum* (rewriting the narrative); and the *media museum* (reorganising the modes of digital production).

At each turn digital technology appears to have challenged a tenet, a defining characteristic of what a museum is. Be it the notion of the museum as creative cabinet. Be it the museum's privileging of the material world. Be it the idea of a museum visit as a framed experience. Or be it the emphasis on fixity and stability, and the authorship and authority of the curator. In each case the evidence (rather, that is, than the official record or commercial hype) suggests this disruption has been difficult for the museum to accommodate, the dilemma hard to work through, and the change a slow process.[2] However, it is equally evident that digital technology has had a catalytic effect on the museum project over the last forty years, widening the horizon of possibilities. It is likely that in the 1960s and 1970s the striving for professionalism and the need for greater efficiency in response to the new demands on collections would eventually have necessitated the need for clear standards in documentation. But it was the advent of automated computer processes in cognate disciplines and institutions that provided the trigger and the impetus for this change. Similarly, the management of complex images such as photographic negatives and film, the curation of ephemeral items such as performance art, and the collecting of non-material assets such as oral testimony, all, in time, would have demanded that the museum re-evaluate its notion of 'object' and 'collection' in the face of modernity. And yet, the digital media revolution that accompanied these re-evaluations quickened their pace and visibility by attracting new funds, drawing in new commentators and introducing new practices. The unique hybrid qualities of the e-tangible (owing something and nothing to both tangibles and intangibles) also drove these thought processes on even further. Likewise, the growth of museum publications, the development of 'outreach' programmes, and the emergence of professional museum marketing all worked to dissolve some of the thresholds that surrounded the traditional walled museum, and worked to extend the idea of the 'museum experience' beyond just a visit to a single physical site. However, again, it has been the computer (or more specifically networked hypermedia) and its ability to support multi-channel two-way communication at a distance that has perhaps pushed the boundaries of the museum the furthest. It has been the Web that has challenged not just *where* but *when* a museum visit can take place, and on whose terms, creating a new arena where many museums today have more of their audience on-line than on-site. And certainly, the new learning practices introduced at the end of the last century (valuing personalised meaning making, the intelligences and the experiences of the individual visitor) and the institution's reinvented sense of social responsibility and the audience empowerment that followed, have all, of course, contributed to a more visitor-centred and 'responsive' museum experience, where visitors are encouraged to interact and participate within the museum. But perhaps it has only been with the arrival of intelligent software (adjusting and building content on the fly) and media communication and production tools (both in the space of the museum and in the visitor's own personal space – be it at work, at study, at home) that a vibrant sense of personalisation and dialogue has taken place, and that museums have seen their assets genuinely added to, developed and reinterpreted by their visitors.

In each case (be it in the systematisation of documentation, the re-definition of 'object', the rescripting of the 'visit', or the acceptance of outside interpretation) digital technology may not have been the only cause or the unique factor. However, in every case it is hard not to conclude that the effect of digital technology has been catalytic, significant and lasting. It would be an exaggeration to suggest that the computer has been the cause of the recent 'reimagining', 'rethinking', 'reshaping' and 'reframing' of the museum. However, from the evidence we have seen, the new digital technologies appear always to have been at the heart of this change. Always posing new dilemmas for the museum, always, we might say, constructively disruptive.

Long before the digital era, museums had always adapted to the social contexts in which they have found themselves, and they had always seen their actions and priorities codified by the intellectual disciplines, information systems and display techniques of their times. Under the influence of just another of these new technologies, we have been – and indeed we remain – witnesses to yet another *recoding* of the museum.

Notes

1 Museum/computer: a history of disconnect?

1 For instance, faced with opposition from workforce unions, the University Museum in Oxford was unable to make use of government schemes (such as the Manpower Services Commission, or the Youth Training Scheme) to provide personnel to input data. See King (1989).

2 In fact 'incompatibility' is the word that Thomas Hoving (1968: vii) used in his address to the first major conference on museum computing, in New York in 1968, to describe the gap he perceived between technology and the humanities that, to him, partly explained the uneasy adoption of computers by his curatorial colleagues. Likewise, it was problems of machine 'compatibility' that John Cutbill elaborated upon in his key paper on the development of machine-based information retrieval in 1970. It is with both these senses of cultural and technical (in)compatibility that I use this term throughout this book.

3 Just a brief survey of the various editions of *The Story of Art* shows that this issue certainly was of concern to Gombrich. In his twelfth edition (1971), he wrote how 'modern production methods' offer 'fresh opportunities' to the art historian. Similarly, at the front of the fourteenth edition (1984) he alluded to his, and his publisher's, drive to 'keep in step with technical developments' (Gombrich 1995: 10, 11).

4 Among some seriously detailed technical discussion on functionality and use, Chenhall (1975: 93–234) also includes subject-specific, if brief, histories of some of the key cataloguing systems that were dominating the US sector at the time, such as SELGEM and GRIPHOS.

5 Unsurprisingly for a book that engages so directly with technology, some passages seem dated to today's reader, such as those on DVDs, digital preservation, the nature of museum Web sites, and IPR. Inevitably, this is a sacrifice that all of us who attempt to write freshly about a 'new technology' make. However, the remarks the book makes on the nature of the information age, the potential of new media, the locus of the museum, the 'network of knowledge' (Keene's term), accuracy and integrity, multimedia production, the nature of institutional change, the importance of skills and training, and strategic development of new technologies in museums, are all valuable and persuasive. See Keene (1998: 3, 10, 17, 26, 56, 89, 91 and Chapter 8 *passim*). Likewise Keene's comments on 'portable curators' today seem prophetic (ibid.: 111).

6 In terms of how unacceptable some of his language appears today, see McLuhan (2001: 5, 18).

2 From the 'day book' to the 'data bank': the beginnings of museum computing

1 Vance (1973: 49), for instance, gestures towards how 'interest in the application of computer technology to museum documentation began to stir in Germany', also in 1963.

2 It is perhaps important to note that by 1965 the Smithsonian was by no means alone in these early in-roads into automation. For instance, at that time a pilot study had also begun at the University of Oklahoma with museums in the State of Oklahoma, to devise

a workable system for inventorying ethnological collections. The work had included a feasibility study into the role of 'automatic data processing systems' and the most efficient means for the storage and retrieval of data, the findings of which had been presented by A. F. Ricciardelli at the symposium on information management in the natural sciences, in Mexico, in December 1967. See Smithsonian Institution (1968b). Similarly, in the UK, the Imperial War Museum had since 1963 been exploring how human agency could be replaced by machines in the indexing of its collections of film, photography, books, papers and other objects, and discussion had led them to the adoption of IBM 80-column punched cards. See Roads (1968).

3 However, the museum's decisions to proceed with the project were evidently based on more than just Squires's case. An independent report on the current functionality and future potential of the information retrieval system developed at the National Museum of Natural History had also been commissioned by the museum's director, and was submitted in May 1970 by Manfred Kochen of the Mental Health Research Institute at the University of Michigan, James Rohlf of the Department of Biology, SUNY Stony Brook, and William Helgeson from the General Electric Company.

4 This name was a truncated version of the term 'SELf GEnerating Master'.

5 This description is found in an undated leaflet entitled *The SELGEM System for Information Management: An Introduction*. See the Smithsonian Institution Archives, accession 95–169, box 1.

6 Indeed, it could be argued that the mixed success in recent years of the application of the Dublin Core metadata standard to the museum sector may relate to the fact that this standard (originating largely from the library and archive community) does not, in its somewhat 'flat' form, recognise some of the complexities and semantics a museum curator might see between the system's 'element set'.

3 Disaggregating the collection

1 Laurencich-Minelli terms these 'alternative microsymmetry' (alternating dissimilar objects) and 'repeating macrosymmetry' (the thematic grouping of objects).

2 For a discussion of the plan of Cotton House prepared by Sir Christopher Wren's office after 1702, see Tite (1994: 80–1).

3 The manuscript he refers to is BL Add. MS 35213. See Tite (1997: 186).

4 Evidence for this comes from BL MS Harl. 6018, fo. 150. See Sharpe (1979: 78).

5 For the seminal study of Camillo's theatre see Yates (1966: 155). Set within a stronger museological context also see Hooper-Greenhill (1992: 97–101).

6 For an eye-witness account from a practitioner who heard Bearman's keynote address to the 15th Annual Meeting of the Museum Computer Network in October 1987, in which evidently he came out with the fateful line that 'computing in museums is a disaster', see Fletcher (1987).

7 The disappearance of the curator's hand from electronic records is an interesting point. With a handwritten index card, accession register items or day book additions, each entry could be connected to specific individuals and, consequently, understood as unique record *events* in time and space. Curators who can recognise other curators' 'hands' can read into those records other layers of meaning, as records are immediately linked to personalities and moments and all that entails (Cooper 2005; Lloyd-Baynes 2005). In this context we can historicise the museological significance as well as the subject-specific or object-specific significance of each entry. All of this is meaning that can potentially be lost in the standard text of the electronic files. This, indeed, is one of the reasons why the National Museum of the American Indian has scanned a hundred years' worth of handwritten catalogue cards (Bridge 2005), and why many other museums now have more of an audit trail through many of the fields in their systems that allow them to trace who has entered what piece of information.

8 Even in a relatively new institution such as the Museum of London, established in the

1970s, each of its departments kept for over a decade its own individual data standard (Metcalfe 1987).
9 The acronym MODES stands for 'Museum Object Data Entry System'.
10 I think here of the conceptual linkages of the CIDOC Conceptual Reference Model (CRM), as a tool for integrating cultural information. The CRM is a top-level ontology for the semantic integration of cultural information.

4 Recalibrating authenticity

1 What writing in digital heritage is yet to do is think through the political and ideological implications of deploying Benjamin's thesis in these discussions on media reproducibility. Commonly, the contexts in which his ideas are used are bereft of the political discourse in which his arguments were actually intended. As enticing as we might find Benjamin's mantra on aura and the authentic, we should perhaps always keep in mind when quoting it so liberally that the assumptions and intentions that lie beneath are more radical and targeted than our more passive usage might at first imply. Research and writing in digital heritage (compared to its sister subjects, still in its infancy) is yet to confront and think through this level of politicisation. Moreover, the case of Benjamin and his theory of 'aura' is a salutary reminder of how much intellectual baggage may come with the ideas that we may choose to transport from other contexts.
2 For a somewhat sceptical review of the conference see Robson (1996).
3 Central to studies in liminality (and rites of passage) is the challenging work of anthropologist Victor Turner. In particular see Turner (1977).
4 Quoting an 1887 report from the British Association for the Advancement of Science, see Tony Bennett (1998): 'A museum without labels is like an index torn out of a book; it may be amusing, but it teaches very little.'

5 Rescripting the visit

1 Peponis and Hedin note, interestingly, that tabular classification was the governing spatial principle within the Bird Gallery, despite the fact that the museum was founded some twenty-two years after the publication of *The Origin of Species*. See Peponis and Hedin (1982: 23).
2 This is a much-quoted passage used by Impey and MacGregor (1985), as well as Macdonald (1998: 7) and Hooper-Greenhill (1992: 78).
3 See Lefebvre (1991: 176, 182, 194–205, 213–17, 208, 301, 325 and 374).
4 However, the first part of the book was written as a summary of the thesis as a whole, so that it could be published and promoted in *L'Homme et la société* (January–June 1974), pp. 15–32. See Shields (1999: 162).
5 For a concise summary of this and the other realms of the Lefebvrean triad see Shields (1999: 160–7).
6 For quite obvious reasons, André Malraux's notion of the 'museum without walls' (*musée imaginaire*) has proved a tempting conceit for many commentators on the impact of the Internet on cultural heritage. See, for instance, Hazan (2003) and MacDonald (1992).
7 For a list of some of the early adopters see Taylor and Ryan (1995).
8 See for instance the quarterly studies by UK National Statistics, specifically its Omnibus Survey, in which 2,000 households in Great Britain have provided information periodically about Internet access. See http://www.statistics.gov.uk.

7 Reorganising production

1 However, it is worth noting that in the case of Leicester, curators would soon be benefiting from training and support, and four years later encouragingly were showing an interest in

developing their own computer systems. This had, by 1990, 'raised the popularity of computers in the Museum' (MCG 1990).

2 Roberts's paper (which drew from his 1994 MBA dissertation, involving thirty-four returned questionnaires) concluded that 'in smaller museums, this has tended to develop as part of the overall curatorial and administrative role, while in larger museums it has been supported as part of the documentation and registration initiative or in its own right'.

3 The initial postal survey was of approximately 8,000 individuals representing as many museums, of which more than 1,200 responded, and 320 indicated involvement in a computer-assisted collections management project. Ultimately, information was received on more than 300 individual projects (Sarasan 1981).

4 For a series of perspectives on the establishment of MDA that captures well the information (as well as the misinformation) that was circulating in the UK sector at the time, see the debate between N. Tebble, on the one hand, and M. Porter and F. Villett on the other, printed in Council for Museums and Galleries in Scotland (1977).

8 Computers and compatibility

1 The paper Hoving refers to here was by Jeanette Wakin, Assistant Professor, Department of Middle East Languages and Culture, at Columbia University.

2 In terms of evidence, it is perhaps important also to note that to hear and see these concerns and fears we have had to look beyond formal reports and marketing rhetoric, and instead listen to the curators themselves, in person, or in their correspondence, or in their minutes, or in their mutually supportive and frank exchanges as communities of practice. There may, in other words, be lessons here for us on where we might go to source evidence in the future as we continue to write our histories of museum computing.

Bibliography

Abbott, R. (1999) *The World as Information: overload and personal design*, Exeter: Intellect.

Abungu, L. (2002) 'Access to digital heritage in Africa: bridging the digital divide', *Museum International*, vol. 54, no. 3: 29–34.

Addis, M., Martinez, K. and Lewis, P. (2005) 'New ways to search, navigate and use multimedia museum collections over the Web', in J. Trant and D. Bearman (eds) *Museums and the Web 2005: proceedings*, Toronto: Archives & Museum Informatics. Online. Available HTTP: <http://www.archimuse.com/mw2005/papers/addis/addis.html> (accessed 25 January 2007).

Adegoroye, D., Arch, N., Hamer, J., Houlihan, M., Lavis, D., King, V., et al. (2000) *Skills Foresight in the Cultural Heritage Sector 2000–2010*, Bradford: Cultural Heritage National Training Organisation.

Alison, R. (1590) *A Plaine Confutation of A Treatise of Brownisme,* London: Thomas Scarlet.

Allden, A. (1987) 'Reports received: British Museum, London', *Museums Computer Group Newsletter*, vol. 3: 3.

Alshejni, L. (1999) 'Unveiling the Arab woman's voice through the net', in W. Harcourt (ed.) *Women@Internet: creating new cultures in cyberspace*, London and New York: Zed Books.

Anderson, D. (1999) *A Common Wealth: museums in the learning age,* London: Department of Culture, Media and Sport.

Anderson, M. (1997) 'Introduction', in K. Jones-Garmil (ed.) *The Wired Museum: emerging technology and changing paradigms*, Washington, DC: American Association of Museums.

Appleton, J. (2001) 'Museums: pushing the wrong buttons?', *Spiked*, 4 May 2001. Online. Available HTTP: <http://www.spiked-online.com/Printable/00000002D09D.htm> (accessed 26 May 2007).

Bachelard, G. (1994) *The Poetics of Space*, trans. M. Jolas, Boston: Beacon Press.

Bandelli, A. (1999) 'Virtual spaces and museums', *Journal of Museum Education*, vol. 24, nos. 1 and 2. Online. Available HTTP: <http://homepage.mac.com/bandelli/CV/articles/virtual.pdf> (accessed 28 May 2007).

Barnes, R. C. M. (1964) *The Present State of Information Retrieval by Computer*, United Kingdom Atomic Energy Authority research group report, Harwell, Berkshire: Atomic Energy Research Establishment.

Barrell, R. (1624) *The Spirituall Architecture, or The Balance of Gods Sanctuary,* a sermon preached at Paul's Cross the 16 November 1623, London: Augustine Matthew and John Norton.

Battro, A. M. (1999) 'From Malraux's imaginary museum to the virtual museum', paper presented to Xth World Federation of Friends Congress, Sydney, September 13–18, 1999. Online. Available HTTP: <http://www.byd.com.ar/vm99sep.htm> (accessed 28 May 2007).

Bearman, D. (1995) 'Standards for networked cultural heritage', *Archives & Museum Informatics*, vol. 9, no. 3: 279–307.

—— (2007) Interview with the author, 14 April 2007.

Bearman, D. and Trant, J. (1999) 'Interactivity comes of age: museums and the World Wide Web', *Museum International*, vol. 51, no. 4: 20–4.

—— (2006) *Survey of Museum Web Implementation, 2005*, Toronto: Archives & Museum Informatics. Online. Available HTTP: <http://www.archimuse.com/research/mwbenchmarks/report/mwbenchmarks2005.html> (accessed 28 May 2007).

Belsey, A. and Belsey, C. (1990) 'Icons of Divinity: portraits of Elizabeth I', in L. Gent and N. Llewellyn (eds) *Renaissance Bodies: the human figure in English culture c. 1540–1660*, London: Reaktion Books.

Benjamin, W. (1999) 'The work of art in the age of mechanical reproduction', in H. Arendt (ed.) *Illuminations*, London: Pimlico.

Bennett, N. A. and Jones, T. (2001) 'Building a Web-based collaborative database: does it work?', in D. Bearman and J. Trant (eds) *Museums and the Web 2001: proceedings*, Toronto: Archives & Museum Informatics. Online. Available HTTP: <http://www.archimuse.com/mw2001/papers/bennett/bennett.html> (accessed 25 January 2007).

Bennett, T. (1995) *The Birth of the Museum: history, theory, politics*, London: Routledge.

—— (1998) 'Speaking to the eyes: museums' legibility and the social order', in S. Macdonald (ed.) *The Politics of Display: museums, science, culture*, London and New York: Routledge.

Bergomatis, G. G. (1562) *The Castle of Memorie*, trans. W. Fulwood, London: Rouland Hall.

Berners-Lee, T. and Fischetti, M. (1999) *Weaving the Web: the past, present and future of the World Wide Web by its inventor*, London: Orion.

Besser, H. (1997) 'The changing role of photographic collections with the advent of digitization', in K. Jones-Garmil (ed.) *The Wired Museum: emerging technology and changing paradigms*, Washington, DC: American Association of Museums.

—— (2000) 'Digital longevity', in M. K. Sitts (ed.) *Handbook for Digital Projects: a management tool for preservation and access*, Andover, MA: Northeast Document Conservation Center.

Black, A. (1996) *A New History of the English Public Library: social and intellectual contexts 1850–1914*, London and New York: Leicester University Press.

Boast, R. (2005) Interview with the author, 12 December 2005.

Borges, J. L. (1964) 'The library of Babel', in D. A. Yates and J. E. Irby (eds) *Labyrinths: selected stories and other writings*, New York: New Directions Publications.

Bowen, J. (1997) 'The Virtual Library museums page (VLmp): whence and whither?', in D. Bearman and J. Trant (eds) *Museums and the Web 97: selected papers*, Pittsburgh: Archives & Museum Informatics.

Bowen, J., Bridgen, R., Dyson, M. and Moran, K. (2001) 'On-line collections access at the Museum of English Rural Life', in D. Bearman and J. Trant (eds) *Museums and the Web 2001: proceedings*, Toronto: Archives & Museum Informatics. Online. Available HTTP: <http://www.archimuse.com/mw2001/papers/bowen/bowen.html> (accessed 25 January 2007).

Bowles E. A. (1968) 'Introduction to the work of the conference', in *Computers and their Potential Application in Museums*, Metropolitan Museum of Art, New York: Arno Press.

Brears, P. (1987) 'Leap forward with SHIC', *SHCG News*, no. 16: 3.

Brewer, C. (1986) 'Reports received: Hancock Museum, Newcastle', *Museums Computer Group Newsletter*, no. 2: 2.

Bridge, D. (1970) 'Prepare specimen record on paper tape', unpublished internal report, 18 May, Smithsonian Institution Archives, accession 95–169, box 1.

—— (1985) Memorandum to R. A. Dierker, E. H. Lytle, D. Bearman et al. on computer security problems at the Museum Support Center, 15 September, Smithsonian Institution Archives, accession 95–169, box 3.

—— (2005) Interview with the author, 6 December 2005.

British Museum (2004) Press release announcing the opening of *The Mummy: the inside story*, July 2004 until January 2005, London: British Museum. Online. Available HTTP: <http://www.thebritishmuseum.ac.uk/newsroom/current2004/mummy.html> (accessed 8 November 2005).

Bullis, H. R. (1967) 'Bionumeric code application in handling complex and massive faunal data', *Systematic Zoology*, vol. 16, no. 1: 52–5.

Burgin, V. (1996) *In/Different Spaces*, Berkeley, Los Angeles and London: University of California Press.

Burnett, J. (1986) 'Reports received: Royal Museums of Scotland, Edinburgh', *Museums Computer Group Newsletter*, no. 2: 4.

Callery, B. G. and Thibadeau, R. (2000) 'Beyond label copy: museum-library collaboration in the development of a smart Web exhibit', in D. Bearman and J. Trant (eds) *Museums and the Web 2000: proceedings*, Toronto: Archives & Museum Informatics. Online. Available HTTP: <http://www.archimuse.com/mw2000/papers/callery/callery.html> (accessed 25 January 2007).

Cameron, F. (2003) 'The next generation: "knowledge environments" and digital collections', in D. Bearman and J. Trant (eds) *Museums and the Web 2003: proceedings*, Pittsburgh: Archives & Museum Informatics. Online. Available HTTP: <http://www.archimuse.com/mw2003/papers/cameron/cameron.html> (accessed 25 May 2007).

Cameron, F. and Kenderline, S. (eds) (2007) *Theorising Digital Cultural Heritage: a critical discourse*, Cambridge, MA and London: MIT Press.

Cannon-Brookes, P. (1984) 'The nature of museum collections', in J. M. A. Thompson, D. A. Bassett, D. G. Davies, A. J. Duggan, D. G. Lewis and D. R. Prince (eds) *Manual of Curatorship: a guide to museum practice*, London: Butterworths.

Castells, M. (2001) 'Museums in the information era: cultural connectors of time and space', *ICOM News*, special issue, vol. 54, no. 3: 4–7.

Chadwick, J. and Boverie, P. (1999) 'A survey of characteristics and patterns of behavior in visitors to a museum Web site', in D. Bearman and J. Trant (eds) *Museums and the Web 1999: selected papers from an international conference,* Pittsburgh: Archives & Museum Informatics. Online. Available HTTP: <http://www.archimuse.com/mw99/papers/chadwick/chadwick.html> (accessed 28 May 2007).

Chan, S. (2007) 'Tagging and Searching: serendipity and museum collection databases', in J. Trant and D. Bearman (eds) *Museums and the Web 2007: proceedings*, Toronto: Archives & Museum Informatics. Online. Available HTTP: <http://www.archimuse.com/mw2007/papers/chan/chan.html> (accessed 25 May 2007).

Chenhall, R. G. (1975) *Museum Cataloging in the Computer Age*, Nashville, TN: American Association for State and Local History.

—— (1988) *Museum Collections and Today's Computers*, New York and London: Greenwood Press.

Chenhall, R. G. and Homulos, P. (1978) 'Museum Data Standards', *Museum News*, vol. 56, no. 6: 43–8.

Chere, Y. A. and Polyakov, A. O. (1978) 'Museum cataloguing and the computer', in *ICOM Committee for Conservation: 5th Triennial Meeting, Zagreb*, Paris: ICOM.

Chimonides, J. (1987) 'Reports received: British Museum – Natural History, London', *Museums Computer Group Newsletter*, no. 3: 3.

CHIN (1992) *Network News: newsletter of the Canadian Heritage Information Network*, no. 3.

—— (1994) *Network News: newsletter of the Canadian Heritage Information Network*, no. 5.

—— (1995) *Network News: newsletter of the Canadian Heritage Information Network*, no. 7.

Chippindale, C. (1991) 'Report on the MCG meeting, Cambridge University Museums, October 1990: Cambridge University Museum of Archaeology and Anthropology', *Museums Computer Group Newsletter*, autumn 1991: 3–4.

Chun, S., Cherry, R., Hiwiller, D., Trant, J. and Wyman, B. (2006) 'Steve.museum: an ongoing experiment in social tagging, folksonomy, and museums', in J. Trant and D. Bearman (eds) *Museums and the Web 2006: proceedings*, Toronto: Archives & Museum Informatics. Online. Available HTTP: <http://www.archimuse.com/mw2006/papers/wyman/wyman.html> (accessed 25 May 2007).

Clark, J. W. (1894) *Libraries in the Medieval and Renaissance Periods: the Rede Lecture delivered June 13 1894*, Cambridge: Macmillan and Bowes.

Colson, F., Colson, J., Parry, R. and Sawyer, A. (2003) 'Cutting off the king's head: images and the (dis)location of power', in A. Bolvig and P. Lindley (eds) *History and Images: towards a new iconology*, Turnhout: Brepol.

Computer Services Center (1981a) unpublished CSC staff meeting minutes, 11 February, National Museum of American History, Smithsonian Institution.

—— (1981b) unpublished CSC staff meeting minutes, 17 March, National Museum of American History, Smithsonian Institution.

—— (1982a) unpublished CSC staff meeting minutes, 29 March, National Museum of American History, Smithsonian Institution.

—— (1982b) unpublished CSC staff meeting minutes, 22 April, National Museum of American History, Smithsonian Institution.

Cook, S., Graham, B. and Martin, S. (eds) (2002) *Curating New Media: third Baltic international seminar, 10–12 May 2001*, Gateshead: Baltic.

Cooper, M. (1993) 'Reports from members: Nottingham Museums', *Museums Computer Group Newsletter*, autumn 1993: 10–12.

—— (1996) 'MCG Meeting: Museum of London 14 May 1996', *Museums Computer Group Newsletter*, spring 1996: 1–4.

—— (2005) Interview with the author, 18 November 2005.

—— (2007) *The Natural History Register Project 1999–2006 and its Reconciliation with the Baseline Database*, internal report, Nottingham City Museums and Galleries.

Copp, C. (1986) 'Computing at Bristol Museum: report of a meeting 25th/26th September 1986', *Museums Computer Group Newsletter*, no. 2: 1–2.

Costigan, J. T. (1999) 'Forests, trees, and Internet research', in S. Jones (ed.) *Doing Internet Research: critical issues and methods for examining the Net*, Thousand Oaks, CA, London, and New Delhi: Sage.

Council for Museums and Galleries in Scotland (1977) *News: newsletter of the Council for Museums and Galleries in Scotland*, no. 18.

Cowtan, R. (1872) *Memories of the British Museum*, London: Richard Bentley and Son.

Coxall, H. (1991) 'How language means: an alternative view of museum text', in G. Kavanagh (ed.) *Museum Languages: objects and texts*, Leicester: Leicester University Press.

Creighton, R. and King, R. (1969) 'The Smithsonian Institution Information Retrieval (SIIR) System for biological and petrological data', *Smithsonian Institution Information Systems Innovations*, vol. 1, no. 1.

—— (1974) 'The Status of SELGEM Development', draft report, 12 November, Smithsonian Institution Archives, accession 95–169, box 2.

Crooke, E. M. (2000) *Politics, Archaeology and the Creation of a National Museum of Ireland: an expression of national life*, Dublin: Irish Academic Press.

Crovello, T. and MacDonald, R. D. (1969) 'Index of EDP-IR project in systematics', Smithsonian Institution, Smithsonian Institution Archives, accession 95–169, box 1.

Croxford I. (2006) 'Wireless networking at the Victoria & Albert Museum', in J. Trant and D. Bearman (eds) *Museums and the Web 2006: proceedings*, Toronto: Archives & Museum Informatics. Online. Available HTTP: <http://www.archimuse.com/mw2006/papers/croxford/croxford.html> (25 January 2007).

Cubitt, S. (1998) *Digital Aesthetics*, London, Thousand Oaks, CA, New Delhi: Sage Publications.

Cutbill, J. L. (1970) 'A format for the machine exchange of museum data', in J. L. Cutbill (ed.) *Data Processing in Biology and Geology*, Systematics Association special volume, no. 3: 255–74.

—— (1971a) Letter to J. F. Mello, 12 November, Smithsonian Institution Archives, accession 95–169, box 8.

—— (1971b) *The CGDS Program Package*, Cambridge research on data processing in geology, report no. 2, Cambridge: Department of Geology, Sedgwick Museum.

—— (1971c) *Data Collection and Conversion Methods*, Cambridge research on data processing in geology, report no. 3, Cambridge: Department of Geology, Sedgwick Museum.

Dawson, D. (1998) 'Aquarelle – access to European Culture Heritage', *Museums Computer Group Newsletter*, spring 1998: 4–5.

Department for Education and Employment (DfEE) (1997) *Connecting the Learning Society: national grid for learning*, UK Government Consultation Paper, London: DfEE.

DeRoux, K. (1998a) 'Exhibit labels: some basic guidelines for small museums', Alaska State Museum, *Bulletin*, no. 5. Online. Available HTTP: <http://www.museums.state.ak.us/Bulletin/labels1.html> (accessed 25 January 2007).

—— (1998b) 'Basic techniques for making and mounting exhibit labels', Alaska State Museum, *Bulletin*, no. 6. Online. Available HTTP: <www.museums.state.ak.us/Bulletin/makinglabels.html> (accessed 25 January 2007).

Devaraj Urs, D. (1974) 'Inaugural address', in O. P. Agrawal (ed.) *Documentation in Museums: proceedings of the 1973 all India museums conference held at Mysore September 19–23, 1973*, New Delhi: Museums Association of India.

Dickins, B. (1998) 'Digital imaging', *Museum Practice*, vol. 3, no. 3: 47–8.

Dierking, L. D. and Falk, J. H. (1998) 'Audience and accessibility', in S. Thomas and A. Mintz (eds) *The Virtual and the Real: media in the museum*, Washington, DC: American Association of Museums.

Dietz, S., Besser, H., Borda, A., Geber, K. and Levy, P. (2004) 'Virtual Museum (of Canada): the next generation, Cultural Heritage Information Network'. Online. Available HTTP: <http://www.chin.gc.ca/English/Members/Next_Generation/pdf.html> (accessed 21 May 2007).

DigiCULT (2002) *The DigiCULT Report: technological landscapes for tomorrow's cultural economy – unlocking the value of cultural heritage*, Luxembourg: Office for Official Publications of the European Commission.

Doran, J. (1974) 'What computers can't do for archaeologists', *Computer Applications in Archaeology*, proceedings of the annual conference organized by the Computer Centre, University of Birmingham.

Dowling, H. G. and Gilboa, I. (1967) 'A punch-card approach toward the retrieval of information in herpetology', paper presented at Symposium on Information Problems in Natural Sciences, Mexico, Smithsonian Institution Archives, accession 95–169, box 13.

Druckrey, T. (1996) 'Introduction', in T. Druckrey (ed.) *Electronic Culture: technology and visual representation*, New York: Aperture.

Duby, G. (ed) (1988) *A History of Private Life: II – Revelations of the Medieval World*, Cambridge, MA, and London: The Belknap Press.

Eccles, S. (1993) 'Reports from members: Glasgow', *Museums Computer Group Newsletter*, autumn 1993: 6.

Economou, M. and Ross, S. (1998) 'A study of information and communication technology funding policy for the Heritage Lottery Fund', *Museums Computer Group Newsletter*, spring 1998: 3–4.

Eisenstein, E. (1980) *The Printing Press as an Agent of Change: communications and cultural transformation in early-modern Europe*, Cambridge: Cambridge University Press.

Eitner, L. (1975) 'Art history and the sense of quality', *Art International*, no. 19: 75–80.

Ekarv, M. (1994) 'Combating redundancy: writing texts for exhibitions', in E. Hooper-Greenhill (ed.) *The Educational Role of the Museum*, London and New York: Routledge.

Ellin, E. (1967a) 'Computer Network Project', 26 February, Smithsonian Institution Archives, RU 7432, Box 19, MCN correspondence, 1967–June 1968.

—— (1967b) 'Computer Network Project: report of the 2nd meeting of the museum consortium', 9 March, Smithsonian Institution Archives, RU 7432, Box 19, MCN correspondence, 1967–June 1968.

—— (1967c) Memorandum to A. Chapman, F. Dockstader, R. Koch and W. Wilkinson, 18 April, Smithsonian Institution Archives, RU 7432, Box 19, MCN correspondence, 1967–June 1968.

—— (1967d) 'Museums announce project for first computerised archive of art', press release, The Museum of Modern Art, 8 December, Smithsonian Institution Archives, RU 7432, Box 19, MCN correspondence, 1967–June 1968.

—— (1968a) 'An international survey of museum computer activity', *Computers and the Humanities*, vol. 3, no. 2: 65–86.

—— (1968b) Letter to J. B. Hightower, 1 May, Smithsonian Institution Archives, RU 7432, Box 19, MCN correspondence, 1967–June 1968.

—— (1968c) Letter to H. Laue, 20 September, Smithsonian Institution Archives, RU 7432, Box 19, MCN correspondence, 1967–77.

—— (1969), 'Museums and the computer: an appraisal of new potentials', *Computers and the Humanities*, vol. 4, no. 1: 25–30.

Elliot, C. (1986) 'Computing at four museums around London: report of a meeting 3rd–4th April, 1987: National Army Museum', *Museums Computer Group Newsletter*, no. 3: 2.

Evans, J. (1621) *The Palace of Profitable Pleasure,* London: W. Stansby.

Evans, R. J. (1997) *In Defence of History,* London: Granta Books.

Evelyn, D. (1980) Memorandum to all staff, 13 November, National Museum of American History, Smithsonian Institution.

Fahy, A. (1991) 'Micro Gallery unveiled at The National Gallery', *Museums Computer Group Newsletter,* autumn 1991: 5–7.

—— (1995) 'New technologies for museum communication', in E. Hooper-Greenhill (ed.) *Museum, Media, Message,* London and New York: Routledge: 82–96.

Feeney, M. and Ross, S. (1993) *Information Technology in Humanities Scholarship: British achievements, prospects, and barriers*, British Library R&D Report 6097, Didcot: The Isis Press.

Fernandes, A. R., Pires, H. C. and Rodrigues, R. (1998) 'A Virtual Interactive Art Gallery', in D. Bearman and J. Trant (eds) *Museums and the Web, 1998, Conference Proceedings,* Toronto: Archives & Museum Informatics. CD-ROM.

Fiennes, C. (1888) *Through England on a Side Saddle in the Time of William and Mary,* London: Field & Tuer.

Fleming, D. (2007) Interview with author, 9 February 2007.

Fletcher, A. (1987) 'Reports received at Liverpool meeting, October, 1987', *Museums Computer Group Newsletter,* no. 4: 3–5.

Flew, T. (2002) *New Media: an introduction,* Oxford: Oxford University Press.

Foster, R. A. (1984) 'The larger provincial museums and art galleries', in J. M. A. Thompson, D. A. Bassett, D. G. Davies, A. J. Duggan, D. G. Lewis, and D. R. Prince (eds) *Manual of Curatorship: a guide to museum practice,* London: Butterworths.

Frost, C. O. (2002) 'Where the object is digital: properties of digital surrogate objects and implications for learning', in S. G. Paris (ed.) *Perspectives on Object-Centred Learning in Museums,* Mahwah, NJ: Lawrence Erlbaum Associates.

Futers, K. (1997) 'Tell me what you want, what you really, really want: a look at Internet user needs', *EVA'97: proceedings*, Paris: EVA.

Gates, B., Myhrvold, N. and Rinearson, P. (1996) *The Road Ahead,* Harmondsworth: Penguin.

Gautier, T. G. (1976) 'Data standards at the National Museum of Natural History', Smithsonian Institution Archives, accession 95–169, box 8.

—— (1978) 'Automated collections documentation system at the National Museum of Natural History, Smithsonian Institution, Washington, DC', Smithsonian Institution Archives, accession 95–169, box 9.

Gere, C. (1997) 'Museums, contact zones and the Internet', in D. Bearman and J. Trant (eds) *Museum Interactive Multimedia 1997: cultural heritage systems design and interfaces. Selected papers from ichim97,* Pittsburgh: Archives & Museum Informatics.

—— (1999) 'Hypermedia and emblematics', in W. Vaughan (ed.) *Computing and Visual Culture,* London: CHArt.

Gilbert, W. (1640) *Architectonice Consolationis: or the art of building comfort*, London: John Legatt.

Gill, T. (1996) *The MDA Guide to Computers in Museums*, Cambridge: The Museum Documentation Association.

Gilmore, E. and Sabine J. (1994) 'Writing readable text: evaluation of the Ekarv method', in E. Hooper-Greenhill (ed.) *The Educational Role of the Museum*, London and New York: Routledge.

Goldman, K. H. and Wadman, M. (2002) 'There's something happening here, what it is ain't exactly clear', in D. Bearman and J. Trant (eds) *Museums and the Web 2002: selected papers from an international conference*, Pittsburgh: Archives & Museum Informatics, 2002. Online. Available HTTP: <www.archimuse.com/mw2002/papers/haleyGoldman/haleygoldman.html> (accessed 28 May 2007).

Gombrich, E. H. (1995) *The Story of Art*, 16th edn, London: Phaidon.

Gordon, S. (1996). *Making the Internet Work for Museums*. Cambridge: The Museum Documentation Association.

Grant, A. (2003) *Evaluation of Digital Cultural Content: analysis of evaluation material*, Cultural Content Forum, November 2003. Online. Available HTTP: <Online. Available HTTP: <http://www.thebritishmuseum.ac.uk/newsroom/current2004/mummy.html> (accessed 27 May 2007).

Grassl, C. O. (1936) 'Visualizing our herbaria', *Museums Journal*, vol. 36: 373–84.

Greengrass, M. (1993) 'Interfacing Samuel Hartlib', *History Today*, no. 43 (December): 45–9.

Gurian, E. H. (1991) 'Noodling around with exhibition opportunities', in I. Karp and S. P. Lavine (eds) *Exhibiting Cultures: the poetics and politics of museum displays*, Washington, DC, and London: Smithsonian Institution Press.

Hazan, S. (2001) 'The virtual aura: is there space for enchantment in a technological world?', in D. Bearman and J. Trant (eds) *Museums and the Web 2001: selected papers from an international conference*, Pittsburgh: Archives & Museum Informatics. Online. Available HTTP: <http://www.archimuse.com/mw2001/papers/hazan/hazan.html> (accessed 27 May 2007).

—— (2003) 'The virtual aura: the technologies of exhibition and the exhibition of technologies', *Museological Review*, 10: 16–30.

Hein, H. (2000) *The Museum in Transition: a philosophical perspective*, Washington, DC: Smithsonian Institution Press.

Heller, J. and Wasserman, S. P. (1967) *A Computer Network for Research in the Arts and the Humanities: a proposal*, Smithsonian Institution Archives, RU 7432 / Box 19 / Museum Computer Network.

Hetherington, K. (1996) 'The utopics of social ordering: Stonehenge as a museum without walls', in S. Macdonald and G. Fyfe (eds) *Theorizing Museums: representing identity and diversity in a changing world*, Oxford and Malden, MA: Blackwell and The Sociological Review.

Hirschi, K. D. and Screven, C. (1996) 'Effects of questions on visitor reading behaviour', in G. Durbin (ed.) *Developing Museum Exhibitions for Lifelong Learning*, London: The Stationery Office.

Hislop, R. (1967) 'Information retrieval and computer printed indexes', *Museums Journal*, no. 67: 91–105.

Hollister, C. C. (1968) Letter to E. Ellin, 24 May, Smithsonian Institution Archives, RU 7432, Box 19, MCN correspondence, 1967–77.

Holm, S. A. (1993) *Let's Set the Record Straight: a report on the state of documentation in the museums of the West Midlands, with suggestions for tackling some of the problems encountered*, Bromsgrove: West Midlands Area Museum Service.

Homans, T., Winterkorn, J., Harris, F. and Kelliher, H. (1995) 'John Evelyn's archive at the British Library', *The Book Collector*, summer 1995: 147–209.

Hooper-Greenhill, E. (1992) *Museums and the Shaping of Knowledge*, London and New York: Routledge.

—— (1994) 'Communication in theory and practice', in E. Hooper-Greenhill (ed.) *The Educational Role of the Museum*, London and New York: Routledge.

—— (2000) *Museums and the Interpretation of Visual Culture*, New York: Routledge.

Hoving, T. (1968) 'Museums, computers and the future', in *Computers and Their Potential Application in Museums*, Metropolitan Museum of Art, New York: Arno Press.

Hughes, K. (2007) 'A museum is not an iPod', *The Guardian*, Saturday 20 January 2007: 31.

Huhtamo, E. (2002) 'On the origins of the virtual museum', Nobel Symposium (NS120) *Virtual Museums and Public Understanding of Science and Culture*. Stockholm, Sweden, May 2002. Online. Available HTTP: <http://www.nobel.se/nobel/nobel-foundation/symposia/interdisciplinary/ns120/lectures/huhtamo.pdf> (accessed 27 May 2007).

Humphrey, P. S. and Clausen, A. C. (1976) *Automated Cataloguing for Museum Collections: a model for decision and a guide to implementation*, Lawrence, KS: Association of Systematics Collections.

Hunt, L. (1989) 'Introduction: history, culture and text', in L. Hunt (ed.) *The New Cultural History*, Berkeley, Los Angeles and London: University of California Press.

Huxley, A. (1994) *Brave New World Revisited*, London: Flamingo.

IBM Federal Systems Division and Ellin, E. (1969) *An Information System for American Museums: a report prepared for the Museum Computer Network*, Gaithersburg, MD: International Business Machines Corporation. Smithsonian Institution Archives, RU 7432 / Box 19.

Impey, O. R. and MacGregor, A. G. (1985) *The Origins of Museums*, Oxford: Clarendon Press.

Information Systems Office (1968) *The MARC Pilot Experience: an informal summary*, Washington, DC: Library of Congress.

Ingram, N. (1986) 'Documentation in social history', *SHCG News*, no. 12: 5.

Irwin, R. (1958) *The Golden Chain: a study in the history of libraries*, an inaugural lecture delivered at University College London 21 November 1957, London: H. K. Lewis & Co.

James, B. (1995) 'The age of the museum is here, even virtually', *International Herald Tribune*, 14 August 1995. Online. Available HTTP: <http://www.iht.com/articles/1995/08/14/bumper.t.php> (accessed 25 May 2007).

Jardine, L. (1997) *Worldly Goods: a new history of the Renaissance*, London and Basingstoke: Macmillan.

Jay, M. (1993) *Downcast Eyes: the denigration of vision in twentieth-century French thought*, Berkeley, Los Angeles and London: University of California Press.

Johnstone, C. (1989) 'Extending SHIC to popular culture', *SHCG News*, no. 21: 6–7.

Jones, M. M. (1991) *Gaston Bachelard: subversive humanist*, London and Madison, WI: University of Wisconsin Press.

Jones-Garmil, K. (ed.) (1997) *The Wired Museum: emerging technology and changing paradigms*, Washington, DC: American Association of Museums.

Katz, S., Kahanov, Y., Kashtan, N., Kuflik, T., Graziola, I., Rocchi, C., Stock, O. and Zancanaro, M. (2006) 'Preparing personalized multimedia presentations for a mobile museum visitors' guide: a methodological approach', in J. Trant and D. Bearman (eds) *Museums and the Web 2006: proceedings*, Toronto: Archives & Museum Informatics. Online. Available HTTP: <http://www.archimuse.com/mw2006/papers/katz/katz.html> (accessed 25 January 2007).

Kaufman, T. C. (1988) *The School of Prague: painting at the court of Rudolf II*, Chicago: University of Chicago Press.

Kavanagh, G. (1990) *History Curatorship*, Leicester: Leicester University Press.

Keene, S. (1998) *Digital Collections: museums and the information age*, Oxford: Butterworth-Heinemann.

Kember, S. (1998) *Virtual Anxiety: photography, new technologies and subjectivity*, Manchester and New York: Manchester University Press.

Kemp, M. (1990) *The Science of Art: optical themes in Western art from Brunelleschi to Seurat*, New Haven, CT, and London: Yale University Press.

Kennedy, A., Prior, D., Sawyer, A. and Pratty, J. (2006) 'Getting archives on-line: innovative concepts in interactive content bringing to life the Gunpowder Plot of 1605', in J. Trant and D. Bearman (eds.) *Museums and the Web 2006: Proceedings*, Toronto: Archives & Museum Informatics. Online. Available HTTP: <http://www.archimuse.com/mw2006/papers/kennedy/kennedy.html> (accessed 27 May 2007).

Kentley, E. and Negus, D. (1996) 'Writing label copy', in G. Durbin (ed.) *Developing Museum Exhibitions for Lifelong Learning*, London: The Stationery Office.

King, G. (1989) 'Computing in three of the University Museums in Oxford: University Museum, Oxford', *Museums Computer Group Newsletter*, no. 6: 3.

Kittler, F. (1996) 'Museums on the digital frontier', in *The End(s) of the Museum*, Barcelona: Fundació Antoni Tàpies: 67–80.

Knell, S. (2000) *The Culture of English Geology, 1815–1851: a science revealed through its collecting*, Aldershot: Ashgate.

—— (2003) 'The shape of things to come: museums in the technological landscape', *Museum and Society*, vol. 1, no. 3: 132–46.

Koch, R. H. (1967) Letter to J. B. Hightower, 7 April 1967, Smithsonian Institution Archives, RU 7432, Box 19, MCN correspondence, 1967–June 1968.

Kochen, M., Rohlf, F. J. and Helgeson, W. B. (1970) 'Report on the NHIR computer system for the National Museum of Natural History Smithsonian Institution', Smithsonian Institution Archives, accession 95–169, box 9.

Koujalgi, V. S. (1974) 'Presidential address', in O. P. Agrawal (ed.) *Documentation in Museums: proceedings of the 1973 all India museums conference held at Mysore September 19–23, 1973*, New Delhi: Museums Association of India.

Kuhn, T. S. (1970) *The Structure of Scientific Revolutions*, International Encyclopedia of Unified Science, vol. 2, no. 2, 2nd edn, Chicago and London: Chicago University Press.

Lammy, D. (2005) Speech at the launch of the 'Digitisation Action Plan for Europe', Bristol, 16 November 2005. Online. Available HTTP: <http://www.culture.gov.uk/Reference_library/Press_notices/archive_2005/dcms160_05.htm> (accessed 27 May 2007).

Langston, D. J. (1982) 'Time and space as the lenses of reading', *Journal of Aesthetics and Art Criticism*, vol. 40, no. 4: 401–14.

Laurencich-Minelli, L. (1985) 'Museography and ethnographical collections in Bologna during the sixteenth and seventeenth centuries', in O. Impey and A. MacGregor (eds) *The Origins of Museums: the cabinet of curiosities in sixteenth- and seventeenth-century Europe*, Oxford: Clarendon Press.

Lefebvre, H. (1991) *The Production of Space*, trans. D. N. Smith, Oxford and Cambridge, MA: Blackwell.

Levenson, J. A. (1998) 'Digital imaging and issues of authenticity in the art museum', in S. Thomas and A. Mintz (eds) *The Virtual and the Real: media in the museum*, Washington, DC: American Association of Museums.

Lewis, G. (1965) 'Obtaining information from museum collections and thoughts on a national index', *Museums Journal*, vol. 65: 12–22.

—— (1967) 'Report of a colloquium held at the City Museum Sheffield, in April 1967. Session 1: introduction', *Museums Journal*, vol. 67: 88–91.

—— (2007) Interview with the author, 20 April 2007.

Library of Congress (1965) *Proceedings of the Second Conference on Machine-Readable Catalog Copy, Library of Congress, November 22, 1965*, Washington, DC: Library of Congress.

—— (1966) *Proceedings of the Third Conference on Machine-Readable Catalog Copy, Library of Congress, February 25, 1966*, Washington, DC: Library of Congress.

—— (1968) *Proceedings of the Fourth Conference on Marchine-Readable Catalog Copy, Library of Congress, December 4, 1967*, Washington, DC: Library of Congress.

Light, R. (2005) Interview with the author, 19 December 2005.

Lister, M., Dovey, J., Giddings, S., Grant, I. and Kelly, K. (2003) *New Media: a critical introduction*, London and New York: Routledge.

Lloyd-Baynes, F. (2005) Interview with the author, 14 December 2005.

Loader, B. (1989) 'Reports received: Royal Botanic Gardens, Kew', *Museums Computer Group Newsletter*, no. 6: 4–5.

Lyman, P. and Besser, H. (1998) 'Defining the problem of our vanishing memory: background, current status, models for resolution', in M. MacLean and B. H. Davis (eds) *Time and Bits: managing digital continuity*, Los Angeles: The J. Paul Getty Trust.

Lynch, C. (2000) 'Authenticity and integrity in the digital environment: an exploratory analysis of the central role of trust', in *Authenticity in a Digital Environment*, papers based on those presented at a workshop January 2000, Washington, DC: Council on Library and Information Resources.

McCall, M. (1992) 'Advanced revelation: a critical review', *Museums Computer Group Newsletter*, spring 1992: 5–6.

—— (1993) 'Reports from members: Luton Museum Service', *Museums Computer Group Newsletter*, autumn 1993: 7–8.

McCutcheon, D. (1993) 'MCG Meeting, British Museum, October 1992', *Museums Computer Group Newsletter*, spring 1993: 2–3.

—— (1995) 'British Museum: Collections Data Management Section (CDMS)', *Museums Computer Group Newsletter*, spring 1995: 2.

MacDonald, G. (1992) 'Change and challenge: museums in the information society', in L. Karp, C. Mullen Kreamer and S. D. Lavine (eds) *Museums and Communities: the politics of public culture*, Washington, DC: Smithsonian Press: 158–81.

MacDonald, G. and Alsford, S. (1991) 'The museum as information utility', *Museum Management and Curatorship*, no. 10: 305–11.

Macdonald, S. (1998) 'Exhibitions of power and powers of exhibition: an introduction to the politics of display', in S. Macdonald (ed.) *The Politics of Display: museums, science, culture*, London and New York: Routledge.

MacDowell, M. and Richardson, J. (2005) 'Multi-purposing museum media: Quilt Treasures oral history and documentary Web portraits', in J. Trant and D. Bearman (eds.) *Museums and the Web 2005: proceedings*, Toronto: Archives & Museum Informatics. Online. Available HTTP: <http://www.archimuse.com/mw2005/papers/macdowell/macdowell.html> (accessed 27 May 2007).

Macfarlane, A. (1991) 'Report on the MCG meeting, Cambridge University Museums, October 1990: The Naga Videodisc and Cambridge Database System', *Museums Computer Group Newsletter*, autumn 1991: 2–3.

McKay, T. (1982). 'A hierarchy of labels', *Exchange,* a newsletter published by the Wisconsin Historical Society, vol. 24, no. 4. Online. Available HTTP: <http://www.wisconsinhistory.org/localhistory/articles/labels.asp> (accessed consulted 25 January 2007).

McKitterick, D. (1997) 'From Camden to Cambridge: Sir Robert Cotton's Roman inscriptions, and their subsequent treatment', in C. J. Wright (ed.) *Sir Robert Cotton as Collector: essay on an early Stuart courtier and his legacy*, London: The British Library.

McLaren, S. B. (1988) 'Review of: *A Guide to Museum Computing*, by David W. Williams, Nashville, American Association for State and Local History Press, 1987', *Collection Forum: the Journal of the Society for the Preservation of Natural History Collections*, vol. 4, no. 2: 77–8.

MacLeod, S. (ed.) (2005) *Reshaping Museum Space: architecture, design, exhibitions*, London: Routledge.

McLuhan, M. (2001) *Understanding Media: the extensions of man*, London and New York: Routledge.

Manguel, A. (1996) *A History of Reading*, London: HarperCollins.

Manning, R. (1969) 'Automation in museum collections', *Proceedings of the Biological Society of Washington*, vol. 82: 671–86.

Manovich, L. (1999) 'Database as symbolic form', *Convergence*, vol. 5, no. 2: 80–99.

—— (2001) *The Language of New Media*, Cambridge, MA, and London: MIT Press.

Marshall, F. (1986) 'Reports received: Leicestershire Museum Service', *Museums Computer Group Newsletter*, no. 2: 3.

—— (1987) 'Reports received: Leicester Museum, Leicester', *Museums Computer Group Newsletter*, no. 3: 3–4.

—— (1989) 'Reports received: Leicestershire Museums', *Museums Computer Group Newsletter*, no. 6: 4.

—— (1991a) 'Report on the MCG meeting, Plymouth City Museum & Art Gallery, June 1991', *Museums Computer Group Newsletter*, autumn 1991: 1–2.

—— (1991b) 'Conference Report: multimedia in European museums, Olympia, June 1991', *Museums Computer Group Newsletter*, autumn 1991: 8.

—— (1992) 'Report on the MCG meeting, Newcastle-upon-Tyne, November 1991', *Museums Computer Group Newsletter*, spring 1992: 1–3.

—— (2005) Interview with the author, 29 November 2005.

Martin, P. (2004) 'Contemporary popular collecting', in S. Knell (ed.) *Museums and the Future of Collecting*, Aldershot: Ashgate.

Mattelart, A. (2003) *The Information Society: an introduction*, London: Sage.

Mello, J. F. (1969) 'Paleontologic data storage and retrieval', *Proceedings of the North American Paleontological Convention: September 1969*, part B: 57–71.

Metcalfe, I. (1987) 'Computing at four museums around London: report of a meeting 3rd–4th April, 1987: Museum of London', *Museums Computer Group Newsletter*, no. 3: 1.

Metropolitan Museum of Art (1968) *Computers and their Potential Application in Museums*, New York: Arno Press.

Miller, K. (2002) 'Museums and virtuality', *Curator*, vol. 45, no. 1: 21–33.

Moffett, J. (1989a) 'Report on the Museum Computer Network Conference, Santa Monica, California, October 1988', *Museums Computer Group Newsletter*, 5: 6–10.

—— (1989b) 'Computing in three of the University Museums in Oxford: Ashmolean Museum, Oxford', *Museums Computer Group Newsletter*, 6: 2.

—— (1992a) 'MCG Meeting, Hampshire County Museums Service, Winchester, and Wiltshire Museums' Sites & Monuments Record, Trowbridge, June 1992', *Museums Computer Group Newsletter*, autumn 1992: 1–3.

—— (1992b) 'Data and Image Processing in Classical Archaeology, held in Ravello, Italy, April 1992', *Museums Computer Group Newsletter*, autumn 1992: 7.

Montaner, J. M. (1990) *New Museums*, London: Architecture and Technology Press.

Morse, L. E. (1968) 'Construction of identification keys by computer', *American Journal of Botany*, no. 55: 737.

Mowat, L. and Edwards, L. (1989) 'Computing in three of the University Museums in Oxford: Pitt Rivers Museum, Oxford', *Museums Computer Group Newsletter*, no. 6: 2.

Murray, D. (1904) *Museums: their history and their use*, Glasgow: James MacLehose and Sons.

Murray, N. and Werner, A. (1987) 'Computing at four museums around London: report of a meeting 3rd–4th April, 1987: Museum of London – Museum in Docklands', *Museums Computer Group Newsletter*, no. 3: 1.

Museums Computer Group (MCG) (1990) 'Computing at Leicestershire Museums, Arts and Records Service', *Museums Computer Group Newsletter*, no. 7: 1–3.

National Museum of American History (1987) *MIRDS: Museum Information Retrieval and Documentation System*, Washington, DC: Smithsonian Institution.

Nuttall, A. (2000) 'History of the MDA', internal unpublished report, Cambridge: MDA.

Office of Computer Services (1975) unpublished final report on computer services at the Smithsonian Institution', Smithsonian Institution Archives, accession 95–169, box 2.

Orgel, S. (1980) *The Renaissance Imagination: essays and lectures by D. J. Gordon*. Berkeley, Los Angeles and London: University of California Press.

Orna, E. and Pettitt, C. (1980) *Information Handling in Museums*, London: Bingley.

—— (1998) *Information Management in Museums*, Aldershot and Vermont: Gower.

Pachter, M. (2002) 'Why museums matter', keynote presentation to MDA conference, Birmingham, July 2002.

Paine, C. (1982) 'To all curators', *SHCG News*, no. 1: 2.

Painter, W. (1556) *The Palace of Pleasure*, London: Henry Denham.

Panofsky, E. (1991) *Perspective as Symbolic Form*, New York: Zone Books.

Parry, R. (1999) 'The Careful Watchman: James I, didacticism and the perspectival organisation of space', in G. Jaritz (ed.), *Disziplinierung im Alltag des Mittelalters und der frühen Neuzeit*, Vienna: Der Österreichischen Akademie der Wissenschaften.

—— (2001a) 'Including technology', in J. Dodd and R. Sandell (eds) *Including Museums: perspectives on museums, galleries and social inclusion*, Leicester: RCMG.

—— (2001b) 'Overcoming the shock of the new: changing the agenda for digital learning', *Biology Curator*, 20, 20–4.

—— (2002) 'Virtuality, liminality and the space of the museum', in *MDA Information*, vol. 5, no. 5, 67–70.

—— (2005) 'Digital heritage and the rise of theory in museum computing', *Museum Management and Curatorship*, vol. 20, no. 4: 333–48.

Parry, R. and Arbach, N. (2005) 'The localized learner: acknowledging distance and situatedness in on-line museum learning', in J. Trant and D. Bearman (eds), *Museums and the Web 2005: proceedings*, Toronto: Archives & Museum Informatic. Online. Available HTTP: <http://www.archimuse.com/mw2005/papers/parry/parry.html> (accessed 25 January 2007).

Parry, R. and Gogan, M. (2005) 'Visualising early modern space: a role for spatial theory and digital media', paper presented to 'Thinking Space in Early Modern England' conference, Warwick, March 2005.

Parry, R. and Hopwood, J. (2004) 'Virtual reality and the soft museum', *Journal of Museum Ethnography*, no. 16: 69–78.

Parry, R. and Sawyer, A. (2005) 'Space and the machine: adaptive museums, pervasive technology and the new gallery environment', in S. MacLeod (ed.) *Reshaping Museum Space: architecture, design, exhibitions*, London and New York: Routledge.

Pearce, S. M. (1995) *On Collecting: an investigation into collection in the European tradition*, London and New York: Routledge.

—— (2005) Interview with the author, 14 December 2005.

—— (2007) 'William Bullock: inventing a visual language of objects', in S. Watson, S. MacLeod and S. Knell (eds) *Museum Revolutions: how museums change and are changed*, Abingdon and New York: Routledge.

Peponis, J. and Hedin, J. (1982) 'The layout of theories in the Natural History Museum', *9H*, no. 3: 21–5.

Peters, J. A. and Collette, B. B. (1968) 'The role of time-share computing in museum research', *Curator*, vol. 11, no. 1: 65–75.

Pettitt, C. (1986) *Museums Computer Group News*, no. 1, September 1986.

—— (2005) Interview with the author, 30 November 2005.

Philips, Pamela (1995) 'Sedgwick Museum, Department of Earth Sciences, University of Cambridge', *Museums Computer Group Newsletter*, spring 1995: 3–4.

Philips, P. (1987) 'Computing at the National Museums on Merseyside: report of a meeting 16th–17th October, 1987: Computing in the NMM', *Museums Computer Group Newsletter*, no. 4: 1.

—— (2005) Interview with the author, 13 December 2005.

Platt, H. (1594) *The Jewell House of Art and Nature*, London: Peter Short.

Poole, N. (2007) 'Are museums doing IT right?', *Museums Computer Group Newsletter*, spring 2007: 2–5.

Poster, M. (1990) *The Mode of Information: poststructuralism and social context*, Cambridge: Polity.

Pratty J. (2006) 'The inside out Web museum', in J. Trant and D. Bearman (eds) *Museums and the Web 2006: proceedings*, Toronto: Archives & Museum Informatics. Online. Available HTTP: <http://www.archimuse.com/mw2006/papers/pratty/pratty.html> (accessed 25 May 2007).

Price, S. (1618) *The Beauty of Holines: Or The Consecration of a House of Prayer, by the Example of our Saviour*, London: B. A. for Richard Meighen.

Purchas, S. (1623) *The Kings Tower and Triumphant Arch of London*, London: W. Stansby.

Radford, G. P. and Radford M. L. (2005) 'Structuralism, post-structuralism, and the library: de Saussure and Foucault', *Journal of Documentation*, vol. 61, no. 1: 60–78.

Radley, A. (1991) 'Boredom, fascination and mortality: reflections upon the experience of museum visiting', in G. Kavanagh (ed.) *Museum Languages: objects and texts*, Leicester, London and New York: Leicester University Press.

Ramelli, A. (1987) *The Various and Ingenious Machines of Agostino Ramelli*, New York: Dover Publications.

Ravelli, L. (2006) *Museum Texts: communication frameworks*, Abingdon and New York: Routledge.

Ray, J. (2005) Interview with the author, 9 December 2005.

Rellie, J. (2004) 'One site fits all: balancing priorities at Tate Modern', in D. Bearman and J. Trant (eds) *Museums and the Web 2004: proceedings*. Toronto: Archives & Museum Informatics. Online. Available HTTP: <http://www.archimuse.com/mw2004/papers/rellie/rellie.html> (accessed 25 January 2007).

—— (2006) '10 years on: hopes, fears, predictions and gambles for UK museums on-line', in J. Trant and D. Bearman (eds) *Museums and the Web 2006: proceedings*. Toronto: Archives & Museum Informatics. Online. Available HTTP: <http://www.archimuse.com/mw2006/papers/rellie/rellie.html> (accessed 31 July 2007).

Renfrew, C. (1967) 'The requirements of the research worker in archaeology', *Museums Journal*, vol. 67: 111–13.

Reynolds, R. (1997) 'Museums and the Internet: what purpose should the information supplied by museums on the World Wide Web serve?', unpublished Master's thesis, University of Leicester.

Roads, C. H. (1968) 'Data recording, retrieval and presentation in the Imperial War Museum', *Museums Journal*, vol. 67, no. 4: 277–83.

Roberts, D. A. (1984) 'The development of computer-based documentation', in J. M. A. Thompson, D. A. Bassett, D. G. Davies, A. J. Duggan, D. G. Lewis and D. R. Prince (eds) *Manual of Curatorship: a guide to museum practice*, London: Butterworths.

—— (1985) *Planning the Documentation of Museum Collections*, Duxford: The Museum Documentation Association.

—— (1997) 'The development of organisational structures and documentation and information technology specialization in museums', in G. Libnow, A. Belz, I. Kalenda and C. Kupper (eds) *Quality and Documentation, CIDOC Annual Meeting 1997*, Nuremberg: Germanisches Museum.

—— (2005) Interview with the author, 21 November 2005.

Roberts, D. A. and Light, R. (1980) 'Museum documentation: progress in documentation', *Journal of Documentation*, 36(1): 42–84.

—— (eds) (1984) *Microcomputers in Museums*, MDA occasional paper 7, Duxford: Museum Documentation Association.

Robson, J. (1996) 'Today Pompeii, tomorrow the Caves of Lascaux', *The Independent*, Monday 5 February 1996: section 2, 8–9.

Roles, J. (1995) 'My Brighton: unlocking access', in A. Fahy and W. Sudbury (eds) *Information: the hidden resource. Museums and the Internet*, proceedings of the seventh international conference of the MDA, Cambridge: The Museum Documentation Association.

Ruffin, J. (1967) Unpublished internal report on records of collections in the Museum of History and Technology, Smithsonian Institution.

Sandell, R. (2007) *Museums, Prejudice and the Reframing of Difference*, London and New York: Routledge.

Sandell, R. and Dodd, J. (1998) *Building Bridges: guidance for museums and galleries on developing new audiences*, London: Museums and Galleries Commission.

Sarasan, L. (1981) 'Why computer projects fail', *Museum News*, vol. 59, no. 4: 40–9.

Saumarez Smith, C. (2000) 'What the future holds for the past', *The Daily Telegraph*, Saturday 16 December 2000, A9.

Schaefer-Jacobs, D. (2005) Interview with the author, 7 December 2005.

Scheicher, E. (1985) 'The collection of Archduke Ferdinand II at Schloss Ambras: its purpose, composition and evolution', in O. Impey and A. MacGregor (eds) *The Origins of Museums: the cabinet of curiosities in sixteenth- and seventeenth-century Europe*, Oxford: Clarendon Press.

Scholtz, S. (1974) *Data Structure and Computerized Museum Catalogs*, Museum Data Bank Research Report no. 2, New York: Museum Data Bank Committee.

Scott, D. (1976) *The Yogi and the Registrar*, Museum Data Bank Research Report no. 7, New York: Museum Data Bank Committee.

Seal, A. (2005) Interview with the author, 14 December 2005.

Sedden, B. A. (1987) 'Reports received: Birmingham Museum, Birmingham', *Museums Computer Group Newsletter*, no. 3: 3.

Semper, R. J., Wanner, N., Jackson, R. and Bazley, M. (2000) 'Who's out there? A pilot user study of educational Web resources by the Science Learning Network (SLN)', in D. Bearman and J. Trant (eds) *Museums and the Web 2000: proceedings*, Toronto: Archives & Museum Informatics. Online. Available HTTP: <www.archimuse.com/mw2000/papers/semper/semper.html> (accessed 27 May 2007).

Serrell, B. (1996) *Exhibit Labels: an interpretive approach*, Walnut Creek, CA: Altamira Press.

Sharpe, K. (1978) *Faction and Parliament: essays on early Stuart history*, Oxford: Clarendon Press.

—— (1979) *Sir Robert Cotton, 1586–1631: history and politics in early modern England*, Oxford: Oxford University Press.

Shields, R. (1999) *Lefebvre, Love and Struggle*, London and New York: Routledge.

—— (2000) 'Performing virtualities: liminality on and off the "Net"', paper presented to 'Virtual Society? The social science of electronic technologies'. Online. Available HTTP: <http://virtualsociety.sbs.ox.ac.uk/events/pvshields.htm> (accessed 27 May 2007).

Shneiderman, B. (2000) 'Universal usability', *Communications of the ACM*, vol. 43, no. 5: 84–91.

Simpson, D. (2005) *Digital Preservation in the Regions: sample survey of digital preservation preparedness and needs of organizations at local and regional levels*, London: Museums, Libraries and Archives Council.

Sledge, J. (2005) Interview with the author, 7 December 2005.

Smith, L. (2000) *Building the Digital Museum: a national resource for the learning age*, Cambridge: The National Museums Directors' Conference, Resource and MDA.

Smithsonian Institution (no date) *The SELGEM System for Information Management: An Introduction*, promotional leaflet, Smithsonian Institution Archives, accession 95–169, box 1.

—— (1967) 'Proposal for research and related activities submitted to the US Commissioner of Education for support through authorization of the Bureau of Research: an information storage and retrieval system for biological and geological data', 9 May, Smithsonian Institution Archives, accession 95–169, box 1.

—— (1968a) 'Proposal for research and related activities submitted to the US Commissioner of Education for support through authorization of the Bureau of Research: an information storage and retrieval system for biological and geological data. Part II', 28 October, Smithsonian Institution Archives, accession 95–169, box 1.

—— (1968b) 'Symposium on information problems in natural sciences', *MUDPIE*, no. 3: 1–2.

—— (1969a) 'First MUDPIE conference', *MUDPIE*, no. 6: 1.

—— (1969b) 'GIPSY', *MUDPIE*, no. 8: 1.

—— (1970) 'Museum Computer Network', *MUDPIE*, no. 11: 1.

Šola, T. (1997) *Essays on Museums and their Theory: towards the cybernetic museum*, Helsinki: Finnish Museums Association.

—— (2004) 'Redefining collecting', in S. Knell (ed.) *Museums and the Future of Collecting*, Aldershot: Ashgate.

Soper, J. H. and Perring F. H. (1967) 'Data processing in the herbarium and museum', *Taxon*, no. 16: 13–19.

Speroni, M., Bolchini, D. and Paolini, P. (2006) 'Interfaces: "do users understand them?"', in J. Trant and D. Bearman (eds) *Museums and the Web 2006: proceedings*, Toronto: Archives & Museum Informatics. Online. Available HTTP: <http://www.thebritishmuseum.ac.uk/newsroom/current2004/mummy.html> (accessed 25 January 2007).

Spiess, K. P. (1981) 'NMAH computerisation of object information: inventory data – current flow', unpublished internal document, National Museum of American History, Smithsonian Institution.

—— (1986) 'Computers in museums: selected great moments from 1965 through 1985', unpublished paper, National Museum of American History.

Squires. D. (1966) 'Data processing and museum collections: a problem for the present', *Curator*, vol. 9, no. 3: 216–27.

—— (1968) *An information storage and retrieval system for biological and geological data*, quarterly report 9/21/68–12/21/68, Project no. 7–1159, Washington, DC: Smithsonian Institution Archives, accession 95–169, box 1.

—— (1969a) *An information storage and retrieval system for biological and geological data*, interim report, Project no. 7–1159, Washington, DC: US Department of Health, Education, and Welfare, Office of Education, Bureau of Research.

—— (1969b) 'Memorandum for the record: trip report – England (1969)', Smithsonian Institution Archives, accession 95–169, box 1.

—— (1970) Letter to HEW Project Staff, 3 August, Smithsonian Institution Archives, accession 95–169, box 1.

Steamson, M. (2002) 'DigiCULT experts search for the e-archive permanence', in G. Geser, J. van Kasteren, P. Kop, J. P. Salzburg, S. Ross, M. Steamson et al. (eds) *Integrity and Authenticity of Digital Cultural Heritage Objects: thematic issue 1*, DigiCULT project, Information Society Technologies Programme, European Commission.

Stiff, M. (1999) 'The 24-Hour Museum project: now and in the future', *Museums Computer Group Newsletter*, spring 1999: 4–5.

—— (2005) Interview with the author, 25 November 2005.

Stone, A. R. (1996) 'Preface', in T. Druckrey (ed.) *Electronic Culture: technology and visual representation*, New York: Aperture.

Stone, S. M. (1984) 'Documenting collections', in J. M. A. Thompson, D. A. Bassett, D. G. Davies, A. J. Duggan, D. G. Lewis and D. R. Prince (eds) *Manual of Curatorship: a guide to museum practice*, London: Butterworths.

Strong, R. (1995) *Art and Power: renaissance festivals 1450–1650*, Woodbridge and Rochester, NY: The Boydell Press.

Suszynski, N. J. (1969) 'Recent advances in source data automation', *Smithsonian Institution Information System Innovations*, vol. 1, no. 3: 1–18.

Swinney, H. J. (1976) *Characteristics of History Museum Activity and their Influence on Potential Electronic Cataloguing*, Museum Data Bank Research Report no. 8, New York: Museum Data Bank Committee.

Taube, M. (1966) 'Information technology: problems and promises', *Library Journal*, vol. 91 no 5: 1155–8.

Taylor, J. H. and Ryan, J. (1995) 'Museums and galleries on the Internet', *Internet Research: Electronic Networking Applications and Policy*, vol. 5, no. 1: 80–8.

Thomas, S. and Mintz, A. (eds) (1998) *The Virtual and the Real: media in the museum*, Washington, DC: American Association of Museums.

Tinkler, M. and Freedman, M. (1998) 'Online exhibitions: a philosophy of design and technological implementation', in D. Bearman and J. Trant (eds) *Museums and the Web, 1998, Conference Proceedings*, Toronto: Archives & Museum Informatics. CD-ROM.

Tite, C. (1994) *The Manuscript Library of Sir Robert Cotton*, The Panizzi Lectures 1993, London: The British Library.

—— (1997) 'A catalogue of Sir Robert Cotton's printed books', in C. J. Wright (ed.) *Sir Robert Cotton as Collector: essays on an early Stuart courtier and his legacy*, London: The British Library.

Trant, J. (1998) 'When all you've got is "The Real Thing": museums and authenticity in the networked world', *Archives & Museum Informatics*, no. 12: 107–125.

Trant, J., Bearman, D. and Richmond, K. (2000) 'Collaborative cultural resource creation: the example of the Art Museum Image Consortium', in J. Trant and D. Bearman (eds) *Museums and the Web 2006: proceedings*, Toronto: Archives & Museum Informatics. Online. Available HTTP: <http://www.thebritishmuseum.ac.uk/newsroom/current2004/mummy.html> (accessed 25 January 2007).

Turner, V. (1977) 'Frame, flow and reflection: ritual and drama in public liminality', in M. Benamo and C. Caramello (eds) *Performance in Postmodern Culture*, Milwaukee: Centre for Twentieth-Century Studies, University of Wisconsin.

The 24 Hour Museum (2003) *Museum Sector Web Statistics 2003*. Online. Available HTTP: <http://www.24hourmuseum.org.uk/etc/formuseums/TXT21448_gfx_en.html> (accessed 28 May 2007).

Vance, D. (1968) Letter to E. Ellin, 2 July, Smithsonian Institution Archives, RU 7432, Box 19, MCN correspondence, July 1968–71.

—— (1973) *Computers in the Museum*, New York: IBM Corporation.

—— (1974) *What are Data?* Museum Data Bank Research Report no. 1, New York: Museum Data Bank Committee.

Vance, D. and Heller, J. (1971) 'Structure and content of a museum data bank', *Computers and the Humanities*, vol. 6, no. 2: 67–84.

van Dijk, J. J. M. (1999) *The Network Society: social aspects of new media* (London, Thousand Oaks, CA, New Delhi: Sage Publications.

Vanns, M. (1984) 'SHIC progress report', *SHCG News*, no. 7: 4.

van Ossenbruggen, J., Amin, A., Hardman, L., Hildebrand, M., van Assem, M., Omelay-enko, B. et al. (2007) 'Searching and annotating virtual heritage collections with Semantic-Web techniques', in J. Trant and D. Bearman (eds) *Museums and the Web 2007: proceedings*, Toronto: Archives & Museum Informatics. Online. Available HTTP: <http://www.archimuse.com/mw2007/papers/ossenbruggen/ossenbruggen.html> (accessed 23 April 2007).

Vigh, P. (2002) 'Hacking culture', in D. Bearman and J. Trant (eds) *Museums and the Web 2002: selected papers from an international conference*, Pittsburgh: Archives & Museum Informatics, 2002.

Wallace, M. (1995) 'Changing media, changing messages', in E. Hooper-Greenhill (ed.) *Museum, Media, Message*, London and New York: Routledge.

Walley, G. (1986) 'Reports received: Natural History Museum, Wollaton Hall, Notting-ham', *Museums Computer Group Newsletter*, no. 2: 3.

Walsh, P. (1997) 'The Web and the unassailable voice', *Archives & Museum Informatics*, vol. 11, no. 2: 77–85.

Wenger, E., McDermodt, R. and Snyder, W. M. (2002) *Cultivating Communities of Practice: a guide to managing knowledge*, Cambridge, MA: Harvard Business School Publishing.

White, H. (1978) 'The historical text as literary artefact', in R. Canary and H. Kozicki (eds) *The Writing of History: literary forms and historical understanding*, Madison and London: University of Wisconsin Press.

Whiting, A. F. (1966) 'Catalogues: damn 'em: an inter-museum office memo', *Curator*, vol. 9, no. 1: 85–7.

Williams, D. W. (1987) *A Guide to Museum Computing*, Nashville, TN: American Associ-ation for State and Local History.

Winston, B. (1998) *Media Technology and Society: a history – from the telegraph to the Internet*, London and New York: Routledge.

Witcomb, A. (2003) *Re-imagining the Museum: beyond the mausoleum*, London and New York: Routledge.

Worthington, R. (2005) Interview with the author, 9 December 2005.

Wotton, H. (1968) *The Elements of Architecture*, Charlottesville: University Press of Virginia.

Yates, F. (1966) *The Art of Memory*, London: Routledge and Kegan Paul.

Žižek, S. (1996) 'From virtual reality to the virtualization of reality', in T. Druckrey (ed.) *Electronic Culture: technology and visual representation*, New York: Aperture.

Zorich, D. M. (2003) *A Survey on Digital Cultural Heritage Initiatives and Their Sustainability Concerns*, Washington, DC: Council on Library and Information Resources.

Index

Related titles from Routledge

Archaeological Theory and the Politics of Cultural Heritage

Laurajane Smith

'Smith's stunning book will change the discipline.' *Larry J. Zimmerman, University of Iowa*

This controversial book is a survey of how relationships between indigenous peoples and the archaeological establishment have got into difficulty and a crucial pointer to how to move forward from these problems.

With lucid appraisals of key debates such as NAGPRA, Kennewick and the repatriation of Tasmanian artefacts, Laurajane Smith dissects the nature and consequences of this clash of cultures. Smith explores how indigenous communities in the US and Australia have confronted the pre-eminence of archaeological theory and discourse in the way the material remains of their past are cared for and controlled, and how this has challenged traditional archaeological thought and practice.

Essential reading for all those concerned with developing a just and equal dialogue between the two parties, and the role of archaeology in the research and management of their heritage.

ISBN10: 0-415-31832-7 (hbk)
ISBN10: 0-415-31833-5 (pbk)

ISBN13: 978-0-415-31832-7 (hbk)
ISBN13: 978-0-415-31833-4 (pbk)

Available at all good bookshops
For ordering and further information please visit:
www.routledge.com

The Engaging Museum
Developing Museums for Visitor Involvement

Graham Black

'*The Engaging Museum* charts a logical path from audience development to interpretation in the gallery, synthesising much thinking of the last 20 years into a textbook of practical value to the student and museum professional.' *Simon Knell, University of Leicester*

'As an academic textbook it serves us well, fully developing each topic, and is replete with supporting information and quotes by reputable sources recognized as being on the cutting edge of visitor studies and museum educational curriculum and evaluation.' *David K. Dean, Museum of Texas Tech University*

'Graham Black gets to the core of what a museum might aspire to in visitor-centred experience, including interpretive planning based on research, a defined audience and multi-layered opportunities for visitors. He has put into print our goals and aspirations – a truly inspirational read.' – *Adera Causey, Hunter Museum of American Art, Chattanooga*

This very practical book guides museums on how to create the highest quality experience possible for their visitors. Creating an environment that supports visitor engagement with collections means examining every stage of the visit, from the initial impetus to go to a particular institution, to front-of-house management, interpretive approach and qualitative analysis afterwards.

This holistic approach will be immensely helpful to museums in meeting the needs and expectations of visitors and building their audience base and includes:

- chapter introductions and discussion sections
- supporting case studies to show how ideas are put into practice
- a lavish selection of tables, figures and plates to illustrate the discussion
- boxes showing ideas, models and planning suggestions to guide development
- an up-to-date bibliography of landmark research.

The Engaging Museum offers a set of principles that can be adapted to any museum in any location and will be a valuable resource for institutions of every shape and size, as well as a vital addition to the reading lists of museum studies students.

ISBN10: 0-415-34556-1 (hbk)
ISBN10: 0-415-34557-X (pbk)

ISBN13: 978-0-415-34556-9 (hbk)
ISBN13: 978-0-415-34557-6 (pbk)

Museum Basics
Second edition

Timothy Ambrose and Crispin Paine

Museums throughout the world have common needs and face common challenges. Keeping up-to-date with new ideas and changing practice is considerably demanding for small museums where time for reading and training is often restricted. *Museum Basics* has therefore been written for the many museums worldwide which operate with limited resources and few staff. Drawing from a wide range of practical experience, the authors provide a basic guide to all aspects of museum work, from museum organisation, through collections management and conservation, to audience development and education. Organised on a modular basis with over 100 Units, *Museum Basics* can be used as a reference to support day-to-day museum management and as the key textbook in pre-service and in-service training programmes. It is designed to be supplemented by case studies, project work and group discussion. This second edition has been fully updated and extended to take account of the many changes that have occurred in the world of museums in the last decade. It includes a glossary, sources of information and support as well as a select bibliography.

ISBN10: 0-415-36633-X (hbk)
ISBN10: 0-415-36634-8 (pbk)

ISBN13: 978-0-415-36633-5 (hbk)
ISBN13: 978-0-415-36634-2 (pbk)

Available at all good bookshops
For ordering and further information please visit:
www.routledge.com

Museum Management and Marketing

Richard Sandell and Robert R. Janes

Museum Management and Marketing reflects upon key trends that have emerged in the application of management and marketing method and theory within the museum and highlights innovative new research and thinking. The Reader considers trends and issues in museum management and marketing from diverse critical perspectives, drawing together a selection of high quality intellectually robust and stimulating articles on both theoretical and practice-based learning in the field.

The Reader is divided into three main sections. The first addresses the implications of the rapidly shifting contexts within which museums now operate and considers the fundamental reorientation of museum roles and purposes that have occurred in response to rapid and turbulent change. The second section highlights developments in museum management, exploring issues including leadership, strategic planning, performance measurement and workforce development which have emerged as especially critical to contemporary management thinking and practice. The final section offers wide-ranging perspectives on the increasingly important role of marketing and considers its tremendous potential to shape the relationships which museums have with their audiences and other stakeholders.

Bringing together a collection of key writings concerned with the investigation, study and practice of management and marketing in the museum, this volume will be invaluable to students and museum professionals who wish to develop their knowledge of this ever changing and challenging field.

ISBN10: 0-415-39628-X (hbk)
ISBN10: 0-415-39629-8 (pbk)

ISBN13: 978-0-415-39628-8 (hbk)
ISBN13: 978-0-415-39629-5 (pbk)

Available at all good bookshops
For ordering and further information please visit:
www.routledge.com

Museums and Education
Purpose, Pedagogy, Performance

Eilean Hooper-Greenhill

At the beginning of the twenty-first century (a period of 'liquid' or 'post' modernity) museums are challenged on a number of fronts. The prioritisation of learning in museums in the context of demands for social justice and cultural democracy combined with cultural policy based on economic rationalism forces museums to review their educational purposes, redesign their pedagogies and account for their performance.

The need to theorise learning and culture for a cultural theory of learning is very pressing. If culture acts as a process of signification, a means of producing meaning that shapes worldviews, learning in museums and other cultural organisations is potentially dynamic and profound, producing self-identities. How is this complexity to be 'measured'? What can this 'measurement' reveal about the character of museum-based learning? The calibration of culture is an international phenomenon, and the measurement of the outcomes and impact of learning in museums in England has provided a detailed case study. Three national evaluation studies were carried out between 2003 and 2006 based on the conceptual framework of Generic Learning Outcomes. Using this revealing data *Museums and Education* reveals the power of museum pedagogy and as it does, questions are raised about traditional museum culture and the potential and challenge for museum futures is suggested.

ISBN10: 0-415-37935-0 (hbk)
ISBN10: 0-415-37936-9 (pbk)

ISBN13: 978-0-415-37935-9 (hbk)
ISBN13: 978-0-415-37936-6 (pbk)

Available at all good bookshops
For ordering and further information please visit:
www.routledge.com

Museums and their Communities

Leicester Reader in Museums Studies

Edited by Sheila Watson

Museums and their Communities brings together a collection of readings from practitioners and researchers, working across a range of disciplines, which explore and illuminate the complex and evolving relationships between museums and the diverse communities they represent, serve and with which they engage.

This collection of provocative and stimulating readings draws together thinking, practice and case studies relating to many different kinds of museum. Through wide ranging, international contexts it examines the ways in which museums operate as sites of community representation, identity and memory.

The Reader considers the shifting institutional priorities of the museum from a focus on collections to a growing concern for audience needs and expectations. It reflects on areas of contestation and addresses a number of timely questions which are increasingly challenging museum practitioners and scholars:

- Who are the museum's communities? What needs and challenges do these constituencies present?
- What is the impact upon the museum of competing community interests?
- How do issues of power and control affect communities and influence the messages museums attempt to communicate?

Museums and their Communities provides a focused consideration of the challenges and opportunities facing museums that wish to engage with their community responsibilities.

ISBN10: 0-415-40259-X (hbk)
ISBN10: 0-415-40260-3 (pbk)

ISBN13: 978-0-415-40259-0 (hbk)
ISBN13: 978-0-415-40260-6 (pbk)

Available at all good bookshops
For ordering and further information please visit:
www.routledge.com

New Heritage

New Media and Cultural Heritage

Edited by Yehuda Kalay, Thomas Kvan and Janice Affleck

The use of new media in the service of cultural heritage is a fast growing field, known variously as virtual or digital heritage. *New Heritage*, under this denomination, broadens the definition of the field to address the complexity of cultural heritage such as the related social, political and economic issues. This book is a collection of 20 key essays, of authors from 11 countries, representing a wide range of professions including architecture, philosophy, history, cultural heritage management, new media, museology and computer science, which examine the application of new media to cultural heritage from a different points of view. Issues surrounding heritage interpretation to the public and the attempts to capture the essence of both tangible (buildings, monuments) and intangible (customs, rituals) cultural heritage are investigated in a series of case studies.

Current discourses arising subsequent to the marriage of new media and cultural heritage are explored, such as the ongoing debate regarding the status of the original and the copy. Challenges addressed in creating cultural heritage virtual environments, such as engagement and evaluation, are presented, and lessons learned from case studies of digital applications in both formal and informal learning environments as well as theoretical and technical frameworks are discussed along with the related methodological limitations. This book is essential reading for those people wishing to understand the key debates in 'new heritage' and appraise the growing innovations applied to cultural heritage.

ISBN10: 0-415-77355-5 (hbk)
ISBN10: 0-415-77356-3 (pbk)

ISBN13: 978-0-415-77355-3 (hbk)
ISBN13: 978-0-415-77356-0 (pbk)

Available at all good bookshops
For ordering and further information please visit:
www.routledge.com

Reshaping Museum Space

Edited by Suzanne Macleod

At no other point in their modern history have museums undergone such radical reshaping as in recent years. Challenges to create inclusive and accessible spaces open to appropriation and responsive to contemporary agendas have resulted in new architectural forms for museums, inside and out.

Reshaping Museum Space pulls together the views of an international group of museum professionals, architects, designers and academics highlighting the complexity, significance and malleability of museum space and provides reflections upon recent developments in museum architecture and exhibition design. The problems of navigating the often contradictory agendas and aspirations of the broad range of professionals and stakeholders involved in any new project are discussed in various chapters that concentrate on the process of architectural and spatial reshaping.

Contributors review recent new build, expansion and exhibition projects questioning the types of museum space required at the beginning of the twenty-first century and highlighting a range of possibilities for creative museum design.

ISBN10: 0-415-34344-5 (hbk)
ISBN10: 0-415-34345-3 (pbk)

ISBN13: 978-0-415-34344-2 (hbk)
ISBN13: 978-0-415-34345-9 (pbk)

Available at all good bookshops
For ordering and further information please visit:
www.routledge.com